D0501235

THE VISION OF TRAGEDY

THE VISION
OF TRAGEDY

NEW EDITION, ENLARGED

RICHARD B. SEWALL

NEW HAVEN AND LONDON: YALE UNIVERSITY PRESS: 1980

Set in Caledonia type.
Printed in the United States of America by
The Murray Printing Co., Westford, Mass.

Published in Great Britain, Europe, Africa, and
Asia (except Japan) by Yale University Press,
Ltd., London. Distributed in Australia and
New Zealand by Book & Film Services, Artarmon,
N.S.W., Australia; and in Japan by Harper & Row,
Publishers, Tokyo Office.

Library of Congress Cataloging in Publication Data

Sewall, Richard Benson.
   The vision of tragedy.
   New edition, enlarged.

   Includes bibliographical references and index.
   1. Tragedy. 2. Tragic, The. 3. Tragedy—History
and criticism. 4. Literature—History and criticism.
I. Title.
PN1892.S43   1980   809'.91'6   79-24203
ISBN 0-300-02485-1
ISBN 0-300-02489-4 pbk.

Acknowledgment is made to the publishers and editors involved for per-
mission to reprint in this volume material from three previous studies:
"The Tragic Form," *Essays in Criticism,* October 1954; "The Tragic
World of the Karamazovs," in *Tragic Themes in Western Literature,* ed.
Cleanth Brooks, New Haven, Yale University Press, 1955; and "The
Vision of Tragedy," *The Review of Metaphysics,* Dec. 1956.

Contents

Preface to the New Edition

Since this book was first published, twenty years of teaching and ruminating on tragedy lead me to say more about two works not on my original list: Kafka's *The Trial* and O'Neill's *Long Day's Journey into Night*. Each explores a central area of contemporary experience rife with tragic potential. Each transcends the limits of realism on the one hand and pathos on the other. Each reaches out toward cosmic concerns, the "infinitude of background" without which tragedy "dwindles to a sorrowful tale," as Macneile Dixon once wrote. In Josef K.'s groping through the maze of the Court's bureaucracy, there is much to remind us of our own predicament in an increasingly depersonalized world; and the problem of guilt—the central theme of the novel—is as old as Job and as new as Quentin Compson. In O'Neill's play, the wrangling Tyrones become Everyfamily, prisoners of their own temperaments; there is no way out—except the one no one will take. In *The Trial*, Josef K. glimpses the way; Kafka sees it all the time. O'Neill, telling the story of his own family, sees it, too— but too late. Both books are in a sense confessional. It is as if each author were saying, "This is my own story, and it is tragic." And in the telling, in the transcendence, in the knowledge gained, each becomes (it might also be said) his own tragic hero.

Other contemporary works might have served this further exploration into the nature of tragedy: among novels, the work of Fitzgerald and Hemingway; in drama, the plays of Williams and Miller. But my choice was not in the end arbitrary. Not only are the two works chosen the sturdiest survivors of the dialectic of twenty years of classroom and conference: above all, they round out our study of tragedy in a peculiarly satisfying way. *The Trial*, with its severe focus on the guilty individual, brings us back to Job and the Old Testament God of Judgment. In *Long Day's Journey into Night*, we return to a major concern of the Greeks: the pall of tragedy as it hangs over whole families. Indeed, what O'Neill has done explicitly (and imitatively) in *Mourning Becomes Electra*, he here fashions into something completely his own—a new creation.

1979

Preface to the First Edition

THE vision of tragedy is hardly reducible to easy formulas, and to show how it reveals itself in literature is to risk travesty. It has much to do with mood, feeling, tone—it is a sense of life, not a doctrine. In a work of literature it is pervasive, implicit, inhering in every detail, every phrase, metaphor, character, and action, each one qualifying and being qualified by every other. Wherever was there a single line sufficiently explicated? The chapters that follow are suggestive only, indicating major lines of development, certain themes, meanings, images that have lived and still live in the tragic imagination of our tradition—in short, tokens only of the increment of meaning from the Poet of Job to William Faulkner.

There is nowhere in the book a single, precise, extricable definition of tragedy. But the well-disposed reader should emerge with a fairly clear notion of what tragedy is (even of what *a* tragedy is) and what it is not; to what extent it differs from, and on occasion includes, other modes and genres, like comedy, satire, melodrama, or the literature of pathos. Other terms that function inevitably in every discussion of tragedy—the tragic hero, action, catharsis—are similarly treated. The movement of the book is, loosely speaking, inductive; meanings accrete as the terms reappear in the advancing chapters. Except in the first chapter, they seldom appear apart from specific literary contexts—the flesh and blood situations which constantly expand, qualify, and test academic generalizations.

The aim of the book is to demonstrate a way of exploring literature that will encourage the reader to do the rest on his own, to make his own discoveries, even his own definitions. My endeavor (after some rather solid pronouncements to begin with) has been to keep the discussion tentative and open.

In his heart of hearts, every reader reserves the right to call this or that work a tragedy, or not a tragedy, just as he feels in his heart of hearts that he alone has "felt the anguish of the marrow . . . the fever of the bone." * This, perhaps, is a proper mood to start: "I alone know what a tragedy is." But then comes the long pull through the centuries, the deepening insight, the retreat from solipsism, the sense (as Conrad puts it) that the meaning of a tale is not like the kernel of a nut, to be gotten at in the forthright way of the nutcracker, but enveloping and permeating the whole as a glow brings out a haze. Sobered, he realizes that this, too, is a search and that the most his friend (and his book) can do for him is to report as faithfully as they can the experiences of one who has gone this way before.

Thus, in method, this book works from "the inside out," letting tragedies explain and define tragedy, with as little help from the outside as possible. It is exclusive, using only eight masterworks to stand for a 2500-year tradition. Matters historical and sociological are but briefly treated in introductory passages or transitional chapters. The emphasis is on action, image and theme, "the essence and the descent" * and the shadow that falls between. For such, it seems to me that a few works, treated in some detail, are enough.

The theme of the book is the unity and vitality of the tragic vision from *Job* to the present. The early chapters assemble the elements and prepare the way; the later ones show the central theme in its latter-day variations. The whole is a continuous essay on tragedy, demonstrating finally, I hope, not only the possibility but the existence of true tragic writing in our time.

I would like to be able to acknowledge all my indebtednesses in writing this book, but it is impossible. I began reading and thinking about tragedy long before I thought of writing a book on it, and the sources of many ideas that came to the surface as I wrote are lost, I fear, from my memory. The notes indicate my gratitude to many but perforce not all of my predecessors in this seemingly perennial endeavor of

* T. S. Eliot, *Collected Poems, 1909–1935*, Harcourt, Brace, 1936; reprinted by permission.

the human mind. To those closer at hand, my debt is clear and memorable—and my thanks are immediate: to Ralph Harper, F. W. Bateson, Maynard Mack, Susan Taubes, John E. Smith, Grover Smith, Jr., Adam Yarmolinsky, Laurence Michel, Harry Berger, Thomas Copeland, Louis Martz, and Frank Brady, for encouragement, criticism, favors little and big. To the students of "English 61: Tragedy," who have witnessed my wrestlings with the subject since 1947, for constant stimulus, and shrewd, honest, and sometimes grueling criticism. To my father, who enlarged my biblical knowledge. To my brother John, who read shrewdly. To Marshall Waingrow for last minute guidance and counsel. To my wife, who has forborne. And finally to Paul Weiss, who first suggested the idea and has seen it through with fortitude and patience.

1959

LEAR. Why, thou wert better in thy grave than to answer with thy uncovered body this extremity of the skies. Is man no more than this? Consider him well. Thou owest the worm no silk, the beast no hide, the sheep no wool, the cat no perfume. Ha! here's three on 's are sophisticated; thou art the thing itself. Unaccommodated man is no more but such a poor, bare, forked animal as thou art.

KING LEAR

1

THE VISION
OF TRAGEDY

WHEN at the end of the *Symposium* Socrates insisted to his friends Aristophanes and Agathon that "the genius of comedy is the same as the genius of tragedy, and that the writer of tragedy ought to be a writer of comedy also," the friends, says Plato, were "compelled to assent, being sleepy, and not quite understanding his meaning." It had been a long night, with much wine, and the friends might well have agreed to almost anything. But whether they would have agreed under different circumstances, and just what Socrates' arguments were, are other questions. One would like to know precisely what he said. Or perhaps the affair was a bit of a paradox spun out for his own amusement. For it seems clear—at least it is the thesis of this book—that the genius of tragedy is not the same as the genius of comedy. As for Socrates' notion that every writer ought to be able to do both, there can be no objection. Some few have done both. What he had in mind, perhaps, was the undeniable truth that the highest comedy gains its power from its sense of tragic possibility, and the profoundest tragedy presents a full if fleeting vision, through the temporary disorder, of an ordered universe to which comedy is witness. Without a sense of the tragic, comedy loses heart; it becomes brittle, it has animation but no life. Without a recognition of the truths of comedy, tragedy becomes bleak and intolerable.[1]

But since the Greeks first wrote what they called tragedies and comedies, and Aristotle in the *Poetics* formulated some principles about them, writers have been conscious of the two modes—each with its own demands—as engaging them in different undertakings, involving them in different worlds. They have gauged their predilections and capacities against the demands of each and have deliberately chosen one or the other, or some calculated mixture. They have often been explicit about it. Shakespeare announced his plays as "tragedies" or "comedies," or, when he chose, mixed the modes with the recklessness of Polonius. Marlowe spoke his intention when in the prologue to *Tamburlaine* he asked his audience to view his hero in "the tragic glass." Ben Jonson ventured into tragedy in his own scholarly, methodical way, boasting to have discharged (in *Sejanus*) all the crucial "offices of a *Tragic writer*," which he got from Aristotle. Milton's choice of the tragic form to express his final mood was deliberate and especially significant in relation to the tragic undertones of *Paradise Lost*. Artists are free—but free to choose their own sort of bondage. It is they and not so much the critics who have worked to maintain the integrity of the forms. Their conscious, explicit choices show that in their eyes the forms are real and different and not merely an academic conspiracy.[2] The phenomenon is a powerful example of the fruitful interaction of tradition and individual talent.

Tragedy, traditionally the most exalted of the forms, has exerted on artists of many generations, not only Greek and Elizabethan, a compelling influence. Its effect on the individual talent has sometimes been noble and often disastrous. It requires an independent, radical vision whose lack is as fatal as the lack of a sense of ultimate harmony is in comedy. Sophocles and Euripides, though building on Aeschylus' original insights and to this extent acting in imitation of him, used the form he had established to express their own individual and radical visions. The Elizabethans, whose nervous and independent force worked creatively on whatever form they chose, expanded and improvised to suit their own expressive needs. Since then, as writers not so vitally equipped have attempted to write tragedy, the sense of strain and artificiality is frequent.

2

The French at their best (Racine, for instance) embodied the true tragic vision in a finely disciplined form; but their next best shows how precarious is the balance between creation and imitation. Milton's vision in the masterful *Samson Agonistes* has been called only "spasmodically tragic."[3] In lesser artists, who approached tragedy too analytically or (it would seem) for its prestige, the strain is painfully obvious. The English theater after the Restoration produced plays called tragedies which are informed, rather, by the moral or "heroic" vision. The romantic poets, great admirers though they were of the Greeks and the Elizabethans, showed how far their world actually was from the world of *Oedipus* and *Lear* (which Shelley described as "the deepest and sublimest of the tragic compositions") when they ventured into tragedy. Shelley's preface to *The Cenci* is an earnest little treatise on tragedy; but he tried the form only once.[4] As his wife wrote, "the bent of his mind went the other way." So did Byron's and Tennyson's, although they both wrote what they called tragedies. Goethe was perhaps wisest when he said "the mere attempt to write tragedy might be my undoing."[5]

In the nineteenth century certain of the novelists had the surest sense of the thing itself. Genuine and vital strains of Greek and Hebraic tragic traditions, intensified by the tragic insights of Christianity, appear impressively, for instance, in Hawthorne, Melville, and Dostoevski. Hawthorne, whose sense of kinship with Greek and Elizabethan tragedy he more than once indicated, invested Hester Prynne with some of the hard outlines of Antigone's character and with much of the passion and color of an Elizabethan. Melville shaped Ahab as "a mighty pageant figure, fit for noble tragedies" and had him chase his "Job's whale" to the far quarters of the globe. Both novels show clearly that their authors were sensitive to the problem of making the tragic vision real to nineteenth-century democratic America.[6] Dostoevski opened up a vast new tragic area by his own peculiar synthesis of the basic insights of all the traditions. Ibsen and O'Neill, Conrad, Kafka, and Faulkner (to name only a few) have each in their own way explored the area which he plotted out. Whether they have written "tragedies" is not at present the point, but they

3

seem closer to the tragic spirit than the Romantic and Victorian imitators.

But how can it be said that a novel by Kafka or Faulkner is more truly tragic than *The Cenci*? What is the "true" tragic spirit, the thing itself? Is it right to say that writers choose the form, or does the form in some subtle way choose them? Shelley chose the form—his wife tells how the idea of writing a tragedy had haunted him long before he encountered the story of *The Cenci*—but, quite clearly, he himself was not chosen. Shakespeare's tragedies are grouped in a period of his life when, as far as we can tell biographically, the "bent of his mind" seems to have been that way. Goethe never felt chosen. He realized that the tragic sense of the world and of man's destiny was not his, and he stayed away. There was nothing that he could not have mastered technically; indeed, Shelley showed how far a near-perfect executive form could be from the thing itself. But tragedy demands qualities of vision which neither of them had.

In general, the tragic vision is not a systematic view of life. It admits wide variations and degree. It is a sum of insights, intuitions, feelings, to which the words "vision" or "view" or "sense of life," however inadequate, are most readily applicable. The tragic sense of life, as Unamuno describes it,[7] is a subphilosophy, or a prephilosophy, "more or less formulated, more or less conscious." It reaches deep down into the temperament, "not so much flowing from ideas as determining them." It is an attitude toward life with which some individuals seem to be endowed to high degree, others less, but which is latent in every man and may be evoked by experience. Unamuno finds it characteristic of some nations and not others. Horace Walpole's epigram, "this world is a comedy to those who think, a tragedy to those who feel," has only relative truth, but it is significant in showing how readily the terms become metaphors to describe a view of life, a cast of thought or temperament.[8]

The tragic vision is in its first phase primal, or primitive, in that it calls up out of the depths the first (and last) of all questions, the question of existence: What does it mean to be? It recalls the original terror, harking back to a world that

4

antedates the conceptions of philosophy, the consolations of the later religions, and whatever constructions the human mind has devised to persuade itself that its universe is secure. It recalls the original un-reason, the terror of the irrational. It sees man as questioner, naked, unaccommodated, alone, facing mysterious, demonic forces in his own nature and outside, and the irreducible facts of suffering and death. Thus it is not for those who cannot live with unsolved questions or unresolved doubts, whose bent of mind would reduce the fact of evil into something else or resolve it into some larger whole. Though no one is exempt from moments of tragic doubt or insight, the vision of life peculiar to the mystic, the pious, the propagandist, the confirmed optimist or pessimist—or the confirmed anything—is not tragic.

Nor is the tragic vision for those who, though admitting unsolved questions and the reality of guilt, anxiety, and suffering, would become quietist and do nothing. Mere sensitivity is not enough. The tragic vision impels the man of action to fight against his destiny, kick against the pricks, and state his case before God or his fellows.[9] It impels the artist, in his fictions, toward what Jaspers calls "boundary-situations,"[10] man at the limits of his sovereignty—Job on the ash-heap, Prometheus on the crag, Oedipus in his moment of self-discovery, Lear on the heath, Ahab on his lonely quarter-deck. Here, with all the protective covering stripped off, the hero faces as if no man had ever faced it before the existential question—Job's question, "What is man?" or Lear's "Is man no more than this?" The writing of a tragedy is the artist's way of taking action, of defying destiny, and this is why in the great tragedies there is a sense of the artist's own involvement, an immediacy not so true of the forms, like satire and comedy, where the artist's position seems more detached.[11]

The findings of the anthropologists about the origins of tragedy are not irrelevant here. Even though they cannot be verified historically, they seem psychologically true. The religious ritual out of which it is thought tragedy grew—the dance of mourning in the fall festival at the death of the old year or (as some think) the ritual sacrifice of propitiation— was in itself an action, a response to a condition, a kind of answer to the question of existence. It was an answer in terms of gesture and action rather than language, and represents, perhaps, man's first attempt to deal creatively with pain and fear.[12] Any action at all was better than nothing. It was not until later, when man graduated from the condition of pain and fear to the condition of suffering—which is the condition of pain and fear contemplated and spiritualized—that the response was verbalized in some kind of art form, a dirge or lament. Even in the most sophisticated of forms, literary tragedy, the element of gesture and action is strong, but it is the contemplated and individual response to suffering rather than the instinctive and tribal. Unamuno's fine ancedote about Solon shows elements of both—the primitive response by gesture (weeping) and the comment from the depths of an anguished spirit. "Why do you weep for the death of your son," the skeptic asked Solon, "when it avails nothing?" "I weep," replied Solon, "precisely because it avails nothing." [13]

It is this sense of ancient evil, of "the blight man was born for," of the permanence and the mystery of human suffering, that is basic to the tragic sense of life. It informs all literature of a somber cast—the dirge, the lament, the melancholy lyric or song, the folk ballad of betrayal and death. It colors many scenes in the great epics and hovers about the best comedy as an imminent possibility. The tragedies of the tradition, from Aeschylus to Dostoevski, say this about it: that by most men it must be learned—and learned through direct, immediate experience: that is, through suffering. So universal is this testimony that it can be taken as one of the constants of tragedy, and the starting point. All men must learn to feel what wretches feel. In the lives of many writers of tragedy there is abundant evidence of deep autobiographic meaning in this recurrent theme, a fact of relevance to the sense of innerness and involvement that tragedy possesses above other forms.

Pressing out from this initial phase of the tragic vision, the artist's action or response takes him beyond the lament or the melancholy lyric toward an increasingly complicated dialectic as he contemplates the thrust and counterthrust of man against destiny. Here his cause is one with the philosophers and theologians, the difference being that the artist's dialectic is not of ideas in the abstract but of ideas in action, ideas as lived. His dialectic is not so much with words as with lives, and his focus is not so much man thinking as man acting, man "on the way." Where the philosophers and moralists would generalize on experience, find unity in multiplicity, and reduce experience to viable categories and prescriptions, the tragic artist explores each experience directly, *de novo*, for whatever it may reveal about man's capacities and possibilities. He presses the "boundary-situation" for its total yield. Whatever he finds man capable of, in action and under extremest pressure, is to him the truth, whether it be abject and miserable or sublime and redeeming. This truth constitutes the "discovery" of tragedy.

Historically, literary tragedy has always appeared at the mature period of a culture, not at its beginning. Although it retains the primitive sense of terror at what Joyce called "the secret cause" [14] of suffering, it is in another sense highly sophisticated. It puts to the test of action all the formulations of philosophy and religion. In the three major western cultures—Hebrew, Greek, and Christian—there have come times (our present era may be one of them) when for reasons internal and external, spiritual and sociological, the questions of ultimate justice and human destiny seem suddenly to have been jarred loose again. Often these critical periods, or "moments," come after a long period of relative stability, when a dominant myth or religious orthodoxy or philosophic view has provided a coherent and sustaining way of life. Suddenly the original terror looms close and the old formulations cannot dispel it. The conflict between man and his destiny assumes once more the ultimate magnitude. It appears to be not a matter of accident, a temporary and limited disturbance, but an essential change in the face of the universe. The whole of society is involved, and the stake is survival. Thus the sense of despair in the early chapters of Job's complaint, the sense of doom in Greek tragedy, Gloucester's fears in the first act of *Lear*, and the sense of disintegration in *The Brothers Karamazov*.

In such periods, and in such moods, artists confront the existential question all over again. They ask, like the elderly trader in Conrad's *Lord Jim*, "How to be?" and embody their answers, ambiguous and tentative, in their "boundary-situations." Each age has different tensions and terrors, but they open on the same abyss. If each new artist's primary source must be the data of his own experience and observation, he just as surely learns from his fellow artists who have stared into the same depths. What they came up with, the statement of their fictions, constitutes the tradition—a total evaluation expressed in a literary form. As the tradition guides the new vision, the vision tests it, alters its focus and direction or expands its compass. Direction and focus may change, but the vision is constant. How vision forged a form, some major modes the form has taken, and some meanings it has revealed, are the concerns of the following chapters.

2

THE BOOK OF JOB

WE LOOK at a work of literature and call it "optimistic" or "pessimistic" or "epic" or "tragic." The book is there before us, and we find the term to describe it. But the work comes first. It is not right to say that without the vision of life embodied in the Old Testament, and notably in *The Book of Job,* the term "tragedy" would have no substance, for the Greeks invented the term and gave it a great deal of substance. But knowing what we do now about the full depth and reach of tragedy, we can see with striking clarity in the writings of the ancient Hebrews the vision which we now call tragic and in *The Book of Job* the basic elements of the tragic form. The cultural situation, the matrix out of which *Job* came, is the very definition of "the tragic moment" in history, a period when traditional values begin to lose their power to comfort and sustain, and man finds himself once more groping in the dark. The unknown Poet's "action," his redoing of the orthodox and optimistic folktale of the pious and rewarded Job, is (as we can say now) a classic example of the dynamics of tragedy, of vision creating form. And the great figure of his creation, the suffering, questioning, and unanswered Job, is the towering tragic figure of antiquity. More than Prometheus or Oedipus, Job is the universal symbol for the western imagination of the mystery of undeserved suffering.

Of all ancient peoples, the Hebrews were most surely possessed of the tragic sense of life. It pervades their ancient writings to an extent not true of the Greeks. "Judaism," writes Paul Weiss, "is Moses in the wilderness straining to reach a land he knows he never can. For the Christian this truth is but the necessary first act of a Divine Comedy. The history of the universe for the Christian is in principle already told. For the Jew history is in the making. It has peaks and valleys, goods and bads, inseparably together and forever." [15] The Hebraic answer to the question of existence was never unambiguous or utopian; the double vision of tragedy—the snake in the garden, the paradox of man born in the image of God and yet recalcitrant, tending to go wrong—permeates the Scriptures. No case is ever clear-cut, no hero or prophet entirely faultless. The Hebrews were the least sentimental and romantic of peoples. The Old Testament stories are heavy with irony, often of the most sardonic kind. And yet their hard, acrid realism appears against a background of belief that is the substance of the most exalted and affirmative religion, compared to which the religions of their sister civilizations, Egyptian, Babylonian, and even Greek, presented a conception of the universe and man both terrible and mean. [16] The Hebraic view of God, man, and nature, wrought through the centuries out of hard experience and exalted vision, presented to the Poet of Job a rich and full-nerved tradition, containing all the alternatives, for evil as well as good, but founded on the belief in a just and benevolent Creator, in man as made in His image, and in an ordered universe.

Throughout their history as it is unfolded in the Old Testament, the Hebrews showed a strong critical sense, a tendency to test all their beliefs, even Jehovah Himself, against their individual experience and sense of values. This skepticism is at the root of much of their irony, and it implies, of course, a very high estimate of individual man. They had a sufficient confidence in their own native and immediate insights to set themselves, if need be, against their God. This was an affirmation about man, the Deity, and the relationship between the two, which the Babylonians and Egyptians surely never achieved, nor, as a people, did the Greeks. The Hebrews saw man not only as free and rational but free, rational, and righteous even before God. The eating of the apple was in a sense an act of the free critical intelligence. [17] Why should there have been even one prohibition, arbitrary and unexplained?

10

The failure in actual experience of the orthodox teaching that God would reward the righteous and punish the wicked gave rise in later times to a whole literature of dissent, ranging from the disturbed and melancholy psalms, the ambiguous attitude toward the Deity in stories like Jonah, to the complaints of Ecclesiastes and the full-scale protests of Job. It is hard to see why Simone Weil said of the Hebrews that they "believed themselves exempt from the misery that is the common human lot" and that only in parts of *Job* is "misfortune fairly portrayed." [18] Their belief in Jehovah and their hope for a Messiah served rather to intensify their sense of present inequity and to increase the anxiety which permeates this protest-literature.

But another aspect of the Hebraic tragic vision gives it its peculiar depth and poignancy, and it is the very clue to *Job*. It comes from the conception of Jehovah as a person, to be communed with, worshiped, feared, but above all to be loved. In the transactions of the Greeks with their gods, no great amount of love was lost. There was no doctrine of Creation, nor a Creator to be praised (as in psalm after psalm) for his loving-kindness and tender mercies. The Greek gods were fallible, imperfect, finite, and, above all, laws unto themselves; to rebel against them might be disastrous but it involved no inevitable spiritual dilemma or clash of loyalties. But Jehovah, in the eyes of the orthodox Hebrew, was righteous, just, and loving—and a being to whom one could appeal in the name of all these virtues. The protest embodied in *The Book of Job* came not from fear or hate but from love. Job's disillusionment was deeply personal, as from a cosmic breach of faith. However critical of the Deity, Job spoke not in arrogance and revolt but in love, and in this at least he was the true representative of an ancient piety.

The unknown Poet of Job, however, saw the old story of Job not as illustrating the ancient piety—that is, a good man blessing the Lord even in his afflictions and being rewarded for his constancy—but as throwing it into grievous question. All the latent doubts and questionings of his race came to a head. Job had trusted in The Covenant and followed The Code; God had watched over him; God's lamp had lighted his way through the darkness, His friendship had been upon his tent. Job was the beloved patriarch of a large family and a man of consequence in the community. And then, suddenly and unaccountably, the face of the universe changed. It was not only that he suffered misfortunes, lost his property, family, position, and health. Mortal man must face losses; the proverbial wisdom of the Hebrews had taught for generations that man was born for trouble, as the sparks fly upward. The shock of the story for the Poet did not lie there, if we may judge by how he retold it. The succession of catastrophes that befell Job, as the folk story recounts them, was systematic, the result of a wager between God and Satan to test Job. Job, who could know nothing of the wager, suffered at the hands of a God whom to worship and to love had been his daily blessing and who had turned suddenly hateful and malign. There was no mortal cause for his sufferings, nothing in his past to account for these repeated, calculated blows. If he had sinned, he had not sinned that much.

From the depth of an ancient skepticism and a sense of justice which dared to hold Deity itself to account, the Poet saw the story, as we would say, in the light of the tragic vision. The primitive terror loomed close. The resolution of the folk story, by which Job for his piety and suffering was rewarded by twice his former possessions and a new family, was unacceptable. The Poet saw Job's suffering as a thrust of destiny that raised the deepest issues, not to be accounted for by a heavenly wager and bought off by a handsome recompense. The suffering had been real; it could not be taken back; and it had not been deserved.

What to do about it? One can imagine in earlier times the primitive response of propitiation or lament, the wailing at the wall, the sharing of communal grief over inexplicable suffering. In later times, psalmists caught the mood in the most beautiful of melancholy and anguished lyrics; rabbis taught men to regard such suffering as punishment for secret sin or as God's way of testing man's loyalty. So Eliphaz (5:17) interpreted Job's suffering: "Behold, happy is the man whom God correcteth: therefore despise not thou the chastening of the Almighty." [19] Again, none of the ancient Hebrew writers responded to the fact of undeserved suffering more sensitively than Ecclesiastes or was truer to the realities of human misery: "The truest of all men was the Man of Sorrows," wrote Melville, "and the truest of all books is Solomon's, and Ecclesiastes is the fine hammered steel of woe." [20] But it was not for Ecclesiastes to discover the full possibilities of the "boundary-situation," to hammer from the hard steel of woe the full dimensions of the tragic form. He observed, and contemplated, and recorded movingly what he saw. But he stopped, half-way, with pathos—the single-voiced lament, the lyric expression of a reserved and passive acceptance.

The Poet of Job chose still another way, and with him tragic vision is fulfilled in tragic form. His response was dynamic and positive. He saw in Job's story the possibilities of a significant action, not only the lamentable blows that fell upon Job but the counterthrust that makes drama. He imagined Job as striking back in the only possible way when the adversary is Destiny—that is, with words. The Poet did not deal in plotted physical action, as in a Greek play; rather, he conceived of ideas, or inner realities, functioning like actions and as fully freighted with consequences. Although Job and his Counselors do not budge from the ash-heap (which 2:8 suggests as the setting of the drama) and do not exchange blows or even threats of blows, they are actually at death-grips. Each side sees survival at stake. The parts of the drama—character, incident, minor actions—are not clearly articulated as in plays to be performed, but the vital tension and forward movement of formal drama are clear. This method of the Poet's—sustained tension throughout the thrust-and-parry of ideas, the balancing of points of view in the challenge-and-response of argument—is the inner logic, or dialectic, of the tragic form as it appears in fully developed drama.

It is a way, of course, of making an important—and "tragic"—statement about the nature of truth. In tragedy, truth is not revealed as one harmonious whole; it is many-faceted, ambiguous, a sum of irreconcilables—and that is one source of its terror. As the Poet contemplated Job's case, he saw that the single-voiced response—the lament or the diatribe —was inadequate. The case was not clear; at its center was a bitter dilemma, every aspect of which, in the full and fair

13

portrayal of human suffering like Job's, must be given a voice. The Counselors were partly right, and Job was partly wrong. Job was at once justified in complaining against his God, and deeply guilty. There was no discharge in that war. The dramatic form above all others conveys this sense of the jarring conflict of ideas-in-action, gives each its due, and shows how each qualifies and interacts on every other. It conveys directly what Jung called "the terrible ambiguity of an immediate experience." [21] Comedy presents ambiguities but removes their terror; in tragedy the terror remains.

This method, like the tragic vision which was a part of the Poet's racial inheritance, was not new in the literature of the Hebrews. *Job* is merely the fullest development of a racial way of expression observable in the earliest writings. For example, after the single-voiced and full-throated praise of the Creator and the Creation in the first chapter of Genesis, the story of Adam and Eve and the Fall moves into a different mode. Many voices are heard, including the Serpent's. This is one way of saying that even this case was not entirely clear. Kierkegaard, who had a lively sense of the tragic aspect of the Old Testament, shows how Adam and Eve, though guilty, were in part justified. The Almighty had "goaded" them. The story of Abraham and Isaac, which moves forward in a kind of tragic dialectic, has frightening undertones, as Kierkegaard's famous discussion in *Fear and Trembling* shows. Moses, Jonah, and many of the Old Testament heroes and prophets argued with Jehovah, questioned his judgment, criticized his harshness or (as with Jonah) his leniency, in actual dialogue. In such ways the Hebrews surrounded even their most sacred religious figures and truths with an aura of ambiguity and qualification. Ideas, or truth, were not regarded apart, as abstractions or final causes. They were ideas-in-action, lived out and tested by men of flesh and blood. Thus like men they were in a constant process of becoming. Even Jehovah, as we see him in the Old Testament, evolved.

So the Poet of Job, true to his tradition, set his protagonist— Job, or the "Job-idea"— free to run the dialectical gamut, to test it not only against Jehovah but against all the standard human formulations that had traditionally resolved such situations. He gave Job human adversaries as well as divine, to try him at every point. Thus the movement of statement-and-reply between Job and the Counselors, now swift, now slow, gives the sense not of the static opposition of ideas in a debate but of men in action, temperamental and passionate. Job is in turn bitter and despairing, angry and defiant, pensive and exalted. The Counselors, in their turn, console, plead, argue, scold, and threaten. Nothing is left untouched in the furious spirals of the debate. The method allows for the fullest "existential" exploration of the concerns—the nature of man and the universe—without which, after the achievement of *Job* and the Greeks, tragedy is purely nominal. Again, what tragedy seems to be saying—what *Job* and the Greeks made it say—is that we come closest to the nature of man and universe in the test-situation, where the strength or weakness of the individual, to endure or let go, is laid bare. Only then does the final "yea" or "nay" have meaning. When Job in his extremity puts ironically the question of the pious psalmist, "What is man, that thou are mindful of him?" the Poet gives no pat answer. The answer is the total *Book of Job*, all that Job says and becomes, all that the Counselors say and do not become, all that the Voice from the Whirlwind says about man and his place in the universe. The answer is the full drama, not in any one of its parts—least of all in the pious and comforting resolution of the folk story in the last chapter.

No analysis can convey more than the bare structure of the Poet's meaning. But the heart of his meaning, and surely the chief source of the tragic meaning for subsequent artists, is contained in the so-called Poem of Job, all that occurs between Job's opening curse (ch. 3) and 42:6, the last verse before the folk-story conclusion. This is the agon, the passion-scene, where the discoveries are made of most relevance to average, suffering, questioning humanity.

Job in the opening curse is in the torment of despair. The shock of his calamities has more than unbalanced him; it has prostrated him. For "seven days and seven nights" he has sat among the ashes, for "his grief was very great." His world has collapsed, his inherited values have been discredited. He faces at least four possible choices. He may follow the advice of his wife to "Curse God, and die." He may come to terms with his fate and accept it as deserved—the advice which his Counselors later give him. He may accept his fate, whether deserved or not, and contemplate it, like Ecclesiastes, with melancholy equanimity. Or he may strike back in some way, give vent to his feelings and carry his case wherever it may lead. The Poet does not present Job in his tragic moment as weighing these alternatives openly, although in "seven days and seven nights" he has had time to consider them all. But we get no sense of a closely reasoned choice. All we know is that he did not commit suicide (although the thought of it recurs to him later), that he "opened his mouth" and talked, and that he took this action through some mysterious dynamic within himself. There was no goddess whispering encouragement at his shoulder or divine vision leading him on. He was "unaccommodated man," moved in his first moment of bitterness to give up the struggle, but for some reason making a "gesture" first. It is this action, and the action which follows from it, which establishes Job as hero. It had what Aristotle called "magnitude": it involved Job totally, and he was a man of high estate on whom many people depended; it involved Job's world totally, since it questioned the basis of its belief and modes of life; it transcended Job's world, horizontally as well as vertically, as the perennial relevance of Job's problem, from his time to ours, shows. And it involved Job in total risk: "Behold he will slay me; I have no hope." [22]

Although there is little in literature as black as the opening verses of Job's curse, in the speech as a whole there is a saving ambiguity which predicts the main movement of the Poem. This movement, in brief, is from the obsessive egotism (like Lear's or Ahab's) that sees particular misfortune as a sign of universal ruin (and even wills it, for revenge or escape or oblivion) toward a mood more rational, outgoing, and compassionate. Job's first words are of furious, not passive, despair. He has been wounded in his pride, humiliated as well as stricken. He curses life and the parents who gave him life. He would have his birthday blotted from the calendar; he would have all men go into mourning on that day and the light of

16

heaven be darkened. He rages in the worst kind of arrogant, romantic rebellion. Yet gradually there is a change, however slight. The furious commands of the opening verses change to questions: "Why died I not from the womb? why did I not give up the ghost when I came out of the belly?" The plaintive tone leads to one more contemplative, as he thinks not of universal darkness but of rest with all those who have gone before, "the kings and the counsellors of the earth . . . princes that had gold, who filled their houses with silver." He has a word for the weary and oppressed, the small as well as the great. The first-person pronoun changes to the third: "Wherefore is light given to him that is in misery, and life unto the bitter in soul . . . ? Why is light given to a man whose way is hid, and whom God hath hedged in?" Although he returns in the last three verses to a mood of anguish and dread, it is more like the response to a spasm of pain— "For the thing which I greatly feared is come upon me, and that which I was afraid of is come unto me"—than the nihilism of the opening verses.

Thus Job does not abandon life, and as he rallies and reorganizes he opens up new and redeeming reaches of life. In the reverse of the way they expect, the Counselors assist in the process. Their arguments sting and thrust, kindle new energies in him, and compel him to ever greater expressive efforts. The dialectic works beneficently with Job. Eliphaz's first speech (ch. 4) is a curious combination of scolding ("Behold, thou hast instructed many . . . But now it is come upon thee, and thou faintest"), of mystical witness ("Now a thing was secretly brought to me . . . in thoughts from the visions of the night"), and of the proverbial comforts about suffering as the common lot and as a corrective discipline. At the end of the speech Job is thoroughly aroused. He will not abide such half-faced fellowship. He will not be accused of impatience by men who have never had their own patience put to the test. He asks of them neither material aid nor deliverance "from the enemy's hand." What he wants is instruction. "Teach me, and I will hold my tongue: and cause me to understand wherein I have erred." This is a great gain over the nihilism of the Curse. To be sure, as often happens in the long sequences to come, Job relapses in the second half of his answer to Eliphaz (ch. 7) into self-pity and lamentation: "My days are swifter than a weaver's shuttle, and are spent without hope." But the speech ends in a surge of vigor, in defiance not so much of the Counselors as of Jehovah himself.

It is in this passage (7:11–21) that he commits himself to the ultimate risk: "Therefore I will not refrain my mouth; I will speak in the anguish of my spirit; I will complain in the bitterness of my soul." Later, in his first reply to Zophar (ch. 13), it is clear that he understands the full terms of the risk: "Though he slay me, yet will I trust in him: but I will maintain mine own ways before him." But by now Job has come to see his own ways and his own complaints in a different light. He sees his misfortunes not as unique but as typical of man's lot. In one phase of his being, at least, he is becoming a partisan of the human race.[23] "What is man, that thou shouldst magnify him"—only to torment him? He never forgets his own personal grievances, but his thoughts turn ever more outward; he does not "rest in his own suffering." [24] He discourses upon God's capricious ways with all mankind: "He increaseth the nations, and destroyeth them" (12:23); upon the flourishing of the wicked and the oppression of the poor (chs. 21, 24); upon the element of chance in all life (ch. 21). For all his frequent lapses into despair, as sudden pain strikes him or as his thoughts turn back to happier times or forward to an uncertain future, he speaks as one having shouldered the burden of humanity.

But this growing sense of partisanship—like Ahab's, "for all that has maddened and tormented the whole race from Adam down" [25]—is only one phase of Job's experience, the structure of which, as the Poet presents it, represents an ordering of experience which many subsequent tragedies have imitated and all of them shared in part, some emphasizing one aspect, some another. It was not until Job gained some mastery over his despair, chose his course, and began his defense, that the full meaning of his position grew upon him. This realization was to be the source of his greatest suffering, beside which his physical afflictions were easy to bear. In justice he could decry the miseries of the human lot and the baffling ways of the Almighty, but he could not forget that it was Jehovah's hands that had (as he says) "made me and fashioned me together round about . . . [and] granted me life and favour, and thy visitation hath preserved my spirit." He was on the horns of a terrible dilemma—the clue to the nature of his suffering. He saw that what he had done, though justified, was wrong. He had been justified in asserting his innocence and in speaking out for all men who had been afflicted as he had. But it was wrong, as the Counselors repeatedly and rightly dinned into his ears, to defy the God whom he loved. If he could have regarded the idea of Justice abstractly, his suffering would not have involved this peculiar anguish. It was the Person in the impersonal that Job loved and could not repudiate—and which monomaniac Ahab hated and spat upon. It is this agony of dilemma, of the knowledge of the ambiguity of every choice, that, since *Job* and the Greeks, has defined tragic suffering. The capacity for such suffering (and even Ahab "has his humanities" [26]) has ever since been the mark of the tragic figure—he who is caught between the necessity to act and the knowledge of inevitable guilt. Job felt duty-bound to challenge God, Orestes to kill his mother, Hamlet to kill his uncle; and all of them knew guilt. Job had progressed from the experience of mere pain and distress to the experience of suffering.[27]

In the course of the long ordeal, the Poet reveals many personal qualities in Job that have since been appropriated into the tradition of formal tragedy. "The ponderous heart," the "globular brain," the "nervous lofty language" which Melville [28] saw as the qualities of the tragic hero are all in Job. After *Job* and the Greeks, it became part of the function of tragedy to represent, and make probable, figures of such stature. What would break lesser folk—the Counselors, or the members of the chorus—releases new powers in Job. His compulsion toward self-justification sends him far and wide over all the affairs of men, and deep within himself; and the agony of his guilt propels him ever nearer his God. He sets himself in solid debate against the Counselors: "I have understanding as well as you: I am not inferior to you." He answers their arguments in the full sweep of a massive mind, rich in learning and in the closest observation of human life. He resists every temptation to compromise or turn back, like Ahab denying Starbuck, or Hamlet thrusting aside his friends. As he gains in spiritual poise (though his course is very uneven), his mental processes become more orderly. He talks increasingly in legal terms. The universe becomes, as it were, a local court of justice where his "cause" can be "tried." "Behold now, I have ordered my cause; I know that I shall be justified." In one mood he complains that there is no "daysman," or umpire, to judge his case; in another he calls upon God to act as judge against Himself. He speaks of his "witness" and his "record" and longs to have his case recorded in a book—like Othello or Hamlet, wanting his full story told.

Nothing is more revealing of Job's (and the tragic hero's) stature than the contrast which the Poet develops between Job and the Counselors. Job outstrips them in every way. By chapter 28 Job has achieved an ironic reversal of roles: the Counselors who came to teach him are now being taught by him—and on the subject of Wisdom. He fails to convince them of the injustice of his suffering or even of the possibility of a flaw in their pat theology. But in failing to change their minds he demonstrates the littleness of minds that cannot be changed. He grows in stature as they shrink. He knows that he has achieved a vision, through suffering, beyond anything they can know. He has mystical insights, as when he sees into the time, perhaps long after his death, when his Vindicator "will stand up upon the earth," and when "without my flesh I shall see God." [29] On his miserable ash-heap (and this is what the Counselors never see) Job rises to heights he never reached in the days of his worldly prosperity, when in his presence "the aged arose and stood up, the princes refrained talking." His summing up, the Oath of Clearance (chs. 30–31), is orderly and composed. He is the master of his spirit. When the Voice from the Whirlwind begins its mighty oration, the Counselors seem not part of the picture at all. They return in the folk-story conclusion (41:7) only to be rebuked: "the Lord said to Eliphaz the Temanite, My wrath is kindled against thee, and against thy two friends: for ye have not spoken of me the thing that is right, as my servant Job hath."

So far, the meaning of *Job* for the tragic tradition is this: A new dimension of human experience, a new possibility, has been explored and rendered probable. Vision, working on the raw materials of experience, has hammered out a form. New value has been found where it was least expected—in the clearest possible case of unjustified suffering. Suffering itself, as the Poet of Job defines it, has been made to yield knowledge, and the way has been plotted out. After this achievement by the Poet of Job and after the similar achievement by Aeschylus in what may have been the same era of antiquity (the fifth century), the "tragic form" was permanently available. No subsequent artist whose imagination was attracted to this mode of writing could ignore it.

It has seemed to many that in the final stages of *Job*—the speech of Elihu, the Voice from the Whirlwind, Job's repentance, and the folk-story ending—tragic meaning, as the Poet has so far defined it, is swallowed up in mystical revelation or orthodox piety. In one sense it is true that the final phase of Job's experience carries him beyond the tragic domain, and the book as a whole is a religious book and not a formal tragedy. The revelation granted Job, and his repentance, would seem to deny the essence of his previous situation—the agony of dilemma, of the opposing compulsions of necessity and guilt. Certainly no such unequivocal Voice speaks to Antigone or Hamlet or Hester Prynne, who conclude the dark voyage in the light of their own unaided convictions, and live out their dilemmas to the end. But in these final scenes the tragic vision of the Poet is still active. Ambiguities remain, and the central question of the book is unanswered. Also, in the treatment of Job's pride, in the final revelation of how Job learned humility, in the irony with which the "happy ending" of the folk story is left to make its own statement, the Poet includes much that is relevant, as we can now see, to the tragic tradition.

At the end of his Oath of Clearance, Job had achieved a state of what Aristotle called catharsis. He had challenged the Almighty, made his case, and purged his spirit. He was in a

21

Hamlet-like state of readiness. In taking him beyond catharsis into abject repentance and self-abhorrence, the Poet makes of him a religious rather than a tragic figure; but the Poem as a whole makes an important statement about pride, which the Greeks were to make repeatedly, though from a different perspective. According to the Poet, and to the Greek tragedians, pride like Job's is justified. It has its ugly and dark side, but it was through pride that Job made his spiritual gains and got a hearing from Jehovah himself. The Lord favored Job's pride and rebuked the safe orthodoxy of the Counselors. The pride that moved Job is the dynamic of a whole line of tragic heroes, from Oedipus to Ahab. It is always ambiguous and often destructive, but it is the very hallmark of the type.[30]

Although the speech of Elihu (chs. 32–37) is generally regarded as not the work of the original Poet of Job, and although it repeats tiresomely much of what the other Counselors had said, it has the distinction of dealing not so much with Job's past sinfulness as with his present pride. Elihu, young, fiery, and a little pompous, is shocked that the Counselors have allowed Job in his pride to have the last word, and he sets out to humble him. Job's eyes have been blinded by pride, and his ears deafened: "For God speaketh once, yea twice, yet man perceiveth it not . . . he openeth the ears of men, and sealeth their instruction, that he may withdraw man from his purpose, and hide pride from man." "Why dost thou strive against him?" Elihu suggests a way of learning humility that is a curious blend of religious insight and the wisdom of tragedy. Job must see in God's chastisement not only discipline and a just judgment, but he must see that in his affliction there is "delivery"—through suffering he may learn: "He delivereth the afflicted by their affliction, and openeth their ear in oppression." [31] But not only this: Job must see with his own eyes. More than the other Counselors, Elihu turns Job's eyes outward. As if to prepare Job for the revelations of the Voice from the Whirlwind (in this respect Elihu's speech is a firm dramatic bridge between Job's "Oath of Clearance" and the climactic chapters of the book), Elihu asks him to contemplate the magnificence of the external universe. "Stand still," he says, "and consider the wondrous works of God." He rhapsodizes on the lightning, the thunder, and the wind; and he sees God's concern for men even in the snow, ice, cold, and rain,

> Whether it be for correction, or for his land,
> Or for lovingkindness . . . [32]

The main movement of Job's experience, from the morbid concern for his own suffering toward membership and partisanship in the human family, is extending even farther outward. He must now experience the Infinite or the Absolute. Even though in formal tragedy there is no such apocalypse as Job presently experiences, the direction is the same. Through suffering, as Aeschylus wrote, men learn—not only their littleness and sinfulness but the positive and creátive possibilities of themselves and the world they live in. They learn them, in *Job* as in later tragedy, not from Counselors or friends, but directly, on their pulses. As in the long debate with the Counselors Job made many discoveries about himself and the human realm, so now the Voice from the Whirlwind opens up for him the vast economy of the universe. In this new perspective, the question "Why did I suffer?" loses its urgency.

The question loses its urgency—Job never asks it again— but it is never answered. To the Poet, in contrast to the teaching of the Counselors or *The Book of Proverbs* or the first Psalm, the universe was not reasonable and not always just. He did not see it as a sunny and secure place for human beings, where to prosper one only has to be good. Even after the Voice ceased, Job was no nearer an understanding of what justice is than when he began his complaints. Unjustified suffering must be accepted as part of a mystery; it is not for man to reason why. The universe is a realm of infinite complexity and power, in which catastrophe may fall at any time on the just as well as the unjust. There may be enough moral cause-and-effect to satisfy the members of the chorus or the Counselors. But all the hero can do, if he is visited as Job was, is to persevere in the pride of his conviction, to appeal to God against God, and if he is as fortunate as Job, hear his questionings echo into nothingness in the infinite mystery and the glory.

Even the folk-story ending contains a tantalizing ambiguity. Few people go away happy at the end of *Job*, or if they do they miss the point. Of course, the sense of frustration is largely eliminated by Job's rewards. God is good; justice of a sort has been rendered; the universe seems secure. We are inclined to smile at how neatly it works out—the mathematical precision of the twofold restoration of Job's possessions and his perfectly balanced family, seven sons and three daughters —a sign perhaps that we are in the domain of something less elevated than Divine Comedy. But the universe seems secure only to those who do not question too far. Can a new family make up for the one Job lost? What about the faithful servants who fell to the Sabeans and Chaldeans? These questions the folk story ignores, and its reassuring final picture also makes it easy to forget Job's suffering and his unanswered question. Although the irony of the folk conclusion seems unmistakable, it was no doubt this easy piety, like the pious emendations to the bitterness of Ecclesiastes, that made *The Book of Job* acceptable to the orthodox for centuries. Actually, it is a "dangerous" book.[33] Although the Hebrews had their recalcitrant figures, capable, like the Poet of Job, of deep penetration into the realm of tragedy, they are rightly regarded as the people of a Covenant, a Code, and a Book. This is one reason, perhaps, why they never developed a tragic theater, where their beliefs and modes of living would be under constant scrutiny. Their public communication was through synagogue and pulpit; their prophets and preachers proclaimed the doctrine of obedience to divine law, and the rabbis endlessly proliferated the rules for daily life. The rebellious Job was not typical. For the most part, their heroes were lonely, God-summoned men whose language was that of witness to the one true light.

3

OEDIPUS THE KING

THAT no such light shone upon the Greeks is a clue at once to the nature of their tragic vision and to the form in which it found expression in their drama. Both vision and form differ in important ways from the Hebraic, reflecting basic differences in the two cultures. Indeed, western culture has often been regarded, especially since Matthew Arnold's famous distinction between Hebraism and Hellenism, as an uneasy dualism of Hebraic mysticism and moral intensity, and the more expansive and humane tendencies of the Greeks. On the one hand are prophet, preacher, and pulpit; on the other, philosopher, scientist, artist, and theater. But the tragic voice of the two peoples is in important ways one. In both it proceeds from the existential vision, the radical response to the life-situation, and in both it is an aspect of the religious consciousness. Suffering is inquired into, made articulate, and creatively appropriated. There is (characteristically) the same centering of meaning in the symbolic hero, whose suffering and discovery provide the structural pattern. The mood is one of exploration and anxiety, and the accomplished form speaks through dilemma and ambiguity.

But Greek dramatists achieved a technical medium, of course, more supple, flexible, and inclusive than the confessional-homiletic style of *Job*. They wrote under different skies and in a climate more favorable to the full development of the tragic form. The humanistic focus of their culture, the peculiar relationship between men and gods, and the institution of the

25

theater sent their achievement far beyond the one full-scale Hebraic tragic achievement of *The Book of Job.*

Compared with the orthodox Hebrew universe, that of the Greeks was stark. They had no One God, no Code, Covenant, or sacred Scriptures. Though they knew their gods had a part in every breeze that blew, in every vital force, and in every human action, the nature of the divine participation in human affairs was unpredictable. There was cause for thanksgiving, as over a happy birth, a safe voyage, or a good harvest; but no one knew why at any moment happiness or safety or plenty might be denied. The ways of the gods were reflected in the precarious and uncertain conditions of existence. Legend told of changes of dynasty even in heaven. Though some gods behaved better than others toward men, the Greeks expected perfect justice from none of them. Even the wise Athena, in the famous case of Orestes, based her vote not on the merits of the case but on personal grounds. In such a universe, one must proceed warily and avoid extremes. Piety consisted in doing nothing to anger the gods, and in pleasing, or appeasing, them through offerings. They were not jealous as Jehovah was jealous when he commanded the Hebrews to have no other gods before him, but often in petty, human ways. They liked gifts, they hated to be jilted, and they worked off their spite shamelessly on mortals or on each other. Except for a hero like Odysseus or Orestes, who for his qualities was favored by god or goddess as ordinary men were not, a Greek's fondest wish was that the gods would leave him alone. A Greek could take no comfort in considering himself as made in the image of God, only a little lower than the angels, and part of a divine, just, and beneficent Creation. Fate, to which in a mysterious way the gods themselves were subject, was an impersonal force decreeing ultimate things only, and unconcerned with day-by-day affairs.[34]

Beyond this, Greek theology did not go. The State could regulate religious festivals and in time of political tension try a Socrates for "atheism." But, as Charles Seltman has pointed out,[35] there was no rabbinate or priestly hierarchy or Church militant to teach or preach or declare dogmatic truth. Socrates was simply a troublesome critic and alleged misleader of youth. The Homeric tales helped mold and guide the Greek imagination, but each individual, each new poet or philosopher, made of them what he could. They contained many useful truths—how heroes behaved, what the heroic virtues were, and how to be a good Greek—but not The Truth of revelation. The Greeks could be said to have had an "open society" as the Hebrews, with their Decalogue and prophecy, did not.

This "dangerous freedom" added a unique terror to the Greek tragic vision but at the same time made the Greek drama possible. The terror lay in this: that, in extremity, individual man was singularly unaccommodated and alone; he could not trust in the goodness of God or abide under the shadow of the Almighty; he could expect no recompense for a blameless life, nor, if he had sinned, could he put any hope, like Job's Counselors, in repentance and a contrite heart. But if there was no such orthodoxy to comfort and sustain, there was none, either, to confine or circumscribe. Greek culture nourished, as the Hebraic did not, an atmosphere peculiarly hospitable to drama, which became at its height an important medium of instruction in the deepest matters of human life and destiny. Here the Greek could witness the disparate elements of his life brought together in a viable aesthetic—if not moral—synthesis. What the materials of Greek religion—myth, legend, folklore—did with these disparate elements was so contradictory or sketchy that for the thoughtful Greek (Seltman suggests) it must have given cause for little more than "quiet speculation or gentle amusement." [36] But the very formlessness of these materials gave good cause, also, to the Greek tragic theater, where in the presence of the gods themselves the tragedies brought them into formal and vital relationship with the affairs of men. The poets submitted their culture to the same critical and creative process that the Poet of Job had exercised on the folk story. Out of the contradictions and conflicting claims of legend and myth, which in actual practice they saw making havoc of the lives of men, they too hammered out a new form.

From internal evidence, at least, the tragedies are witness to a "tragic moment" in Greek history similar to that discernible in *Job*. Like all such moments, it is to be accounted for in no simple terms. The political and social reforms of Pisistratus in the Sixth Century strengthened Athens in all ways, and gave it a new sense of its dignity and power. His encouragement of the arts and the institution of the great festivals, at which, in the next century, the dramatic contests were held, prepared the way externally for tragedy. The victory at Marathon gave to the Athenians the same spur and tonic that Elizabethan England knew after the Armada. National vitality and nerve, essential to creativeness of any sort, were high. The threat from the east, though successfully overcome, brought about a crisis in Athenian affairs in which, as in any war-situation, traditional values were brought into new focus; a new way of thinking and a new self-consciousness emerged. Athenian democracy under Pericles, who built the Parthenon and the Propylaea and counted Sophocles among his friends, provided the ideal milieu for their expression. Untold new possibilities were at hand, new discoveries imminent. In war, politics, trade, and the manual arts, the Greeks were learning what they could do; they were preparing to learn from the tragedians (and the philosophers) who they were.

But the immediate situation does not alone account for what Greek tragedy actually said when Aeschylus, in the early years of the fifth century, began writing plays. Also, there is little in pre-Aeschylean literature that could be regarded as preparing for the tragedies, as the long tradition of "dissent" in Old Testament literature could be said to have prepared for Job. It is thought that Aeschylus built formal tragedy on the simple structure of village folk drama and Dionysiac song, which gave expression in some of their phases to the folk sense of affliction and of the need to propitiate the powers that brought it. His famous addition of the second actor was a gain not only in technique but in substance; it made dramatic action possible, of course, but more important it showed that Aeschylus recognized a kind of truth—"tragic" truth—that can be conveyed only through dramatic action, or the dialectic, as we have called it, of the play. In Homer he had at hand ample "tragic" truth, as well as examples of superb narrative and dramatic writing. But again, there is little in Homer to account for the peculiar treatment Aeschylus gave his materials. Simone Weil, whose essay on the *Iliad* is unsurpassed in its insight into the tragic aspect of Homer, shows the world of that epic as dominated by force, blind and mechanical, which reduces men to things and destroys them indiscriminately. Through indirections—image, metaphor, the stark recording of so many fatal actions—Homer gives a sense of loss and waste and doom, even while he shows his heroes as capable of courage and loyalty, and his gods as often benign. But human suffering is in general presented as unrelated and haphazard. There is no frontal assault on underlying causes, no sense that the future can differ from the past or present.[37] No Homeric hero asks Job's radical questions. "We men are wretched things," says Achilles wearily, "and the gods who have no cares themselves have woven sorrow into the very pattern of our lives." [38] Simone Weil says truly that, although the question of justice "enlightens" the *Iliad*, it never "directly intervenes in it." [39] For some reason, perhaps to be explained as much by the radical vision of a single man as by external conditions or pressures, the question of justice came strikingly to the fore in the Greek tragic drama. Aeschylus, in major insights so much like the Poet of Job that he has been called the most Hebraic of the Greek tragedians, was the first to subject the idea of justice to the full dialectic of action. It became a recurrent theme in all Greek tragedy, from *Prometheus* and the *Oresteia* to *Medea* and *The Bacchae*. The question "Why does man suffer?", was seen to lead to all other questions, and thence to the nature and destiny of man.

Without the Hebraic effort toward transcendence—"I will lift up mine eyes unto the hills"—and the obsessive sense of guilt which, as with Job, tended toward introversion, the Greek vision focused on the immediacy of experience, and on the nature of man, more sharply and objectively than did the Hebraic. The three tragedians are true to their Homeric background in this respect, that they keep a sharp eye on the present. Though the radical, metaphysical question "Why?" is implicit, and often explicit, in all their fictions, the dramatic medium in which they worked kept their attention centered on the "who," the "what," and the "how" of the action.

29

Aeschylus, the most theological and moral, presses the stark and bloody legends toward some degree of resolution or harmony between gods and men. He would wring at least some approximation of justice from the adventurer-gods. His Job-like Prometheus calls upon the heavens to be more just—and (if we can trust what tradition records about the last acts of the trilogy) they were. At the end of the *Oresteia* tensions and ambiguities remain, but Athena finally intercedes to cast some light on the dark ways of men. In the dialectical pressures, in "the constant grinding conflict" of the trilogy's action, human character is revealed as no Greek before Aeschylus revealed it. The dark ways are plotted thoroughly. But for all their enormous vitality and depth, the characters have a static quality, slip a little too easily into categories, and seem manipulated toward a preconceived general truth—and a truth that leads beyond, or above, tragedy.

Again, if it were not for Euripides' depth of insight and sure sense of values, it could be said that he looks the other way, below tragedy. He shows in grueling detail the disintegration of human character or the wreck of human lives under the stresses which the gods seem willfully and cruelly to place upon them. In every action, every passion, every step he takes, man is vulnerable. The gods may wreck him for their sport or their jealousy, or sit idly by while he wrecks himself. Euripides makes it clear where the major blame lies; in such a world the ideal of justice is ironic, and man's freedom is marginal.

Sophocles, often called the purest artist of the three, seems truest to the "givenness," the one most inclined to leave the question open. Aeschylus never begs the question, but he moves beyond it toward mysticism and revelation; and Euripides' tendency is toward nihilism and denial. Sophocles neither preaches nor rails. In the destructive element, he would say (with Conrad's Stein), "How to be?" Man is free but fated, fated but free. In the boundary-situation what happens? What qualities does he reveal? Through suffering what does he learn—not about the gods, for they are simply "given," but about himself? Let us carry out the action (Sophocles seems to say) to its uttermost limits, explore the farthest reaches of human possibilities; only then can we pose the question of justice. If the answer is "tragic," it is at the same time heroic—in a way which Sophocles (and Homer) peculiarly defined. *Oedipus the King* is Sophocles' farthest penetration into these mysteries, and the nuclear Greek tragedy.

The story of Oedipus, like the story of Job, is of a man plunged suddenly from prosperity and power to ruin and ignominy. We see both heroes at the height and the depth of their worldly fortunes. Oedipus, whom in the first scene the Priest calls "the first of men," to whom all knees are bent, is at the end polluted, blind, banished from the land he ruled and loved and from the people who lovingly obeyed him. Job had complained of his former friends, "They abhor me, they flee from me," and this was to be part of Oedipus' anguish. Both stories raise the same problem and state it in its extreme form: is there justice in a world where, for no reason clear to the ethical understanding, the worst happens to the best? ("That inscrutable thing," cried Ahab, "is chiefly what I hate.") [40] Oedipus, no more than Job, could be held accountable for his sufferings. He had faults, like Job, of temper and pride, and he made mistakes in judgment. But Sophocles does not present him as, a priori, a guilty man. The slaying of his father was done in ambiguous circumstances and in ignorance of Laius' identity, nor did he know that Jocasta was his mother when he married her. The play, like Job, presents a mystery— the stubborn and destructive stuff of experience as man meets it "on the way." Why do such things happen? All attempts to rationalize the play, to remove "the secret cause," fail. Oedipus' search for his own identity is of course capable of large extension. "Who am I?" is a variant of Job's "What is man?" and the answer is not that Oedipus is a sinner being punished by righteous gods, or an innocent man being destroyed by malign gods, or a man trapped by subconscious sexual jealousy of his father, or—as the Chorus says finally— a man who is better off dead. [41] The answer, as in *The Book of Job*, is in all that Oedipus says, does, and becomes; all that each lesser character and the Chorus say and do and do not become; all that is implicit in image and metaphor; all that is revealed through the rapid and relentless dialectic of the action.

As with *Job*, no analysis can convey more than a part of the rich meaning of the play. What emerges is not a doctrine or a system; it is rather an impression or sense of life. The hard, discrete particularities are brought into a kind of unity, but it is ambiguous, precarious, unfinal. We are left with images that cling, that fascinate and horrify, attract and repel, whose meanings cannot be stated precisely or ever fully reckoned. The meanings change and accrue with the advancing action—and afterwards in our thoughts. Sophocles, accepting the terms of Oedipus' situation as in the old story, sets him free, though fated, as the Poet set Job free to "open his mouth" in the midst of his afflictions. Oedipus speaks as much through actions as words, and the precise or full meaning of what he does is forever beyond our reach. What mysterious dynamic within him impels him to pursue his quest so tenaciously? No god was at his shoulder, as when Apollo told Orestes to murder his mother. Why did he blind himself? As he gives reason after reason, each one loses its cogency. At the end of the play much remains to praise, much to blame, and much to wonder at. What we thought impossible has happened. The destructive element has yielded more than destruction.

The first of the images that cling, and the play's first intimation of the human condition, is the plague-stricken city of Thebes. It stands to the play as the afflictions of Job stand to *The Book of Job*. It is the permanent backdrop of the play, the steady reminder of the precariousness of our lot, of the blight man was born for. The play opens at the point of crisis in the city's affairs. Normal life is suspended and survival is threatened. Prayer and sacrifice have been unavailing. The people turn in despair to Oedipus, who saved them from a similar fate once before. But against this setting another situation unfolds, involving Oedipus not as king and savior but as an individual human being, a situation so horrible in its possibilities that the people, engrossed in this new revelation, all but forget their own afflictions. In this doubly destructive element, Sophocles has set his protagonist, Oedipus or the "Oedipus-idea" (which is Man), free, like Job, to run the full dialectical gamut, in order to test him not only against the brute stuff of fate but against all the standard human pressures and claims, within and without: the unruly passions and compulsions which, like Job's, twist his course this way and that, and the conflicting, distracting voices of his fellow beings, each with its own claim and justification. The course differs from Job's. The dramatist leads Oedipus gradually toward the ultimate test, and much is revealed on the way. Without Job's peculiar sense of religious dependence and yearning, Oedipus is more on his own. He walks a lonelier path, through a starker world. What he finally does and says and becomes is the product of his own human stuff. And like all human stuff as seen in the tragic vision, it is a strange mixture of guilt and innocence, beauty and ugliness, goods and bads "inseparably together and forever."

But first, save for Oedipus' brief opening interrogation, we hear the voice of the suppliant citizens, speaking through the Priest. Out of their own helplessness they have come to appeal to Oedipus to rid them of the "fiery demon gripping the city." They are the poor and oppressed (for whom Job had compassion), the eternal, pathetic victims "as long as the world lasts," and they can only report and lament the dark world they find themselves in.

> Sorrows beyond all telling—
> Sickness rife in our ranks, outstripping
> Invention of remedy—blight
> On barren earth,
> And barren agonies of birth—
> Life after life from the wild-fire singing
> Swiftly into the night.[42]

"All's dark," they cry (in the second Ode); "we fear, but we cannot see, what is before us." In their lamentations, they do not once question the nature of things. Like the Job of the folk story, they keep the faith. They accept immediately the Oracle's explanation that their land is polluted by the presence of the slayer of Laius, and long for his capture. But they never

33

suggest that the terrible pestilence is unjust to them. In the third Ode, when, to add to their anxieties, the awful truth about Oedipus is becoming clear, even then they say:

> I only ask to live, with pure faith keeping
> In word and deed that Law which leaps the sky . . .

And the Law they refer to is the grim, retributive justice of the gods against presuming mankind, the law which (they think) can be neither questioned nor outdone.

It is hard to imagine a set of conditions more likely to produce a complete spiritual upheaval than that which they face. Their domestic world is in ruins, obviously the work of the unseen powers. Oedipus, who had been their one hope, the man who could do no wrong, is now the target of dreadful suspicions which, if true, would spell his downfall and threaten the stability of the State. The angry exchanges between Oedipus and Teiresius show leadership as all but bankrupt. Oedipus reveals ominous qualities they hardly could have expected, if we can judge by their earlier homage and supplication. In the encounter with Creon, Oedipus is even more arrogant and suspicious and hot-tempered, until Jocasta has to separate them like quarreling children. These shocking revelations lead the Chorus only to reiterate the old, hard doctrine of *hubris* and to call piously upon Zeus.

> Who walks his own high-handed way, disdaining
> True righteousness and holy ornament;
> Who falsely wins, all sacred things profaning;
> Shall he escape his doomed pride's punishment? . .

> Zeus! If thou livest, all-ruling, all-pervading,
> Awake; old oracles are out of mind;
> Apollo's name denied, his glory fading;
> There is no godliness in all minkind.

The present experience merely confirms their stock knowledge, that he who would grasp for more than the common lot invites the correction of the gods.

It is to their credit, perhaps, that when they see Oedipus in the final scene, blood streaming from his eyes, their moraliz-

ing is stifled by their horror and compassion. Perhaps they see
that it does not quite fit the case; their tact, at least, is superior
to that of Job's Counselors. But still there is no outcry against
the gods, only two brief queries.

> Horror beyond all bearing!
> Foulest disfigurement
> That ever I saw! O cruel,
> Insensate agony!
> What demon of destiny
> With swift assault outstriding
> Has ridden you down? . . .

> Those eyes—how could you do what you have done?
> What evil power has driven you to this end?

The suddenness of Oedipus' fall, the twofold nature of his
suffering—"once in the body and once in the soul"—and the
name rather than the nature of the evil power that goaded
him on: these are the limits of the Chorus' response to the
awful things they have witnessed. Their final comment, which
is the last speech of the play, shows them numbed and nihilistic. "Behold: this was Oedipus, greatest of men." This is life;
no man is happy until he is dead.

But the simple, syllogistic response of the Chorus, like
that of Job's wife, is only a part of the complicated synthesis
of the play, only one possible response to the hard truth of
existence. It is only one of the many images or voices, which,
interacting, qualifying one another, welling up from and defining the central action of the play, contribute to the total
meaning. To the questions "How to be?" "In the destructive
element, what becomes a man?" the answer of the Chorus is
plaintive and unheroic. As an inevitable part of Oedipus'
racial consciousness it must be regarded as, for him, too, a
constant compelling alternative to action. It is stated most
stridently by Jocasta when she sees where Oedipus' action is
leading: "In God's name," she cries, "if you want to live, this
quest must not go on." Like Job, Oedipus turns a deaf ear to
such counsel: "I must pursue this trail to the end."

To the Greeks, every action was a risk because it might

invite the displeasure of a god; but, such was the tragic aspect of existence, man had to act. Great actions, the kind about which tragedies were written, involved great risks; and, since they inevitably involved a degree of *hubris*, they were ambiguous. Oedipus had always been a man of action. He had killed a man, not (as Sophocles has him describe the circumstances) altogether unjustly. He had violated no graven Law about killing; the victim happened to 'be his father and a king, and for these facts alone does Oedipus admit his pollution. Again, he had solved the riddle of the Sphinx, a "good" act, except that, as we see him in the opening scene, he is ominously confident of his ability to solve all other riddles. His marriage to the king's widow had been approved by the people and entered into only after he thought himself free and clear of the Oracle's prophecy. The Chorus had rejoiced in his action in the crisis of the Sphinx, and they longed for his active help in their present need. But as the truth unfolds and they see him as prideful and overweening, they apparently wish that he had not acted at all. They even call on Zeus to correct his pride.

But the play as a whole does not pass this judgment. It presents Oedipus' actions, past and present, in all their multiple meanings—and one meaning is that such actions as his cannot be prejudged, or judged so simply. *Hubris* is not "sin." It is the mysterious dynamic of all tragic action, dangerous because it involves a challenge to the powers that be, but not (in the tragic view) morally good or bad. It may lead to destruction—indeed, it so often has that the folk will have none of it; but without it, no man acts or suffers or learns. And it is the distinctive mark of the hero. Jocasta, urging Oedipus to desist, asks, "Have I not suffered enough?" But in determining to pursue the trail to the end, to take all risks and bear all consequences, Oedipus sets himself apart from her, the Chorus, and all others around him. The hero of epic (by way of contrast) takes a different sort of risk and invites a different sort of suffering. He would sack a city, or found one, and he faces the possibility of failure. He stands to lose friends, kinsmen, and his own life. But his goal is external and clear; and though he may be tempted, there is no doubt about what

36

his choice should be. His suffering has little in it of dilemma or enigma; it is not, characteristically, spiritual suffering. In continuing the quest of his own identity, Oedipus (like Job) defies the best advice of his time and plunges into a darkness. He knows he is not wholly right, but proceed he must. A man without *hubris* would have humbly acquiesced in his fate and let it unfold as it would. There would have been no significant action. Oedipus wants to wrench from fate its full truth, and at once. He will take whatever comes, and so he acts.

Oedipus' action, his relentless pursuit of the truth about the slayer of Laius, culminating in the cataclysmic stroke of his self-blinding, stirs from their long-dormant state a host of loyalties and disloyalties, beliefs and disbeliefs, goods and evils; sets them in new perspective; and reveals new and more endurable truth about them. His action sets other actions going, some mean, some beautiful, both in himself and others. Each action reveals the doer more clearly for what he is, and the world he lives in more clearly for what it is. Oedipus' own qualities of suspicion, arrogance, and temper, which worry the Chorus and infuriate Teiresias and Creon, appear in a different light as these actions unfold, no more definitive of his character than Job's early bitterness and despair defined Job.

Teiresias (the first to be drawn into the action), though justly indignant (as far as the play tells us) at Oedipus' threats and accusations, appears as a good prophet but no hero. For pity's sake he would have withheld the truth and retained the status quo. Better for man not to know either the worst or the best about his nature. Teiresias is a specialist and a conservative. His business is to tell the future, not to comment on it. We hear from him nothing more about the justice of Oedipus' lot than from the Chorus. Creon, too, speaks rightly in his own defense against the angry charges of Oedipus. But he too is a specialist, and his speciality is circumspection. He is the professional moderate. Why should he have plotted against Oedipus when he is entirely satisfied with his life as it is? "What more could any moderate man desire?" he asks Oedipus. "I stand in all men's favour, I am all men's friend." His defense is his record and his character: middle of the road, safe and sane. After Oedipus' self-blinding, he conducts him-

37

self, and the situation, correctly, firmly, and with some compassion, but no more than prudence permits. It seems little
more than another episode to him, his first problem as king.

Jocasta is the central figure in this pattern of evasion in
which Oedipus himself operates up to a certain point. Her
first action, at Oedipus' birth, was to expose the child on the
slopes of Mt. Cithaeron in an effort to escape the prophecy
of the Oracle. Though no Greek could have told her whether
the action was right or wrong, he might have told her it was
useless. Neither she nor Oedipus, when he tried to evade the
prophecy by judicious change of residence, seems to have
been involved in serious impiety. No one accuses them of trying to controvert the will of the gods. In the final scene, this
theme is strikingly absent from the comments of the Chorus;
and when Oedipus questions Creon's suggestion of consulting
the oracle about what to do with him, he is met only with this
terse rejoinder, "Now even you will trust the God." But during
the rising action of the play, Jocasta's wifely concern was to
keep Oedipus from trouble, to still his worries; and so she
persistently tried to discount the authority of the Oracle. The
closer Oedipus gets to the truth, the more frantic she becomes;
until, in her moment of jubilation when the Messenger reports
the death of Polybus, Oedipus' supposed father, she slips into
a cynicism which denies all divine order whatever:

> Fear? What has a man to do with fear?
> Chance rules our lives, and the future is all unknown.
> Best live as best we may, from day to day.
> Nor need this mother-marrying frighten you;
> Many a man has dreamt as much. Such things
> Must be forgotten, if life is to be endured.

Oedipus, though tempted under the first shock of Teiresias' charge and, later, by Jocasta's blandishments, never goes
so far. The charge that he was Laius' slayer had come suddenly, like Job's afflictions, and had had the same unbalancing
effect. Oedipus had struck back in a fury of self-protection.
The reverent tones in which he had first addressed Teiresias
as the all-knowing prophet, "our only help and protector,"

had turned suddenly to vituperation and countercharge. As with Job, the black bile of his nature had been started. But, again like Job, it was not long before he gained control of himself. In the midst of his destiny, he asserts his freedom. He proceeds like a prosecuting attorney against himself, ferreting out the truth from every bit of evidence. Not one hint will he reject, not one bit of the prophecy—like "this mother-marrying"—will he ignore. He would like to have agreed with his wife:

> If she [my mother] were dead, you might have spoken so
> With justice; but she lives; and while she lives,
> Say what you will, I cannot cease to fear.

But he is soon past the point of temptation: "I cannot leave the truth unknown." When finally the truth *is* known, the ultimate distinction is made between him and Jocasta. Unable to accept the terms of so horrible a reality, she makes the supreme evasion of taking her life. Oedipus lives on to bear out his destiny to the end.

In all this, the question of justice—the justice of Oedipus' fate—is not once directly raised, even by Oedipus himself, who of all the people in the play would seem to have had the right to raise it. Twice he comes close. Early in the play, when he first becomes aware of his vulnerable state, he says:

> Can it be any but some monstrous god
> Of evil that has sent this doom upon me?

And in the final scene when the Chorus asks him why he put out his eyes, his answer is, "Apollo laid this agony upon me." But there is no such open defiance of the heavens as in Job's complaints or in Prometheus' quarrel with Zeus. Instead of Prometheus' thundering "I was wronged!" Oedipus accepts his fate: "Be it so." He is like all the others in the play (even the Chorus) in feeling, apparently, the futility of verbal protest.

But there is no doubt of the desperate injustice which the play as a whole presents. As Kitto points out, the injustice done to Oedipus is the apex of a pyramid of ironies and injustices—and of the most grievous kind: evil happens to those who intend the best.[43] Out of pity the Shepherd spared the infant Oedipus—for such a fate. The Messenger, thinking to bring the best news, brought the worst. Teiresias wished to remain silent but was forced to speak. Jocasta, thinking to allay her husband's fears, dropped the one hint—that the killing of Laius took place where three roads met—which set in operation the whole train of events. Oedipus, searching for the slayer of Laius for the good of his city, brought ruin upon himself, death to his queen, and the prospect of a dreary life for his daughters. In the play no word is said about the efficacy of his sacrifice; no one thanks him for it, nor is he consoled by thoughts of martyrdom. Though Oedipus has faults of temper, no character in the play consciously does evil; and yet all suffer. The general disaster is as uncalled for as it seems crushing.

No play ever presented more starkly the terms of existence, "what it means to be." The messenger who reports Oedipus' blinding might well have spoken for the whole play: "All ills that there are names for—all are here." And yet such is the effect of Oedipus' action that the final impression is not of unmixed evil. Although Oedipus never questions the justice of the gods, he *does* something about it—and, as it were, outdoes it. The sustained action of his quest and the culminating action of his self-blinding set all the other actions, including those of the gods, in a new light. The disparate elements are reordered and recomposed. There emerges a clear hierarchy of values around which man can reorganize his ways—as when, through Antigone's heroic action, the whole Theban society re-forms behind her, or when Hamlet purges Elsinore. And the principles around which the new synthesis takes place are two: man's freedom and his capacity to learn.

Why did Oedipus put out his eyes? Like Job's action it has "magnitude" and is heavy with ambiguities. The scene which the Messenger reports is the most horrible and the most enigmatic of the play: Oedipus snatching the brooches from the bodice of his dead wife and plunging them "from full arm's length" into his eyes, "time and time again,"

40

> Till bloody tears rain down his beard—not drops
> But in full spate a whole cascade descending
> In drenching cataracts of scarlet ruin.

Why this fearful image? Its surface function in the play is relatively clear. It fulfills the prophecy of Teiresias that "He that came seeing, blind shall he go," clinching the ironic theme of the blind Seer who could not, and the King who would not, see. Its very horror shows the ironic inadequacy of the Chorus' final response. Oedipus' own motives are far from clear. He says that he did it to spare himself the sight of the ugliness he had caused, that he could not bring himself to face the people on whom he had brought such suffering. In *Oedipus at Colonus* he tells his son that he did it in a moment of frenzy and not from a sense of guilt. When the Chorus, in the present play, asks him directly why he did it, he says that Apollo had a hand in it. Again, he says he did it so that he might not meet eye-to-eye his father or his mother "beyond the grave." No one reason suffices, nor all of them put together. The act seems compounded of opposite elements: egotism and altruism, self-loathing and self-glorification. As an act of destruction, it shows man at his worst. To the extent that it was "determined," it shows the gods at their worst. But as an act of freedom, it turns out to be curiously creative in unexpected ways, and shows man at his best. What Oedipus insists upon in his reply to the Chorus is that the act was his own:

> Apollo, friends, Apollo,
> Has laid this agony upon me;
> Not by his hand; I did it.

Whatever he may have thought he was doing, the act stands in the play as his culminating act of freedom, the assertion of his ability to act independent of any god, oracle, or prophecy.

The "creativeness" of the act is all that is imaged in the final scene, the colloquy with Creon and the farewell to the daughters, and, as Sophocles was to present it years later, Oedipus' apotheosis in *Oedipus at Colonus*. It lies in all that Oedipus learned, about himself and his world, and in all the

41

others learned in this and the final play. The shrewd "reckoner" (as Bernard Knox shows [44]), for whom at first riddles were easy, in this final reckoning finds that the answer to the question of the city's suffering is himself. The root (Sophocles seems to be saying) is man, and the gods who preside over his destiny have little care for whatever agony he may endure to achieve this knowledge. There is no use seeking any justice in the process, nor does the knowledge, which is hard and "tragic," necessarily compensate for the suffering.

But the knowledge may make the terms of existence more endurable. It brings a greater humility, as in Oedipus' apology and deference to Creon in the final scene and, in the opening scene of *Colonus*, the quiet permissiveness of the once headstrong king, now schooled by suffering. With humility come compassion and a new tenderness—which Lear learned and Ahab rejected. The final image of Oedipus, full of concern for his daughters even as he faces his wretched future, is in sharp contrast to the overconfident and slightly pompous figure of the opening scenes. To those who had looked closely, his limp, as he strode to greet the suppliant citizens, might have been (as Francis Fergusson suggested) telltale; but he must have seemed to them, as he seemed to himself, all-in-all sufficient. Even then, he did not deserve his fate. The important fact is that when it came, he accepted it, acted in accordance with it, and ultimately was saved by it. It was not a Christian salvation, nor were his new humility and love what the Christian understands by these virtues. He is still Oedipus; he still (as he shows at Colonus) believes in himself and is capable of hating his enemies. He is in no sense "born again." But he has enlarged his domain as a human being. He has a new sense of the powers that shape human destiny. Even, like Job, he has a new sense of kinship with them: in *Oedipus at Colonus* he tells Creon that death will not soon take him, that he feels "preserved for some more awful destiny"—the mysterious finale at Colonus.

At the end of the present play, the Chorus look on him with pity and awe, but with loathing. They avoid his blind, groping arms. He is unclean, polluted, and he himself urges Creon to banish him at once, to free the city of his vileness. This is done with dispatch, after a none-too-generous moment of farewell with his daughters: "This is enough," says Creon. "Will you go in?" The Chorus conclude the play with their warning to those who believed they had "solved the riddle" and that felicity was permanent. But at the end of *Colonus,* when Oedipus' full stature is established, the tone is different. Loathing becomes reverence; the moralizing of the Chorus has no more place in the scene than the pious maxims of Job's Counselors after the Voice from the Whirlwind speaks. Although it is perhaps wrong to read the two plays in strict tandem, since many years separated their composition and conditions had changed, the later play has traditionally been regarded as a comment on the earlier, or even an answer to it. In the second play, it is said, the gods make up to Oedipus for their injustice in the first. But the gods, as Cedric Whitman points out, actually have little to do with it. In the second play, Oedipus still risks, suffers, and achieves a more-than-human status through the exertion of his own human capacities—and not through a god's grace. If the apotheosis of Oedipus, like Job's final vision, takes us beyond the realm of tragedy, we still see, in the final scene of the bereaved daughters, real suffering and real loss, mitigated only by the new insight into human capacities which the hero has revealed.

4

THE TRAGIC FORM

THE vision of tragedy as it is revealed through the fully developed form should now be clear. *Job* and *Oedipus* do not exhaust the possibilities, of course; Kitto's book (among others) shows how many distinctions should be made by the specialist on Greek tragedy alone. But in the search for essences these two works are central. Values have been incremental, but each new tragic protagonist (for instance) is in some degree a lesser Job or Oedipus, and each new work owes an indispensable element to the Counselors and to the Greek idea of the chorus. I wish, in this brief interchapter, to restate in summary form the constants of tragedy we have so far established. But first a word about some of the differences between *Job* and *Oedipus* and about the relevance of these differences to the subsequent tradition.

The Book of Job, especially the Poet's treatment of the suffering and searching Job, is behind Shakespeare and Milton, Melville, Dostoevski, and Kafka. Its mark is on all tragedy of alienation, from Marlowe's Faustus to Camus' Stranger, in which there is a sense of separation from a once known, normative, and loved deity or cosmic order or principle of conduct. In emphasizing dilemma, choice, wretchedness of soul, and guilt, it spiritualized the Promethean theme of Aeschylus and made it more acceptable to the Christianized imagination. In working into one dramatic context so great a range of mood—from pessimism and despair to bitterness, defiance, and exalted insight—it is father to all tragedy where the stress is on the inner dynamics of man's response to destiny.

Oedipus stresses not so much man's guilt or forsakenness as his ineluctable lot, the stark realities which are and always will be. The Greek tradition is less nostalgic and less visionary —the difference being in emphasis, not in kind. There is little pining for a lost Golden Age, or yearning for utopia, redemption, or heavenly restitution. But if it stresses man's fate, it does not deny him freedom. Dramatic action, of course, posits freedom; without it no tragedy could be written. In Aeschylus' *Prometheus* Kratos (or Power) says, "None is free but Zeus," but the whole play proves him wrong. Even the Chorus of helpless Sea Nymphs, in siding with Prometheus in the end, defy the bidding of the gods. Aeschylus' Orestes was told by Apollo to murder his mother, but he was not compelled to. The spirit with which he acquiesced in his destiny (a theme which Greek tragedy stresses as *Job* does not) is of a free man who, though fated, could have withdrawn and not acted at all. Even Euripides, who of all the Greek tragedians had the direst view of the gods' compulsiveness in man's affairs, shows his Medea and Hippolytus as proud and decisive human beings. And, as Cedric Whitman says about the fate of Oedipus, the prophecy merely predicted Oedipus' future, it did not determine it. Had Oedipus wished to escape his prophesied future, he might have killed himself on first hearing of it or never killed a man or never married. The fact that he acted at all, with such a curse hanging over him, explains why, perhaps, he is not entirely a stranger to guilt. But the fact remains that Oedipus presides over that mode of tragedy less concerned with judgment (eschatology) than with being (ontology), less with ultimate things than with things here and now; less with man and the gods as they should be than with man and the gods as they are.

In the Christian era, except for an occasional academic exercise or tour de force, there has been no tragedy identifiable as pure Hebraic or pure Greek. When the writers of the Renaissance found models and guides in Greek tragedy, in Aristotle, and in Seneca, they came to them with imaginations inevitably Christianized. What resulted from the amalgam of Hebraic, Greek, and Christian was still a third mode of tragedy—"Christian tragedy"—which added to the traditional

45

modes its own peculiar tensions and stresses. What remained constant and compelling was the ancient tragic treatment of evil; of suffering; and the suggestion of certain values that may mitigate if not redeem.

Evil. The Greek tragedies, the imitations of them by Seneca, and the freer, more humanistic reading of the Old Testament, especially *Job,* brought to the men of the Renaissance not only the aesthetic delight and challenge of beautifully ordered structures and of richly poetic language but a sense of common cause in the face of insoluble mystery that centuries of Christian piety could not still. The Greek plays and *Job,* the products of long traditions and sophisticated cultures, spoke to latent anxieties and doubts which the Renaissance, itself a sophisticated culture and the product of a long tradition, was, in the general "freeing of the imagination" of that period, beginning to seek means of expressing more fully. The Greek plays and *Job* presented a view of the universe, of man's destiny and his relation with his fellows and himself, in which evil, though not total, is real, ever threatening, and ineluctable. They explored the area of chaos in the human heart and its possibility in the heavens. They faced the facts of cruelty, failure, frustration, and loss, and anatomized suffering with shocking thoroughness but with tonic honesty. The Greeks affirmed absolutes like justice and order, but revealed a universe which promised neither and often dealt out the reverse. The Poet of Job showed a universe suddenly gone astray and brought it back to an uneasy balance only by appeal to a religious revelation—and not before giving a full view of his great protagonist, alone and embittered, forced unjustly into a "boundary-situation" not of his own making, where his only real help was himself. In the thirty-two surviving Greek tragedies, in the length of Job's complaints, and in the lesser examples of Hebraic literature of the same cast, this basic theme of the "dark problem" appears in many guises and in varying degrees of emphasis. The focus shifts, but the vision is constant. The range and power of its manifestation in the Hebraic poem and the Greek plays established it as the informing element of tragedy. A way had been found of giving the fullest account of all the forces, within and without, that make for man's destruction, all that afflicts, mystifies, and bears him down, all that he knows as Evil. Aristotle is singularly silent about it, but it is the essence and core of tragedy.

Suffering. But the tragic poets of antiquity had made another great discovery. They had found a way of presenting and rendering credible in a single, unified work of art, and hence at one and the same time, not only all that harasses man and bears him down but much that ennobles and exalts him. They found in dramatic action the clue to the rendering of paradox—the paradox of man, the "riddle of the world." Only man in action, man "on the way," begins to reveal the possibilities of his nature for good and bad and for both at once. And only in the most pressing kinds of action, action that involves the ultimate risk and pushes him to the very limits, are the fullest possibilities revealed. It is action entered into by choice and thus one which affirms man's freedom. And it leads to suffering—but choice of a certain kind and suffering of a certain kind. The choice is not that of a clear good or clear evil; it involves both, in unclear mixture, and presents a dilemma. The suffering is not so much that of physical ordeal (although this can be part of it) but of mental or spiritual anguish as the protagonist acts in the knowledge that what he feels he must do is in some sense wrong—as he sees himself at once both good and bad, justified yet unjustified. This kind of suffering presupposes man's ability to understand the full context and implications of his action, and thus it is suffering beyond the reach of the immature or brutish, the confirmed optimist or pessimist, or the merely indifferent. To the Greek tragedians, as to the Poet of Job, only the strongest natures could endure this kind of suffering—persisting in their purpose in spite of doubts, fears, advice of friends, and sense of guilt— and hence to the Greeks it became the mark of the hero. Only the hero suffers in this peculiar, ultimate way. The others remain passive, make their escape, or belatedly or impulsively rally to the hero's side, like the Sea Nymphs in *Prometheus*. Even murderesses like Clytemnestra and Euripides' Medea, whose monstrous crimes make them anything but heroic in

47

the romantic and moral sense, are dignified by their capacity for this kind of suffering.[45]

Values. Suffering of this kind does more than prove man's capacity to endure and to perceive the ambiguity in his own nature and in the world about him. The Greeks and the Poet of Job saw the suffering endured by these men of heroic mold to be positive and creative and to lead to a reordering of old values and the establishing of new. This is not to say that they recommended it, as in St. Paul's exhortation to "glory in tribulation"; Job never glories in his tribulations, and no Greek hero embraces his destiny gladly. He is characteristically stubborn and resentful. Nor did the tragic writers see these new values as ultimately redemptive. But suffering under their treatment lost its incoherence and meaninglessness. It became something more than a sign of the chaos or malignity at the center of being. They showed that, for all its inevitable, dark, and destructive side, it could lead under certain circumstances not only to growth in the standard virtues of courage, loyalty, and love as they operate on the traditional level, but also to the discovery of a higher level of being undreamt of by the standard (or choric) mentality. Thus Job's challenge to Jehovah, for which the Counselors rebuke him, opened up realms of knowledge—even of truth, beauty, and goodness— of which the Counselors were ignorant. And Oedipus' pride, which makes the Chorus fearful, led to discoveries, human and divine, which make their moralizings seem petty indeed. Tragedy, as the Greek plays defined it and *The Book of Job* did not, stresses irretrievable loss, often signified by death. But suffering has been given a structure and set in a viable relationship: a structure which shows progression toward value, rather than denial of it, and a relationship between the inner life of the sufferer and the world of values about him. Thus the suffering of Job and Oedipus, of Orestes and Antigone and Medea, makes a difference. If nothing else, those about them see more clearly the evil of evil and the goodness of good. The issues are sharpened as never before. Some of the tragedies end more luminously than others. There is nothing like the note of reconciliation at the end of *Medea,*

48

for instance, that there is in the final scenes of the *Oresteia* and *Oedipus*. But Medea, by the end of the play, has (like Clytemnestra) displayed qualities of "a great nature gone wrong," and the play as a whole asserts values that transcend her enormities. The emphasis is on "greatness," and because of her action the dark ways are both more and less benighted than they were before. Though nothing fully compensates (the plays say) there is some compensation. There has been suffering and disaster, and there is more to come. But the shock has to some degree un-shocked us. We are more "ready." [46]

Such is the approach to the question of existence, and such the appraisal of the stuff of experience, that constitute the form of tragedy as the artists of antiquity achieved it. They did not make permanent laws of tragedy, nor did Aristotle, whose distinction lay in seeing that a form was there and in cutting beneath theatricality to give it statement. The *Poetics* was a powerful influence in directing the writers of the Renaissance to the plays. They found them to have well-ordered structures, which, when the time was ripe, they turned to for suggestive models. And, informing these structures, giving them their very shape and body, was that characteristic vision of evil, suffering, and value which we have learned to call tragic.

5

TRAGEDY AND CHRISTIANITY

In POINT of doctrine, Christianity reverses the tragic view and makes tragedy impossible.[47] It announces a joyous miracle, a moment in history that transforms history. "Therefore if any man be in Christ, he is a new creature: old things are passed away; behold, all things are become new." The God for whom Job groped in his suffering— "Behold, I go forward, but he is not there; and backward, but I cannot perceive him"—suddenly demonstrated His nearness and His love. The dark ways became light. The source of all evil was personalized in the Adversary, whose eventual destruction was certain. Suffering was seen to lead not simply to a new human perspective or knowledge but to closer identification with Christ, a new spirituality and intimacy with the divine. Hence St. Paul rejoiced in suffering and urged his followers to seek it out. The old values of action, questioning, resistance, the positive side of pride, were challenged by a new doctrine: accept the mystery; for evil return good; shoulder the cross and walk humbly with the Lord. It is the meek who will inherit the earth, the peacemakers who will see God.

To the sufferers of the earth, this doctrine came as a mighty hope and solace. Death lost its sting; no loss was permanent, no injustice without its heavenly recompense. Indeed, the perfect Christian (as Rousseau once remarked [48]) makes a poor citizen: his concern is the New Jerusalem, not the old. Present evils are negligible in the light of Heaven.

The old tragic problems disappear in this new and perfect knowledge; and the Christian, far from kicking against the pricks or arraigning a deaf heaven, zealously prepares his soul for immortality, and in the prospect of God's benignity is lost in wonder, love, and praise.

Although this was the glorious promise of the Gospels, seeming to remove the tragic from human life, subsequent history behaved in the old tragic ways, and individual man—the man of flesh and blood—not only found himself fighting the old battles, within and without, but found the issues deepened, the enemy more real and tangible, and the stake infinitely greater. For one thing, man was presented with a great new dilemma: to believe or not to believe, a choice charged with terror. To believe meant to be born again, to cast off the old ways—a "hard and bitter agony," a dark night of the soul. This meant suffering of a new kind, unknown to Greek or Hebrew. Not to believe meant to face, alone and unaccommodated, a void of meaninglessness to which the revelations of Christianity had added the ultimate terror: infinity. One could close the door on it or try to fill the void with sturdy philosophy, but once it had become a part of the western imagination it could not be ignored. The possibility was always there. And for the believers, even the saints and mystics, the fathers of the Church, the way was anything but smooth. The tragic note of the mad child's father in the Gospel (Mark 9:24) rings through some of the most exalted confessionals: "Lord, I believe; help thou mine unbelief." "*Insecuritas* is a preparation for Revelation and Revelation in turn nourishes a new *insecuritas*," writes Adriani, and speaks of the drama whose climax was the Crucifixion as one would of the ultimate tragedy: "the infinite peace and infinite torment both present in the episode of Gethsemani."[49] And for a moment on the Cross, as Matthew and Mark describe the scene, even Christ felt forsaken.

The Homeric Greeks, says Walter Otto, had "no myth of the soul." Occasionally, and fleetingly, we see into the inner life of one of their heroes, but "this inwardness itself has no language."[50] The tragedians gave it greater dimension and made it more articulate, but the tragic heroes knew no inner

51

torment like Job's and nothing to compare with the Christian's. If it has been said with some justice that Socrates "discovered" the soul, his discovery hardly brought about the great shift in the individual consciousness that came with Christianity, nor provided anything like the extraordinary discipline that Christianity brought to bear upon the inner life. Neither the Greeks nor Job knew the deep Christian consciousness of sin or the Christian's need for constant self-examination. Though Job approached this state, it took a catastrophe to turn his eyes inward; he never knew the sense of one's love being infinitely inadequate return for Christ's love in dying for man. The Christian is born sinful and lives with the guilt of Adam, preliminary to any action whatever, good or bad. Should he act sinfully, he must accept complete and utter guilt, because he sins not only in full knowledge of the Law and the Covenant, which Job knew, but against the Word made flesh in Christ and his teachings, and against God who promised, through Christ, eternal salvation. Since to the Greeks the hand of a god was in every action, no Greek ever felt himself completely responsible. ("Apollo, friends, Apollo, / Has laid this agony upon me") and hence never knew the overwhelming remorse and wretchedness of soul felt by the sinning Christian, nor, on the other hand, the knowledge of Redemption in the Atonement. The Greek, says Otto, "can remain large and proud, even in his fall. . . . Helen, who deserted husband and child with her paramour and brought indescribable woe upon two peoples, does indeed reproach herself bitterly, but the real blame is accounted Aphrodite's, and Helen remains the great woman she was." [51] The Greek tragedies, in putting greater stress on moral responsibility, involved their heroes in more than occasional self-reproach, but it remained for Christian tragedy to give full dramatic treatment to the guilty and remorseful soul.

Indeed, in Kierkegaard's Christianity (hardly representative, though suggestive), "even the most tried of the tragic heroes walks with a dancing step compared with the knight of faith." "The hero does the deed and finds repose in the universal, the knight of faith is kept in constant tension." He is "kept sleepless, for he is constantly tried." [52] If Kierkegaard's view of the tragic hero seems limited—Agamemnon, his one example, is more of an adventurer than a tragic hero—his testimony to the reality of tension, isolation, and dilemma in the Christian experience shows how much of the tragic remains, to certain sensitivities, in this new dispensation. Instead of negating tragedy, or taking man in one leap of faith "beyond tragedy," Christianity in actual practice, historically, has provided a matrix out of which has come, since the beginnings of the Renaissance, a prodigious amount of tragic expression, not only in literature but in painting, sculpture, and music. It is the religions of the east, whose direction is toward nonbeing, the denial of the individual and of the reality of suffering and death, that have proved inhospitable to tragedy.[53] Kierkegaard's "fear and trembling" comes from the terrifying responsibility, the sense of imminent inadequacy, which Christianity places on the individual. "The knight of faith is obliged to rely upon himself alone. . . . He is the paradox . . . the individual, without connections or pretensions. This is the terrible thing . . ." If the eastern religions tend to make passive what Christians call the soul and reduce the area of feeling and consciousness, Christianity, except for occasional and minor quietistic movements within the Church, enkindles the soul, sensitizes the feelings, and opens up new and terrifying possibilities.

These possibilities seem to have struck western Europe with great force in the period of the Renaissance. The growing humanist culture showed revealing signs at every hand, the outgrowth of tendencies latent in the long Christianizing process that followed the founding of the Church. The task of the early Fathers had been reconstructive. They had to produce from the cultural welter of the Greco-Roman collapse a comprehensive and powerful theology and a Church that could live. Aside from obvious social, political, and economic difficulties, one of the reasons why for many centuries no literary tragedy was produced in western Europe was that the most creative minds were otherwise employed. Eternal salvation was the dominant and absorbing issue. All of life, down to the minutest details of everyday existence, had to be reorganized and reassessed around it. Dogma had to be formulated, argued about, established. An elaborate system of Church organization and discipline had to be evolved and administered. The communicants of the Church—roughly comparable to those who might have attended the theater in Athens—needed no secular reminder of who they were or what existence meant: their priests told them. The celebration of the Mass, the daily reminder of the suffering and death of Christ, had its own "cathartic" effect, filling a need not unlike what Aristotle found in Greek tragedy. Though the Church is witness to a joyous miracle, it never blinked at the hard and bitter struggle of daily living. Its ceremonies are solemn, its teachings often hard; its music, as in the old plain song, melancholy. To the mass of folk who, though nominal communicants, remained (as Powicke suggests [54]) mostly unregenerate pagans, the surface display of the Church, the stories of hellfire and horned devils, provided a simple substitute for a tragic theater. Many of the popular ballads, whose origins probably go back well into the period often thought of as faced solidly toward the New Jerusalem, reveal a hard and Greeklike vision of unredeemed man and a tendency to point to the harsh realities of the *old* Jerusalem, often with a bitterness (and even relish) that no good parish priest could have countenanced.[55]

The conquering of despair, the restoration of what Gilbert Murray called "nerve," the reassertion of the freedom of the will which had been captured by pagan fatalisms were all contributions of the Church toward the burst of individualism that signified the Renaissance. The process by which the world was regained; by which the flesh-denying and even life-denying tendencies within the Church itself were checked or counterbalanced; by which the new determinism of God's Providence (which, as Willard Farnham points out,[56] was hardly different in theory from the old pagan fatalism) was made to allow for individual responsibility—this process was long, slow, and hard, and called for much heroism of its own sort. The crowning works of the Middle Ages—Aquinas, Dante, Chaucer—show a balance of flesh and spirit, of this-worldly and other-worldly concern, seldom elsewhere achieved.

As life during the later Middle Ages became more stable

and opulent and the things of life more fascinating, the Christian view of life as a preparation, of suffering as a discipline, and of death as the entry into the glories of eternal life, lost much of its power as the dominant image. One symptom was the growing interest, not in the end of the journey—the torment of hell or the blessings of heaven—but in the journey itself, the action through which man must go. Dante used a journey as the structural principle of his great *Comedy*. Boccaccio and Chaucer, who both used the journey-structure in their fictions, told stories which treated life not so much as something else (a preparation) but as interesting and fascinating in itself. Suffering and death began to be explored for their own sakes, not as a discipline or a transition. Of the countless paintings of the bleeding and agonized Christ the question has been asked, "Why did these men like to see their Savior suffer and die?" The fashion of the memento mori, the graveyard rendezvous, the enormous popularity of the Dance of Death were all signs of the growing secularist imagination. They reveal an increasing sense, never entirely suppressed in the most pious times, of anxiety and doubt—the original terror coming close again. The miracle and morality plays depicted man's lot through dramatic action—his earthly pilgrimage, the wages of sin, the terrors of death and of the miraculous—and for all their orthodoxy, the note of terror of little man against the infinite often intrudes. As the form became more complex, the plays began to explore more fully the dialectical possibilities of action and the ambiguities of character and situation. Though the conclusions were foregone, the stature of the protagonist, Man, grew. The way was being prepared for the full statement of Elizabethan tragedy.

There were other developments, of course, that sharpened the dilemma of the Renaissance as the new worldliness came into conflict with traditional teaching. On the one hand was the great stored-up potential of the soul, developed through centuries of spiritual discipline in meditation, worship, prayer, confession; on the other were the humanist enterprises that, though good in themselves, had anything but spiritual tendencies. Knowledge became prized more for its own sake and less for the glory of God. Technical skills and

6

DOCTOR FAUSTUS

W. H. AUDEN observed that at the end of a Greek tragedy
we say, "What a pity it had to be this way"; at the end of a
Christian tragedy, "What a pity it had to be this way when it
might have been otherwise." [58] If there is more freedom in
Greek tragedy and more of a sense of fate in Christian tragedy
than this statement suggests, still it points to the true tragic
locus and tone of Marlowe's *Doctor Faustus,* the first major
Elizabethan tragedy and the first to explore the tragic possibilities of the head-on clash of the Renaissance compulsions
with the Hebraic-Christian tradition. His *Tamburlaine,* presumably written in the previous year (1587), for all its scenes
of violence and pathos, was more of a single-voiced statement
of the outward Renaissance thrust, a reckless flouting, without much inner concern, of all that Greeks knew as *hubris* and
fate and all that Christians knew as sin, guilt, and damnation.
Marlowe viewed it as "tragic," perhaps, in its picture of suffering and destruction and in the spectacle of death overtaking
in the end even this mightiest of worldly conquerors.[59] Although there are spiritual reaches and broodings in *Tamburlaine* that Marlowe never got from the Greeks, it was in *Faustus* that he turned the focus inward, saw the soul as the tragic
battlefield, and wrote the first "Christian tragedy."

"Cut is the branch that might have grown full straight."
So says the Chorus in the final speech of *Faustus,* bringing the
play to a typical morality-play or *De Casibus*-story ending
with a warning against such fiendish practices as Faustus followed. "What a pity it had to be this way when it might have

57

been otherwise." The choice which would have made all the difference belonged to Faustus, and he knew it. No god urged him on, no oracle foretold his fate. He sinned, suffered remorse, and was damned. The medieval predecessors of the play had told the same story, with variations, again and again; and insofar as *Faustus* merely repeats the old pattern it is anything but tragic. There is no mystery in this kind of universe; it is all too predictable, and the moral issues are clear cut. The terror, had Faustus only chosen differently, might have been avoided; and we are left comfortable and secure in the knowledge of how to escape his downfall.

But Marlowe did not merely repeat the old pattern, and his universe is not comfortable or secure. The Elizabethan theater invited something like the same kind of aesthetic interest in the direful aspects of human experience that Greek tragedy had stimulated in both artist and spectator. Indeed, knowledge of the Greek form, to humanists like Marlowe, must have had a compulsive force of its own, quite apart from personal predilections—although in Marlowe's case, there is evidence that those predilections were many and strong. That the Greeks had once ordered and presented human experience in such a way, and so powerfully, was an inescapable and compelling fact. Popular taste, which had been nourished on the rudimentary action of the old religious (but increasingly secular) plays, asked to see the full story acted out. With the dramatic treatment of action freed from ecclesiastical control, the way was open for the expression once again of "tragic" truth—the truth of man in action as seen by the free and inquiring artist. Marlowe had said enough in *Tamburlaine* to get himself excommunicated many times over, but he had said it in a play, in a dramatic context, and he was not prevented from writing more plays. If, in *Faustus,* he brings the play to a pious conclusion, the "truth" of the play goes far beyond the Chorus' final piety, just as the meaning of *Oedipus* transcends by far the choric summing up of that play. The voice of the Chorus is not the only voice in *Faustus.* For one thing, no figure of the old moralities talks so much or takes us so deep into his own being as does Faustus—or does so much and so boldly. Faustus in thought and action, brooding, philosophizing, disputing, conjuring, defying God and risking all with a flourish, does not suggest so much the lay figure of the moralities, Everyman, as, (in one of his phases) Adam the knowledge-seeker and (in others) the defiant hero of the Greek tradition—a Prometheus or Tamburlaine.

Thus the "secret cause," the true source of the tragic terror of the story of *Faustus* as Marlowe treated it, does not lie in the Christian moral equation of which Faustus in the end finds himself an inevitable term. The "fearful echoes" that "thunder in his ears" in the interludes between his conjuring exploits are momentarily terrifying to him but not because of the mystery of their origin, which is fifteen centuries of Christian teaching and spiritual discipline. He tells the Scholars (Scene 14) that he suffers from "a surfeit of deadly sin that hath damned both body and soul." Such was the fate of the sixteenth-century German magician whose story Marlowe dramatized. But like the Poet of Job and the Greek tragedians, who found new and tragic meaning in old and orthodox stories, Marlowe interpolated into the old medieval equation the new, mysterious, and terrifyingly ambiguous dynamic of the Renaissance, gave it a fascination and a dignity never realized in previous treatments of the story, and made Faustus, rather than Hamlet, "the first modern man." The story of this twenty-four-year action, telescoped by Marlowe into a few vivid scenes, introduced the modern tragic theme of the divided soul—soon to become "the complicated modern soul" of Dostoevski's analysis—torn between the desire to exploit its new mastery and freedom and (on the other hand) the claims of the old teachings, which to defy meant guilt and a growing sense of alienation. Faustus is tragic because he recognized the dilemma as real. Even as he boasts that his soul is his own, to dispose of as he will, he hears the fearful echoes thundering in his ears.

As with Job and Oedipus, we first see Faustus at the peak of his worldly power and influence. Hs is master of the new knowledges and skills, a famous physician, honored by whole cities, and revered by his students. Why was he restless? Why was he unwilling to remain "but Faustus, and a man"? Why this urge to command "all things that move between the quiet poles"? "The one fixed star" of tragedy, writes Arthur Miller,[60] is the hero's urge to "realize himself" fully in the face of all that would rob him of his just deserts or repress what he feels to be his true nature; and the gauge of his heroism is the magnitude of the risk he is willing to take. In this sense the tragedy of Faustus is the tragedy of Adam, "goaded" (as Kierkegaard saw it) by the knowledge of his freedom into what seemed like the one possibility of self-realization his situation offered. Paradise was not enough. To the orthodox, Adam's action was not only sin but utter folly, just as to the Chorus who begins and ends the play Faustus' action was wholly devilish. This too is the sense of the opening soliloquy, in which Faustus brushes aside all studies but necromancy, the key to the self-realization he craves. Immediately the Good Angel tells him to "lay that damned book aside," and the Angel who bids him "go forward in that famous art" is "Evil."

But to Marlowe (judging from the way he presented it) the case was more complicated and more fascinating. He saw the entire action not only as "Good" or "Evil" would see it but as the man of flesh and blood, the one who takes the risk, sees it and lives it out. What are the inner sources of such an action, what is the feel on the pulse, what is the discovery? The meaning of the play is not only that Faustus' act was sinful and foolish. The meaning is in all that Faustus says and does and becomes; it is the total yield of the "boundary-situation" into which Faustus walks of his own accord, acting out the mysterious tragic dynamic of his times.

If Job began in bitterness, and Oedipus in self-confidence too close to complacence, Faustus' first mood after seizing upon necromancy as his study is one of arrogant and impatient lust for power. It is redeemed, if at all, by the full imaginative run that gives even his petty wishes—"the pleasant fruits and princely delicates"—a kind of poetic validity. Marlowe sets his hero's mind completely free to range forbidden realms, and no voice save Tamburlaine's gives comparable expression to the outward Renaissance thrust.

> All things that move between the quiet poles
> Shall be at my command. Emperors and kings
> Are but obeyed in their several provinces,
> Nor can they raise the wind or rend the clouds;
> But his dominion that exceeds in this
> Stretcheth as far as doth the mind of man.
> A sound magician is a mighty god:
> Here, Faustus, try thy brains to gain a deity!

"How am I glutted with conceit of this!" cries Faustus, as he relishes his promised power over all things great and little, temporal and spiritual. His whirling wishes at first have little pattern, no redeeming cause or ideal—no quest for justice or truth; and as his desires grow more fantastic and vainglorious the spectacle is not pretty. But the opening scenes do not wholly condemn him. His absurd egotisms are mixed with intellectual and humanitarian impulses. He would "resolve all ambiguities," read strange philosophy, clothe the schoolboys in silk, and rid his country of the foreign yoke. When Valdes warns him that he must be "resolute," his courage is tested and he responds like a hero. He is prepared (at the end of Scene 1) to take the ultimate risk: "This night I'll conjure though I die therefore." Later, in Scene 3, he rallies the spirits of the Devil's own messenger, Mephistophilis, whose heart faints as he foresees Faustus' awful future. Rising in his "manly fortitude," he scorns Mephistophilis' warning, rejects all hopes of heaven's joys, and offers his soul to Lucifer for twenty-four years of his heart's desires. With his decision come new energy, new power, new command. However "evil" his course, he has left the apathetic and cynical talk of the opening lines of the play and is now man "on the way."

It is said that the great tragedies deal with the great eccentrics and offenders, the God-defiers, the murderers, the adulterers. But it is not tragedy's primary concern to establish the moral truth or the sociological meaning of the hero's action. It is the orthodox world, and not the tragic artist, which judges (or prejudges) a Job or an Oedipus, a Faustus or a Hester Prynne. To bring his protagonist swiftly to the point of ultimate test, the artist imagines a deed which violently

61

challenges the accepted social and (it may be) legal ways. Hence the fact that tragic heroes are often criminals in the eyes of society, and hence the frequency of the legal trial as a symbolic situation in tragedy from Aeschylus to Dostoevski and Kafka. It is the characteristic emphasis of tragedy written in the Christian era that the "criminals" become "sinners" as well, so that the hero is ranged not only against his society but against God and his own soul. Starbuck could not see why Ahab should go whaling for anything but profit; he was aghast at Ahab's "sin" toward one of God's dumb creatures; and had the *Pequod* ever returned, Ahab would have had to stand trial for his criminal neglect of his charge, as before Starbuck's God he must stand trial for his immortal soul. But *Moby-Dick* is not primarily concerned with Ahab as a criminal or sinner, nor is Marlowe's play primarily concerned with Faustus as the Church or society would regard him. The moral qualities or the sociological aspects of the hero's initial choice are less important than the qualities he shows and the discoveries he makes in the subsequent action. Indeed, as Dostoevski was to show about the increasingly standardized society of his time, for purposes of moral discovery the "criminals and outcasts" provide the richest material for the inquiring artist. Judged in this scale, it was better for Faustus to sell his soul, for Hester to sin with Dimmesdale, and for Raskolnikov to commit murder than that no action at all be joined. Thus (as we have seen) the Greeks respected pride and made it a heroic quality, though they saw its destructive side. Stripped of its eschatology, the Christian doctrine of the *felix culpa*, the fortunate fall of Adam, is akin to the treatment in tragedy of the hero's initial crime or sin.[61] Precarious as such an ethic is, tragedy holds aloof from moral judgment and presents the action in such a way that moral judgment can be only one element, and not the most important, in the total response. Marlowe asks us to view the entire action before judging Faustus, and so presents him that unequivocal moral judgment is impossible.

The strange course begins directly Faustus has made his choice. In the upsurge of his arrogance he feels confident and secure. He ridicules such notions as "hell" and "damnation" and "these vain trifles of men's souls." He is elated with the success of his first conjuring (Scene 3), reproves the faint-hearted Mephistophilis, and sends him to strike the twenty-four-year bargain with Lucifer. In a similar mood, after signing the contract in blood, he calls hell a "fable" and the threat of eternal torment an "old wives' tale." "Ay," says Mephistophilis, "think so, till experience change thy mind." It is Faustus' redeeming quality that experience *could* change his mind and that he is sensitive to every stage of the process. By the time of his second conjuring (Scene 5), even before the signing, he confesses doubts. "Something soundeth in mine ears," he says—a voice that calls upon him to abjure his magic and turn to God again. "Why waverest thou?" he asks himself. "Be resolute." As he comes ever closer to the edge of the known and the tried, a glimpse into the abyss brings a moment of intense self-realization:

> Ay, and Faustus will turn to God again.
> To God? He loves thee not;
> The God thou servest is thine own appetite.

In the dialogue with the Good and Evil Angels, immediately following, the tone with which he speaks of "Contrition, prayer, repentance—what of them?" is hesitant and nostalgic. "Sweet Faustus—" pleads the Good Angel, and Faustus seems for a moment to yield, only to be drawn back to his arrogant ways by the Evil Angel's reminder of honor and of wealth that now lie within his power. "Of wealth!" cries Faustus,

> Why, the signiory of Emden shall be mine.
> When Mephistophilis shall stand by me
> What God can hurt me? Faustus, thou art safe:
> Cast no more doubts.

But the doubts will not vanish, and Faustus lives out his twenty-four-year gamble as the first modern tragic man, part believer, part unbeliever, vacillating between independence and dependence upon God, now arrogant and confident, now anxious and worried, justified yet horribly unjustified. He is forced constantly to renew his choice between two awesome alternatives, and in the opposite phases of the rhythm he sees greater and more glorious heights, and depths of greater

63

terror. Soon the gentle voice that "sounded" in his ears, bidding him abjure his magic and return to God, becomes the fearful thundering echoes: "Faustus, thou art damned!" What he is learning is the truth of his own nature—a truth which it was his peculiar Renaissance compulsion to forget or deny: that he is creature as well as creator; a man and not a god; a dependent, responsible part of a greater whole. He learns that his soul is not a mere trifle cf his own, to use as a commodity, and that "contrition, prayer, repentance," hell and damnation, are not (as the Evil Angel told him)

> . . . illusions, fruits of lunacy,
> That make men foolish that do trust them most.

Like Koestler's Rubashov (in *Darkness at Noon*) he had "forgotten the infinite" and the humbling terror with which it invests all the undertakings of man.

Pressing on in spite of the echoes and the doubts, he reaches levels of perception never gained by the less venturous. Like Job, he was not content with having "heard by the hearing of the ear"; he must see with his own eyes. He has frivolous moments (some of them surely not of Marlowe's conceiving), when he boxes the Pope's ears and gets grapes in January. But the random wishes of his early days of conjuring take a more salutary direction. He does not want so much what power will bring—he never takes the Signiory of Emden, never walls Germany with brass, never clothes the schoolboys in silk. He wants what all men, good and bad, have wanted; to conquer time, space, and ignorance. Above all he wants knowledge: what is hell? where is it? who made the world— "the plants, the herbs, the trees that grow upon the earth"? He cruises hither and yon in the world and above it, exploring all climes and the secrets of the heavens. He delves into the past, makes "blind Homer sing," Amphion play the harp, and Helen appear for a dazzling moment. What Marlowe dramatizes is not only the terror of the black art as the old story told about it and as we see it reflected (in the play) in the eyes of the lesser characters, The Old Man, Wagner, and The Scholars, but the wonder of it—the wonder of the man who dared use it and the wonder of the mysteries it unfolds.[62]

But within the wonder is the terror of its fascination and compulsion, beckoning man into the peculiar dilemma of modern times. On the one hand is human limitation and finiteness, the necessary postulate and the first step in the Christian experience. On the other, with the old catechism wearing thin, it is the compulsion of modern man to deny his limitations, press ever further into the mysteries of a universe which appears steadily to yield more and more of its secrets to his inquiring mind. To rest content with his limitations seems to deny his own God-given powers; and yet to challenge the mystery is somehow evil and portends not only present suffering but, such are the echoes that thunder in his ears, the horrors of eternity.

> Why wert thou not a creature wanting soul?
> Or why is this immortal that thou hast?

asks Faustus in his last despairing moments. To the medieval theology which held that man *is* because he believes, the Renaissance replied that man is because he thinks and acts and discovers. Neither one, as Marlowe presents Faustus' dilemma, is wholly right or wholly wrong. The world of certainties is no longer intact, and we are only a step from the riddles and the eternal questioning that harassed the Karamazovs. In the world of tragedy, the hero can only take the road of experiment. He must follow his bent, take action, and live it through. By contrast, in Goethe's version of the story, Faust has divine sanction. "The Prologue in Heaven" dramatizes a quite different universe, as amidst its harmonies God specifically commends Faust's inquiring mind and authorizes the pact with the Devil. The Goethean Faust knows melancholy and frustration. He gets himself (and Gretchen) into a sad scrape. But he never experiences the terror of the Elizabethan hero's dilemma or takes so bold a risk or suffers his despair. He adjusts himself nicely to Gretchen's death, and in the end his actions are brought into harmony with good nineteenth-century humanitarianism.

The end of Marlowe's play shows, of course, that (like the tragic Karamazovs) Faustus could not live out his idea. But between the disillusioned scholar of the first scene and the agonizing, ecstatic figure of the final scene there is a notable difference. He enters, not alone this time, but with the Scholars; and for the first time in the play he has normal, compassionate discourse with his fellows. His role of demigod over, he is human once more, a friend and befriended. "Ah, gentlemen, hear me with patience," says he who has but recently lorded it over all creation. His friends now seem more "sweet" (as he thrice addresses them) than any princely delicate or Signiory of Emden. Although the thrill of his exploits still lingers— "And what wonders I have done all Germany can witness, yea all the world . . ."—he is humble and repentant. He longs to be able to weep and pray but imagines in his despair that devils draw in his tears and hold his hands as he would lift them up. He confesses to the Scholars the miserable source of his cunning. Knowing his doom is near, he refuses their intercession and bids them "Talk not of me, but save yourselves and depart." They retire, like Oedipus' children at Colonus, for the hero to meet his fate alone. "Gentlemen, farewell," he says as they go. "If I live till morning I'll visit you; if not, Faustus is gone to hell."

If to the orthodox it is more a sinner's fate than a hero's, there is something of the classic apotheosis in Faustus' final moments. He transcends the man he was. He goes out no craven sinner but violently, speaking the rage and despair of all mankind who would undo the past and stop the clock against the inevitable reckoning. The grandeur of conception of his earlier worldly imaginings gains a kind of sublimity.

> Stand still, you ever-moving spheres of heaven,
> That time may cease and midnight never come.

Like Job in the agony of his suffering, he has visions never vouchsafed in his days of prosperity. The nearer to Hell, the closer he is to Heaven:

O I'll leap up to my God! Who pulls me down?
See, see, where Christ's blood streams in the firmament!—
One drop would save my soul—half a drop! ah, my Christ!

He asks no questions now; he sees with his own eyes: first the Christ of mercy, then the God of wrath as He "Stretcheth out his arm and bends his ireful brows." He longs to be hidden under hills, thence to be borne aloft to heaven in the volcano's breath; he would be dissolved into a cloud and thus ascend; he would be turned into a beast with no immortal soul: "All beasts are happy . . ." It is eternity that appals him, the consequence of his living, immortal soul. He curses the parents who engendered him, he curses Lucifer, and (most justly) himself. He does not hide his eyes. "My God, my God, look not so fierce on me!"

> Adders and serpents, let me breathe awhile!
> Ugly hell, gape not—come not, Lucifer—
> I'll burn my books—ah, Mephistophilis!

The Devils lead him off, amidst thunder. If he is more sinning than sinned against, he yet has shown great capacities for good as well as evil, and we cannot feel that perfect justice has been done. Theologically, of course, Faustus in his extremity was mistaken: it is never too late to ask and receive God's mercy and pardon. Or, does Marlowe present him as still unpurged of his pride ("And what wonders I have done all Germany can witness, yea all the world . . ."), a sinner not wholly repentant? He does not completely abase himself in self-loathing (as a good Christian would) nor accept without demur a fate which he knows, according to the contract, is just. Rather, he resists his fate, imagines impossible evasions, clings to every precious second of remaining life. Perhaps Marlowe believed that Faustus was doomed no matter how humble his repentance; or he may have conceived him as so hardened in his rationalism as to believe faith a mere function of reason. But the final scene gives a sense, not so much of the justice and goodness of the universe as of the transcendent human individual, caught in the consequences of a dilemma which, granted the conditions of his times, it was impossible for any imaginative man wholly to avoid.

7

KING LEAR

KING LEAR is another story of a soul in torment, a "purgatorial" story. Again the tragic writer has internalized a commonplace action, the facts of which were legendary and presumably known to Shakespeare's audience. Like the Poet of Job, who dramatized the tragic alternatives to the folk story, and like Marlowe, who saw the elements of tragic dilemma in the story of Faustus, Shakespeare transformed the tale of the mythical, pre-Christian King Lear ("who ruled over the Britons in the year of the world 3105, at what time Joas ruled in Judah") into a dramatic action whose shape and quality define Christian tragedy in its full development. This is not to say (as it should now be clear) that the play accords with Christian doctrine—certainly not the Christian view of death and salvation, although the values of the Christian ethics are abundantly illustrated. Nor does the term "Christian tragedy" make a statement about the author's faith or lack of it. It suggests the meeting in a single dramatic action of the non-Christian (Greek, pagan, or humanist) with the Christian to produce a world of multiplied alternatives, terrible in its inconclusiveness—as, for instance, the "terrifying ambiguity" with which *Faustus* confronts us—in which the certainties of revealed Christianity lose the substance of faith and become only tantalizing possibilities hovering about but not defining the action, like Horatio's "flights of angels" or the "holy water" of Cordelia's tears. Marlowe followed out the old story, even to the devils carrying off Faustus amidst thunder; but his actual Hell is humanist ("Where we are is hell," said Mephistophilis) and, like the Heaven Faustus reached for in the end, functions in the play less as an objective Christian belief than as a way of dramatizing inner reality. The one absolute reality that Faustus discovered, and the absolute reality all tragedy affirms and to which Christian tragedy gives new emphasis and infinite dimension, was the reality of what Christianity calls the soul—that part of man, or element of his nature, which transcends time and space, which may have an immortal habitation, and which is at once the seat and the cause of his greatest struggle and greatest anxiety. Compared with *Faustus*, *King Lear* shows this situation in a much vaster ramification, until it seems to touch the highest ("the gods that keep this dreadful pudder o'er our heads") and the lowliest, and is finally caught up in a Greeklike fate that carries the action to a swift and terrible conclusion.

Recent scholarship has sufficiently demonstrated the main outlines of the Elizabethan world-view which, inherited from the teachings of the medieval theologians, the tragic dramatists now ventured to put to the full test of action.[63] For all the centrifugal, disruptive forces at work in the Renaissance, what remained deep in the imagination of western man was the sense that, in spite of appearances, there was order in the universe which should find its counterpart (and did, when society was in a healthy state) in the ordered life of man on earth. The terrestrial hierarchy was an emblem of the celestial, with king, priest, father (of the family), and master (of servants) exercising each in his area of influence a divinely sanctioned authority. In man the individual, reason was king and the passions were its subjects. Thus the father was God and King in the family, and his children were bound to him by more than filial ties of love and devotion. Below man was the world of animals and below animals the world of inanimate things. This "great chain of being" was, moreover, a sensitive affair. Disorder in any of the parts might affect the whole; weakness in any link might cause a vital break, even to cutting man off from God and the hope of salvation. Marlowe, more openly iconoclastic in *Tamburlaine* than in *Faustus*, was the first of the tragedians to posit a shockingly different universe, whose principles are disorder, strife, and force, where Olympian dethrones Titan when he wills and can, and gives divine sanction to the restless will-to-power in man. So Tamburlaine justifies to Cosroe his bloody conquest:

> The thirst of reign and sweetness of a crown,
> That caus'd the eldest son of heavenly Ops
> To thrust his doting father from his chair,
> And place himself in the empyreal heaven,
> Mov'd me to manage arms against thy state.
> What better precedent than mighty Jove?
> Nature, that fram'd us of four elements
> Warring within our breasts for regiment,
> Doth teach us all to have aspiring minds . . .[64]

In this Marlovian world Tamburlaine defied all principles of order and hierarchy, followed his passion for conquest until there was little left to conquer, and died unrepentant, unpunished by the hand of man or God, and plotting new conquests for his sons. *Lear* shows no such relish of disorder. The tone of the play is of a world where disorder is a fearful threat and so frequent a reality as to suggest a universe where order is illusory or where, at best, it comes only as a momentary longed-for respite from the warlike conditions of existence.

The first actions of the play show hierarchy broken and order imperiled. Lear abdicates, with equivocal provisos, and divides his realm. His youngest and fondest daughter asserts her will against his. In a burst of temper he banishes her and his loyal follower, Kent, who had tried to stay his rashness. His two elder daughters, now emboldened, conspire against him; and in the second scene, as if through spread of contagion, the Earl of Gloucester learns of the supposed treachery of his favorite son, Edgar. Gloucester's despairing soliloquy (I.2) sets the modal background of the play, like the lament of the chorus of Theban citizens in *Oedipus* over their dying city. The series of shocks has given him a glimpse into the depths—a glimpse that throws his world into a new and terrifying perspective. "Love cools, friendship falls off, brothers divide. In cities, mutinies; in countries, discord; in palaces, treason; and the bond crack'd 'twixt son and father. This villain of mine comes under the prediction; there's son against

70

father: the King falls from bias of nature; there's father against child. We have seen the best of our time: machinations, hollowness, treachery, and all ruinous disorders follow us disquietly to our graves." [65] Gloucester is old, gullible, and superstitious; the rest of the play bears out his none-too-sturdy character; but he expresses a sober truth about the reality the play presents. He *had* seen the best of his time, and he and a number of others were soon to be followed to their graves by events then taking shape. All this is dire and (as he says) "strange." His broodings are consistent not only with the subsequent action but with the many other ways by which the play suggests the terror of the human condition. The insistent beast imagery ("Tigers, not daughters . . ."), the pictures of man reduced to beast ("poor, bare, forked animal as thou art"), the thundering chaos of the storm, the scenes of bestial cruelty ("Out, vile jelly!") and of pitiful madness show how precarious order is. This is the destructive element, the blight man was born for.

As before, from Job to Oedipus to Faustus: If this is the condition of existence, what to do about it? "How to be?" The tragic artist sets up a new hierarchy (so to speak), a hierarchy of values or responses, ranging from the choric to the heroic. The Chorus looks on and despairs. Job's wife saw no hope and urged suicide. Jocasta pleaded with Oedipus to withdraw from the action. The Good Angel and the Old Man urged Faustus to desist. Although Gloucester is later drawn into the action and transcends himself, his immediate response is to view, like a true pagan or member of the chorus, the present ominous events as signs of a fateful disturbance in the celestial and human orders. All is dark and foreboding: "These late eclipses in the sun and moon portend no good to us. Though the wisdom of nature can reason it thus and thus, yet nature finds itself scourg'd by the sequent effects." The upshot of such a view, as Edmund promptly points out in sturdy Christian ethical terms, is to lay all our ills to "the charge of a star," "all that we are evil in" to "a divine thrusting on." No tragedy (surely not *Lear*) partakes of such unmixed fatalism. But (on the other hand) the upshot of Edmund's view is, by laying evil to the charge of the sinful will, to turn *Lear* into a morality play. "Tragedy," remarked Paul Tillich,[66] "combines Guilt and Necessity," and the response of the hero is neither to yield to fatalism nor humble himself in total guilt, but to press on in his action to find by experience the truth of his own nature and of the nature of man. This is the "dark problem" that Hawthorne presents in *The Scarlet Letter*, the meaning of the "labyrinth" through which Hester and Dimmesdale thread their precarious way. Lear, soon brought to a very Christian sense of guilt by the nagging of the Fool and the twinges of his conscience, finds that the effects of his original hasty action have ramified beyond the question of his guilt, and that he is involved in consequences (the plot of Goneril and Regan against him) which stir in him very different feelings. Had the play been a Christian play, its rationale might have been satisfied with Lear's "Woe that too late repents" and with his new and more charitable view of the "poor naked wretches" of whom he had taken little care. But the mills of quite unchristian gods seem to be grinding. Lear cannot rest in his own remorse, which at best is never unmixed with hate and hurt feelings. As he feels the pressure from Goneril and Regan ever more insistent, the evil closing in, the question of who is to blame—whether it is the "most small fault" of Cordelia or his own "folly"—ceases to be the issue. Caught up in the action which he had unwittingly precipitated, he refuses to default or compromise (in spite of the pleadings of the Fool) and presses on in heroic pride to justify himself. It is in this mood that he curses Goneril and Regan, vows dreadful vengeance, and plunges into the storm.

Why did Shakespeare choose to dramatize the inferno-purgatory of the subsequent actions? He had a happy ending direct to his hand in the Holinshed account, which tells of the reunion of Lear and Cordelia, the success of their armies, Lear's restoration to the throne, his two-year reign, quiet death, and state burial. Why the painful madness ("A sight most pitiful in the meanest wretch, / Past speaking of in a king!")? the blinding of Gloucester? the death of Cordelia? Why did Oedipus dash out his eyes, or why did the people of the late Middle Ages and the Renaissance like to see their Savior suffer and die? Such questions pose basic aesthetic problems, ranging from the mysteries of the creative process and its motivation to problems of the response of audience and spectator, "catharsis," the taste and temper of whole cultures. "Tragic moment," "involvement," "gesture," "action" suggest aspects of the truth, certainly, but they beg enormous questions. F. L. Lucas once discussed the various theories of tragic pleasure, found none of them satisfactory, and proposed that what we seek is truth—as near the whole truth as we can get, man at his worst and at his best. "Destiny scowls upon him: his answer is to sit down and paint her where she stands." [67]

The temptation with *King Lear,* as with many tragedies written in the Christian era which inevitably include Christian modes, patterns, and terms, is to give the picture a too-Christian hue: to read the play as reconciling the inferno and purgatory in the perfect goodness of Kent's loyalty, Cordelia's Christlike love, Lear's humility, and (some have even suggested) the reunion of father and daughter after death in a Christian Heaven.[68] But "Christian tragedy" is still tragedy. It may turn the Christian conceptions of Hell and Purgatory to metaphoric use as psychological realities; its heroes may "sin," suffer remorse, and (like Lear) know what "repentance" is. But whatever redemption the hero wins is not through Divine Grace but, like the Greek hero, through his own unaided efforts. He has no comforter on the dark voyage, no Heavenly City as his destination, where his bundle of sins drops miraculously from his back. What is Christian about Christian tragedy is not eschatological but psychological and ethical. Hamlet's was a soldier's burial, not a saint's or martyr's. When in the final scene of *Lear* the King enters with Cordelia in his arms, Kent, Edgar, and Albany pronounce a choric verdict on the pitiful spectacle:

> KENT.   Is this the promis'd end?
> EDGAR.   Or image of that horror?
> ALBANY.   Fall and cease!

The Christian hope is shattered. The promised Judgment confuses evil and good, and both perish. The original terror looms close, all the more shocking and disillusioning by virtue of the high promises of the Christian revelation. In one sense, this *is* the end. The Chorus, as at the end of Oedipus, have spoken truly. Cordelia is "as dead as earth," and the best his friends can wish for Lear is that he be allowed to die:

> KENT.   O let him pass! He hates him
> That would upon the rack of this tough world
> Stretch him out longer.

Loss is as irretrievable and final as that of any pagan tragedy.

So the action concludes. But as Sophocles showed in his presentation of Oedipus, or the Poet of Job of his agonizing hero, there is another action, internal, a "counter-action," which functions vitally in the tragic dialectic and comprises an important part of the meaning. The turn which Christianity gave to tragedy being inward, this counter-action—the inner workings of human beings under stress, the discovery (or rediscovery) of "soul" or the lack of it—is more fully developed and given in greater detail in Christian tragedy than any Greek tragedian would have thought justifiable or relevant. The initial action of Scene 1 having been taken, what Lear becomes (rather than what becomes of him), and what each of the other characters becomes or shows himself to be, prove the choric verdict only partly true. The counter-action qualifies the terrible implications of the action and reveals possibilities which make the whole more bearable.

Like Job and Oedipus, Lear shows himself more than sinner, more than sinned against. He does evil, and evil is done to him; but in the course of his ordeal, which in part he brought upon himself, he transcends both these categories. Like the other heroes, he ends victor as well as victim. His victory (as Cedric Whitman calls the victory of Oedipus) is pyrrhic and, like everything else about him, ambiguous. His path toward it is tortuous, revealing goods and bads inextricably mixed. It is a pilgrimage (if the term can be dissociated from its Christian promise), and it is presented with characteristic Renaissance-Christian interest in the journey or the process—an interest which foreshadows the harassing "pilgrimages" of Dostoevski's heroes and of the protagonists of the modern psychological novel.

Lear's pilgrimage commences true to a pattern now familiar. A man is wounded to the quick—not an ordinary man, but for his age and time "the first of men." His estimate of himself, of his position in the state, in society, in his family, his view of man and the universe, are suddenly called in question. Gloucester's dire thoughts are in part Lear's also, as in Cordelia's action and later in Goneril's and Regan's, he sees his universe tottering. His response is not despair but violence —characteristic, as Goneril and Regan assure each other, of the rashness of old age and of a temperament never stable; but characteristic also, as the developing action of the play shows, of the initial response of the hero. His new and shattering knowledge of the irrational and the demonic forces in himself and in the world around him drives him to the edge of madness. He has moments of fearful nihilism. His curses against his daughters and his railings in the storm recall the dark and destructive mood of Job's opening curse or the frenzy of violence in which Oedipus struck out his eyes. But, like Job and Oedipus, he does not stay long in such a mood, which, even at its worst, is ennobled by his appeal to justice beyond and above the world of man. And in his time of stress new and saving qualities appear—not only his remorse but his increasing efforts toward restraint and patience (hard won from his knowledge of the disastrous effects of his own impatience) and his enlarged sympathies for the humble and the oppressed.

As the Chorus said about Oedipus, Lear is "twice-tormented," in body and mind, and his mental suffering is in itself twofold. As he sees the large consequences of his moment of rashness, he feels guilty and innocent at the same time. He is plunged into the middle of Job's problem: effect is out of all proportion to cause; justice has lost its meaning. "I am more sinned against than sinning." Like Job's, his universe has gone awry, and a recurrent theme of the scenes of his madness, or near-madness, is his longing, like Job's, for instruction. He wants to know the reason of things. "Teach me, and I will hold my peace," Job said to the Counselors. Lear in his confusion takes Edgar for a scholar, a "learned Theban," an "Athenian," one who can give him instruction:

> First let me talk with this philosopher.
> What is the cause of thunder?

"What is man that thou art mindful of him?" Job had asked, and Lear's questions are of the same kind, the basic and (as here) often explicit question of all tragedy, "Is man no more than this?" "Is there any cause in nature that makes these hard hearts?" Finding no answer, he would, in his fantasy, himself bring reason and justice to the world, as in his mad "arraignment" of Goneril and "anatomizing" of Regan. This is the theme, too, of his ravings later to the blind Gloucester (IV. 6):

> Thou rascal beadle, hold thy bloody hand!
> Why dost thou lash that whore? Strip thy own back.
> Thou hotly lusts to use her in that kind
> For which thou whip'st her. The usurer hangs the cozener.
> Through tatter'd rags small vices do appear;
> Robes and furr'd gowns hide all. Plate sin with gold,
> And the strong lance of justice hurtless breaks.
> Arm it in rags, a pygmy's straw does pierce it.

He would himself right the fearful unbalance: "None does offend, none—I say none! I'll able 'em." But in another instant this clear insight, even in his madness, into the universal nature of the problem (like the moments, before his mind cracks, of true Christian repentance and enlarged sympathies) reverts to the mad desire for revenge:

> It were a delicate strategem to shoe
> A troop of horse with felt. I'll put't in proof,
> And when I have stol'n upon these sons-in-law,
> Then kill, kill, kill, kill, kill, kill!

The cause of justice and suffering humanity is badly mixed with pride and hate—with Job's nihilism and Ahab's vindictiveness. Even the remnants of reason are gone and passion rules. Lear shouting his "Kill, kill, kill . . ." images the ultimate disaster, when chaos is come again. As with the other heroes, the path is never straight up; the balance is always precarious. Lear is never "born again."

But these are not Lear's final words, nor are they his

responsible words. The dialectic is not played out. In the final moments of the scene he fancies that his friends are his pursuers; he jests madly with them, and runs impishly off the stage, fairly gibbering—"Sa, sa, sa, sa!" We next see him in the French camp, with Cordelia at his bedside and soft music playing to ease his return to consciousness. The scene of his awakening and reconciliation with Cordelia is as close to redemption as tragedy ever gets. Christian images and spirit pervade it. Lear mistakes his daughter for "a soul in bliss" and starts to kneel for her benediction as she asks for his. All is repentance, forgiveness, harmony. Here, if ever in tragedy, we are in the presence of the peace that passeth understanding. But it is wrought out of the dialectic of experience and through no conversion or doctrine or miracle—except it be the one miracle that tragedy witnesses, the miracle of the man who can learn by suffering.

But it was fated that Lear learn too late. Fatefully free, Lear was free to choose his own fate. He became by that action freely fated, and fate must run its course. The peace and harmony of the reconciliation were real but momentary. Nothing saves him—not his own hard-won self-knowledge and humility or Cordelia's richer humanity and more expressive love or Gloucester's regeneration or Edgar's bravery or even Edmund's last-minute repentance. The repeated mischances of the last act seem, like Job's misfortunes, systematic. Edmund repented too late. His message revoking Cordelia's execution arrived too late. Lear slew her executioner, but too late to save her life. There is nothing Christian in Lear's response to this awful fact, and the heaven he invokes as he carries her in is deaf indeed:

> Howl, howl, howl, howl! O, you are men of stones!
> Had I your tongues and eyes, I'd use them so
> That heaven's vault should crack. She's gone for ever.
> I know when one is dead, and when one lives.
> She's dead as earth.

No wonder Edgar sees in the scene a world where time and chance happeneth to all, deserving and undeserving alike.

Although some have pointed to the redeeming fact that

Lear seems to die in an ecstasy of love and hope in his moment of fancy that Cordelia is still alive, the final scene hardly affords such comfort. Nor does the scene say anything about a reunion of father and daughter in a Christian heaven. It says much about loss, decay, suffering, and endurance. "The wonder is," says Kent, "he hath endur'd so long." "The oldest," concludes Edgar,

> . . . hath borne most; we that are young
> Shall never see so much, nor live so long.

It says nothing about salvation, only a wan restoration, after great loss, of a kind of order. The kingdom has, in a sense, been purged—even, indirectly, by Lear, whose defiance of his daughters precipitated the crisis, brought Cordelia back, kept the dialectic of action going and the future still open to possibility. It is not that the "forces for good" triumph over the "forces for evil." Practically speaking, no one triumphs. Lear, Gloucester, and Cordelia die, and they are as dead as Goneril, Regan, and Edmund. Kent sees his own death near. The monstrous and the bestial, the petty and the weak in man have taken a fearful toll, and with these qualities a perverse fate has worked in seeming conspiracy. The play suggests no adequate compensation; there is no discharge in that war, except in death, which, as Edgar pleads for Lear, means only a cessation of pain.

The best that can be said is that human nature, in some of its manifestations, has transcended the destructive element and made notable salvage. Not only Lear, but Cordelia, Gloucester, Edgar, and Albany have grown in knowledge and self-knowledge, have entered a new dimension, achieved a richer humanity. Even the repentant Edmund and the servant who defends Gloucester against his persecutors figure in this repeated pattern. But when Albany says in the concluding moments of the play that "we that are young / Shall never see so much," what does he mean? So much evil? So much suffering and endurance? Or so much nobility, self-sacrifice, and love? (The bodies of Lear and Cordelia are there before him as he speaks.) True to the tragic vision, the play answers these questions ambiguously.

But the play embodies tragic truth in another important way. The goods and bads may be shown as inseparable—that is, eternally present in all human actions and in the nature of the universe—but both are real (good as well as evil), and they are distinguishable. Further, though the good cannot be said to triumph, neither can evil. A balance, however precarious, is maintained. If the play denies the comforts of optimism, it does not retreat into cynicism. Its world is hard; evil is an ever-present wolf at the door. But man is free to act and to learn. If Lear never learned what makes these hard hearts, he learned much about the workings of his own heart. He could have found it all in "the old moral catechism," but such is the nature of modern tragic man that he must learn it (like Faustus) in his own way and on his own pulses. He had heard by the hearing of the ear, but at last he saw. What keeps the atmosphere of the play still sweet is just that substance of traditional knowledge, relearned through agonizing experience, an affirmation in the face of the most appalling contradictions.

8

TRAGEDY AND THE MODERN WORLD

To SAY that, after Shakespeare's great tragedies and the best of the Jacobeans', the next genuine achievement in tragic literature was not to come for two hundred years and in a form other than the drama, is seemingly to ignore the great achievement of Racine, Milton's *Samson,* and the many plays confidently called tragedies by their authors that appear in the annals of the theater in a steady march from the Restoration on down. It is to say, with apparent arrogance, that such writers of self-styled tragedies as Shelley, Byron, Büchner (the author of the striking *Woyzeck*), Tennyson (*Becket*), and Browning (*Sordello*) knew not what they did. Each one of these pieces, certainly, partakes of the elements of tragedy, and such a play as Racine's *Phèdre* might serve as well as *The Scarlet Letter* to illustrate the main line of western tragedy. But in the search for essences selection is pardonable, if not imperative, and the semantic fortunes of the word "tragedy" is another (however illuminating) study.[69] After the English Renaissance and the tragic ambiguities of human passion and reason as presented in Racine's plays, the next "tragic moment" in western culture developed in the mid-nineteenth century. To consider, however briefly, what happened in tragedy after Shakespeare and during the two centuries that followed the closing of the theaters in 1642 is not only to give needed perspective to the peculiarly modern, or contemporary, tragic problem but to throw into sharper relief many of the values essential to tragedy per se.

During the Jacobean years tragic tension in the drama slacked off. It is not that playwrights lost their sense of the Good (Webster was a good moralist), but in the world of their plays it became a decreasingly effective dramatic force. Faustus was amply forewarned and knew, in theory, precisely what he was doing; Lear came to know the full moral meaning of what he had done; such knowledge is powerfully dramatized, as we see both heroes presented through action and word in full moral and spiritual awareness. In the subsequent drama, the stature of man shrinks. Vision becomes clouded, distinctions blurred, and knowledge chimerical. This is the meaning of the frequency in these plays of the imagery of darkness, fog, murk, or mist; of drift (as at sea), maze, labyrinth; of disease, rottenness, poison, and madness. The Duchess of Malfi lived in "a rank pasture, here, i' th' court," amidst a "kind of honey-dew that's deadly," [70] and her little light was soon extinguished. What expresses but one phase of the world of *Faustus* and *Lear* defines the world of *The Duchess of Malfi*. "Knowledge is confounded with knowledge." [71] Man loses his sense of direction and with it his sense of freedom and creative power. "We are merely the stars' tennis-balls," cries Bosola in *The Duchess*, "struck and bandied which way please them." And although Bosola in the end achieved a minor conversion toward compassion and repentance, it is far less definitive of the play than his dying words:

> Oh, I am gone!
> We are only like dead walls or vaulted graves,
> That, ruined, yield no echo. . . .
> In what a shadow, or deep pit of darkness,
> Doth, womanish and fearful, mankind live.

It is not difficult to account for the notoriously short life of the great periods of tragic drama. So powerful is the human urge toward resolution, so deep the longing for "discharge in that war," that few artists have for long been able to sustain, and few audiences endure, the tensions of tragedy. The necessary involvement is demanding, costly. The dark problem must be decided either way or transcended. From the Poet of Job, Aeschylus, Sophocles, and Shakespeare to Melville, Dostoevski, and Faulkner, the tendency has been to modulate into a religious or quasi-religious or comic mood. Thus the more-than-tragic transcendence of the Voice from the Whirlwind in *Job,* the reconciliation that concludes the *Oresteia,* Oedipus' apotheosis at Colonus, the "twilight mood" of *The Tempest.* Melville's final piece was *Billy Budd* with its Christological suggestions; and Faulkner's *Intruder in the Dust,* constructed on a grim and Greeklike theme and plot, modulates finally into a scene of perfect comedy. Or, when the values that sustain tragedy begin to disintegrate and the "nerve" fails, the dramatist (who is to some degree the creature as well as the creator of his times) may resort to another alternative: irony. This is the path (according to Willard Farnham) which Shakespeare followed in some of his later plays beyond "the frontiers of tragedy." [72] This, too, is the characteristic mode of Euripides in those of his plays which all but lose us in a forest of ironic ambiguities. Here the detachment of the artist seems almost complete, and he becomes an anatomist of evil—as Eliot says of Middleton, "without prejudice, without personality." [73] This is the way toward reportage, naturalism, clinical detail, and case history. Or again, the dramatist may make whole plays out of one of the many elements (like irony) which tragedy even at its best holds in uneasy control: pathos, melodrama, the "absurd." All these tendencies, which we are pleased to call "modern," are symptomatic of the default of tragedy and are discernible in the tragic drama of the declining Jacobean stage. Underlying them all is frank despair in the face of the human condition. When the English theater began functioning again with the Restoration, "tragedies" were written and produced; but their approach to the basic questions of human existence was something other than what we have witnessed in our discussion so far. The bent of history went the other way.

Milton's great gesture, in his epics and in *Samson Agonistes,* toward the spiritual reconstruction of his age asserted the very values of which the Jacobean drama signified the decline: freedom, responsibility, guilt, and the possibility of knowledge through suffering. But in his two Christian epics, Milton spoke (as he knew) to a sparse audience, and the tragedy, *Samson Agonistes,* had no effect whatever in re-establishing a tragic theater. The Restoration theater was oriented toward comedy, the heroic play, or tragedy "moralisée." It was no longer a theater of "myth and ritual" touching the life of the whole community at its very center. Many forces were at work, besides the moral and spiritual ones Milton deplored, to create an atmosphere inhospitable to tragedy for many generations to come. A whole sociology is involved here, some components of which were the politics of the Restoration, the developing middle-class economy, the trend toward a reassuring deism in theology, and the increasing confidence in empirical science—all that eventuated, that is, in the Age of Enlightenment with its utopian hope for the human race. In Pope's epigram, "God said, *Let Newton be!* and all was light"; and the light dissipated the mystery and revealed the pattern: Nature's (and God's) plan for man. There still was "tragedy" in individual human lives—anguish, despair, and suffering—as there is in every age. The tragic spirit never dies, but it goes underground, to find sporadic expression in lesser forms (like the melancholy song or lyric, the "blues" of our own day [74]) or on the periphery of the forms currently in fashion. Thus it is discernible in some of the harder edges of Restoration comedy; in the continued interest in Shakespeare's tragedies and in imitations of them; later, in the darker side of life as portrayed in the early novels and in Swift's satire; still later, in the premonitions in verse of what was to develop into the great romantic dissent; even (by the mid-eighteenth century) in the more somber currents of Dr. Johnson's sense of his times and his thoughts on death. But the major drive of the creative minds from the Restoration on went toward strengthening the new hope and confirming the new orthodoxy. Pope could see man as

> A Being darkly wise, and rudely great,
> . . . in doubt to act, or rest;
> In doubt to deem himself a God, or Beast;
> In doubt his Mind or Body to prefer;
> Born but to die, and reas'ning but to err . . . [75]

83

But these doubts were not tragic doubts. The "Plan" is clear
for those who would see it:

> All Nature is but Art, unknown to thee;
> All Chance, Direction, which thou canst not see;
> All Discord, Harmony not understood;
> All partial Evil, universal Good . . .

"Whatever is, is right." Man's function is to know his place in
the universal scheme and adjust himself to it.

The mid-eighteenth-century reform movement in France
and later in England was posited on a similar optimism and
employed a method which was the reverse of the tragic. Under
the impulse of Rousseau, in many ways the pioneer of the
movement, Evil was reduced to evils, which were looked upon
as institutional and therefore remediable. The nature of man
was no longer the problem; rather, it was the better organization and management of men. Individual man was good; society had corrupted him and society could be changed. Thus
by taking thought, the men of the Enlightenment sought to
improve the human condition and applied "the clear and
distinct idea" to social institutions, while in the next generation, the romantic poets appealed to what they regarded as the
primary qualities, the sympathies and affections (quite un-
mysteriously and naturally good) that made for human survival and brotherhood. Both were rebellious in that they
challenged existing institutions; sometimes revolutionary; and
often (like Rousseau) a prey to melancholy. The reformers
lived to despair of seeing their counsels prevail, and the romantics lamented man's failures and his transiency on this
earth. But neither their rebellion nor their despair were
tragic. The old haunting fear and mystery, the sense of paradox and dilemma at the very center of man's nature, had been
replaced—at least officially—by a new and confident dogma.
Man's eyes were turned, not down and in, but outward, upward, and toward the future. Among the poets, private disillusionment could be sublimated by ever more persistent concentration on the ideal or in nostalgic return to the past or in
the healing power of myth and pathos. Occasionally it came
out raw in a brief despondent lyric or in the ironic rejection

of the whole human experiment in such a piece as Byron's *Manfred*. If this mood increased as romantic hopes waned following the political upheavals in France and with the growing concern over the evils of the new industrialism, any major dissenting movement was absorbed in the conservatism and compromise of Victorianism, with its sturdy morality, material expansion and prosperity, and its way of appropriating even the sinister implications of such revelations as Darwin's into its own peculiar optimism.

But dissent there was—and a tragic dissent, as we have now come to use the term. Again a familiar pattern was repeated. Traditional certainties (in this instance the Christian revelation and ethic joined with the optimistic formulations of the Enlightenment and of the Romantics) failed to accommodate individual experience; and the failure was seen as not mere personal disorientation, to be expressed in melancholy lyrics, but as a fault at the very heart of things, recalling the original terror and bringing the nature of man once more into dark question. Mysteries once thought solved, at least officially, returned to haunt the imagination. Matthew Arnold sensed the uneasiness of the age, lamented "this strange disease of modern life," but failed to go beyond its lyric expression. There was no tragic theater at hand to interpret this new crisis. Even what the mid-century regarded as tragedy, according to an anonymous editor of the time, was out of fashion: "Tragedy is becoming every day more unpopular, and operas, vaudevilles, and purely comic performances have almost wholly usurped its place." [76] What also was in fashion, however, was the novel, a vehicle flexible enough to accommodate the new vision (which was as old as Aeschylus and Sophocles); but it remained for artists outside the Victorian domain—in America and Russia—to turn the novel to the uses of tragedy. As often in the history of genres, a vehicle once thought trivial, a device for mere story telling, became—and remained until the theater of Ibsen and O'Neill came to share the function—the closest modern approximation of the Greek and Elizabethan tragic theaters. Hawthorne's *The Scarlet Letter* and Melville's *Moby-Dick* were the first novels in English to express the old vision by means of the new vehicle.

fined myself within the limits of the old Surveyor's half a dozen sheets of foolscap." Meditating upon the simple outlines of Hester's story as the old document recorded it, Hawthorne asked, as it were, the existential questions: What (to Hester) did it mean to be a woman of flesh and blood, caught in that situation of guilt but sanctioned by a kind of inner necessity, the promptings of her own high spirit, which neither she nor her pious lover could repudiate as entirely evil ("What we did had a consecration of its own.")? What did it feel like to live through a dilemma so potent with destructive possibilities? What must have been the impact on a powerful yet sensitive nature? Is there not here, too, a "boundary-situation" sufficient to call in question man's very conception of himself and what he lives by? [77]

Hester's religious heritage and her community pronounced her utterly guilty; she had sinned "in the most sacred quality of human life." She was ostracized, imprisoned, and put on trial for her life: "This woman [said one of her persecutors] has brought shame upon us all, and ought to die. Is there not a law for it? Truly, there is, both in the Scripture and the statute-book." In her extremity, what was she to do? To accept the community's verdict of total guilt would be to renounce the element of "consecration" she knew to be true of her relationship with Dimmesdale; and yet to renounce the community in the name of her consecration was equally unthinkable. She had sinned, and she knew guilt. But hers was no passive nature and, from some mysterious promptings of her own being, she took action in the only way she knew how; in the dim light of her prison cell, she embroidered the scarlet letter—with matchless artistry and in brilliant hue.

That is, she accepted, yet defied. She wore the "A" as the sign of her sin, which she publicly acknowledged—but she wore it on her own terms. Preserving a margin of freedom, she asserted the partial justice of her cause. The letter, when she appeared in public, "had the effect of a spell, taking her out of the ordinary relations with humanity, and enclosing her in a sphere by herself." Facing the Puritan crowd, she could have cursed them—and God—and died, either spiritually, or actually by suicide (she thought of suicide in prison). She

could have revealed the name of her lover and got a mitiga-
tion of sentence, or prostrated herself in guilt and got the
sympathy of the community. Instead, she decided to "maintain her own ways" before the people and her judges—though
it slay her. Her final answer was to live out her dilemma in
full acceptance of the suffering in store.

In the penultimate chapter of the novel, as Hawthorne
prepares for the climactic revelation of the scarlet letter, he
himself sums up the result of his meditations on Surveyor
Pue's brief summary. With Hester and Pearl headed for the
scaffold to join Dimmesdale, "Old Roger Chillingworth," he
writes, "followed, as one intimately connected with the drama
of guilt and sorrow in which they had all been actors, and
well entitled, therefore, to be present at its closing scene."

It had been the work of the Enlightenment, the Romantics, and (in America) the Transcendentalists, so to shift the
perspective on man and his problems as to render needless or
meaningless or irrelevant (as they thought) this "drama of
guilt and sorrow" which Hawthorne saw in the old story.
Emerson was aware of the contrarieties of life and of the soul's
struggle, but neither he nor his fellow Transcendentalists saw
in them the stuff of drama, much less tragic drama. It was for
Hawthorne, who "alone in his time," writes Allen Tate,[78]
"kept pure, in the primitive terms, the primitive vision," to
transmute "the puritan drama of the soul," which for the
faithful ended in the New Jerusalem, into tragic drama. The
essence of Hester's seven-year course is conflict—of Hester
with her self, her society, and her God. The conflict throughout is fraught with ambiguity, with goods and bads inextricably mixed, and constantly and bitterly recognized as such by
Hester. Contrarieties are never resolved, and the issues of the
soul's struggles are unsettled either way. "Is not this better,"
murmured Dimmesdale to Hester after the confession on the
scaffold, "than what we dreamed of in the forest?"—to which
Hester could only reply: "I know not! I know not!"

This is the sum of Hester's seven years of penance and
agonized self-questioning. The Puritan code, which tortured
and yet sustained her, failed in the end to answer her question. And in the multiple ambiguities of action and character,

in the prevailing "tenebrism" of the novel,[79] in the repeated images of the maze, the labyrinth, the weary and uncertain path, Hawthorne sets (by indirection) the Emersonian promise in a harsh and tragic light. Hester and Dimmesdale had "trusted themselves"; their hearts had "vibrated to that iron string." And it was not entirely wrong, the novel says, that they should have done so. But Hawthorne, in the true vein of tragedy, dealt not with doctrinaire injunctions but with actions in their entirety, with special regard, in this instance, for their consequences—a phase to which Emerson was singularly blind. These consequences, Hawthorne saw, are never clear, they involve man not only externally as a social being but internally, to his very depths, and they can be dire. To the question, "In the destructive element, how to be?" the novel presents an ambiguous answer. One answer is the choric comment in the final chapter: "Be true! Be true! Be true!" But that is no more the full meaning of the experience the novel records than the final summing up of the Chorus in *Oedipus,* that no man should be counted happy until he is dead. The answer is in all that the action reveals in all the characters— what they say, do, and become—and in the innumerable suggestions (whose drift I have indicated) of setting and image.

The seven-year action which is precipitated by Hester's Antigone-like independence, or (to the Puritan judges) stubbornness, involved her and those whom it touched intimately in deep suffering and loss of irretrievable values. Hester lost her youth, her beauty, her promise of creativity, and any sure hope she might have had of social or domestic happiness. She lost Dimmesdale, whom a full confession at the outset might have brought to her side, and whose life was ultimately ruined anyway. She was the cause of Chillingworth's long, destructive, and self-destructive course of revenge. She anguished over Pearl's bleak and bitter childhood. Her own loneliness and isolation, especially for one of so warm and rich a nature, was a constant sorrow and reminder of her guilt, a kind of suffering which Antigone or Medea, who in other ways are not unlike her, never knew in similar quality or duration. And in the end, she knew not whether she had done right or wrong. She goes out of our ken, a gray figure (still wearing her scarlet

89

letter, resumed "of her own free will"), and, "wise through dusky grief," giving comfort and counsel to the perplexed or forlorn.

If a major salvage from her experience is this hard-won wisdom of Hester's, it is not the only point of light in the dark world of mysteries and riddles that the novel in general portrays. By her stand Hester asserted her own values against the inherited and inhumane dogma of her community as surely as Prometheus, in Aeschylus' play, asserted his own sense of justice against Zeus. In both instances the suffering of the hero "made a difference." Hester humanized the community that would have cast her out, even put her to death. She forced it to reassess its own severe and absolute dogmas, as Antigone forced a reassessment in Thebes, or Hamlet in Elsinore, or Prometheus on Olympus. She envisioned, and in quiet corners whispered of it to those who would hear, a "brighter period . . . a new truth . . . to establish the whole relation between man and woman on a surer ground of mutual happiness." If Dimmesdale perished because of the ordeal her action plunged him into, it was not before he had achieved a measure of heroic strength and a new insight which in the normal course would never have been his. When he died he was "ready" as he had never been before. At his death Pearl achieved a new humanity: "The great scene of grief in which the wild infant bore a part, had developed all her sympathies; and as her tears fell upon her father's cheek, they were the pledge that she would grow up amid human joy and sorrow, nor forever do battle with the world, but be a woman in it." Hester, Dimmesdale, and now Pearl learned what it is "to be men and women in it"—what it means to be.

Dimmesdale in his faith died praising God—a religious death. Hester lived out her "tragic" existence, giving counsel but, "stained with sin, bowed down with shame," denied the prophetic voice she might have raised, still believing, yet not believing (as witness the "A" which she wore to the end) in herself. "After many, many years," she was buried with her lover, and even her burial, like everything else in her life, was ambiguous. She was buried next to Dimmesdale, "yet with a space between, as if the dust of the two sleepers had no right to mingle." No right to mingle? In the first scene of the novel, Hawthorne had said of Hester's judges: "They were, doubtless, good men, just, and sage. But, out of the whole human family, it would not have been easy to select the same number of wise and virtuous persons, who should be less capable of sitting in judgment on an erring woman's heart, and disentangling its mesh of good and evil." Had Hester's and Dimmesdale's deed a "consecration of its own," or had it not? The Puritan judges said no. Even Hawthorne, speaking through the novel as a whole, suspends judgment. "We know not. We know not." Dimmesdale, the believer, could look forward to the last day "when all hidden things shall be revealed," when "the dark problem of this life" shall be made plain. But in this life he had wandered in a maze, "quite astray and at a loss in the pathway of human existence." So, to a close and scrupulous observer like Hawthorne, it must ever be. The pathway is beset with pitfalls and dubious choices. The shrewd pick their way warily. The passionate are likely to stumble or go wrong, and "good intentions" have no bearing on the inevitable penalty, which often far exceeds the crime. This is hard, but, to the heroic in heart, no cause for despair. There is wisdom to be won from the fine hammered steel of woe; a flower to be plucked from the rosebush at the prison door "to relieve the darkening close of a tale of human frailty and sorrow." To relieve, but not to reverse or redeem.

Henry James said that Hawthorne had "a cat-like faculty of seeing in the dark"; but he never saw through the dark to radiant light.[80] What light his vision reveals is like the fitful sunshine of Hester's and Dimmesdale's meeting in the forest— the tragic opposite of Emerson's triumphant gleaming sun that "shines also today."

10

MOBY-DICK

It is easy to see why Melville, himself a prey to the deepest forebodings about the optimism of his day, recognized at once his kinship of spirit with Hawthorne. "There is a certain tragic phase of humanity which, in our opinion [he wrote], was never more powerfully embodied than by Hawthorne." [81] A year after Hawthorne published *The Scarlet Letter*, Melville dedicated his own most powerful embodiment of this tragic phase, *Moby-Dick*, to Hawthorne, his acknowledged master. Together the two books are witness to the vitality of the tragic vision, which pierces beneath the "official view" of any culture to the dark realities that can never be permanently hidden,[82] and together they mark a recrudescence of the tragic spirit in what would seem an unlikely time, on unlikely soil, and without benefit of tragic theater or tragic audience.

Both authors were aware of the untimeliness of their books. Hawthorne, in the famous letter to his publisher, Fields, spoke of fearing that his novel would "weary very many people and disgust some" by keeping so close, and with so little diversification, to "the same dark idea." Would he have an audience receptive to his peculiar view of things? The Greek and Elizabethan dramatists or Racine or even the Poet of Job could count on an audience culturally predisposed through myth, theater, or racial view to accept at once a drama of direness. Hawthorne had to make his own audience, to lead it by easy stages, as it were, into the dark idea. Hence the familiar, reassuring tone of the Custom House introduction, where the only dire events involve a certain goose of tragic toughness and the routine political loss of a job not worth holding. Hence the whimsical apology, in advance, for the "stern and sombre aspect" of Hester's story—"too much ungladdened by genial sunshine; too little relieved by the tender and familiar influences which soften almost every scene of nature and real life, and, undoubtedly, should soften every picture of them"—an apology which we may well regard as almost wholly tactical.

And hence (among other reasons) the long preliminary phase of *Moby-Dick*, introducing Ishmael, the reassuringly normal one who would go to sea now and again to drive off the spleen, or merely to satisfy "an everlasting itch for things remote"; who would take "the universal thump" with equanimity, and cry three cheers for Nantucket—"and come a stove boat and stove body when they will, for stave my soul, Jove himself cannot." The world of Ishmael's setting forth, like the world of the Custom House, was undimmed by the dark idea and seemingly invulnerable to any Jovian thunderbolts. God was above young Ishmael's world as he packed his bag for Cape Horn and the Pacific; and even as he read on the tablets of Father Mapple's chapel in New Bedford the fate of the whalemen who had gone before him, he "grew merry again." The rest of his story shows how shallow his optimism was, as Melville leads him (and the untragic American audience) by slow degrees, but remorselessly, toward tragic truth.

Ishmael has been called the chorus to Ahab as tragic hero, but this is hardly adequate to describe his total participation in the tragic action. To be sure, the Aeschylean choruses became involved, acted, and suffered as the other choruses in Greek drama for the most part did. But it is significant of Melville's task of rendering his tragedy probable to his age that Ishmael frames and pervades the story as no Greek chorus does. He is a constant link to the known and familiar. He is average, goodhearted humanity, though somewhat more given to meditation than most and (as he says of himself) "quick to perceive a horror." His optimism lies not in his denial that the horror is there but in his hope of being "social with it"—

93

"since it is but well to be on friendly terms with all the inmates of the place one lodges in." Only gradually does this hope come to be fully tested. All the little horrors of the early stages of his adventures are accommodated to his hearty, comic vision. He accepts the wintry and forbidding conditions of his stay in New Bedford with good cheer. The inauspicious omens in Father Mapple's chapel fail to daunt him. He shares his bed with the terrifying Queequeg, and rejoices in the evidence of natural goodness even in this pagan cannibal. Queequeg's rescue of the man overboard on the trip to Nantucket confirms his faith in his new friend and in this "mutual joint-stock world" where Christians and cannibals live and let live. "Dost know nothing at all about whaling, I dare say—eh?" asks Captain Peleg as Ishmael presents himself at the *Pequod* to sign on for the voyage. "Nothing, Sir," he answers handsomely; "but I have no doubt I shall soon learn." Only Peleg's strange confidences about the captain of the *Pequod*—that "grand, ungodly, god-like man, Captain Ahab"—momentarily shake his confidence that there is no horror he cannot be social with. As he hears the story of Ahab's fierce troubles, he is filled "with a certain wild vagueness of painfulness concerning him"—"a sympathy and a sorrow for him, but for I don't know what, unless it was the cruel loss of his leg." But more than that—"a strange awe of him; but that sort of awe, which I cannot at all describe, was not exactly awe; I do not know what it was."

Such were the first intimations to this young novitiate of mysteries not to be resolved by his philosophy, the first hint (as Stephen Daedalus was later to refine on Aristotle's notion of terror) of "the feeling which arrests the mind in the presence of whatsoever is grave and constant in human sufferings and unites it with the secret cause." So far in Ishmael's experience whatever had been grave had not been constant, and what had been constant had not been grave. Pity, of the sort which he felt for Ahab's misfortune, is a passing thing, as he soon confesses: "However, my thoughts were at length carried in other directions, so that for the present dark Ahab slipped my mind."

But the sense of awe, the intimations of terror, were not

to be denied, nor the full terror in store. Queequeg's pagan fanaticisms, his all-day Ramadan, or Fasting and Humiliation, were easy for Ishmael's ready rationalism—"I say, we good Presbyterian Christians should be charitable in these things, and not fancy ourselves so vastly superior to other mortals, pagans and what not, because of their half-crazy conceits on these subjects"—and he pled with his cannibal friend to give over his "prolonged ham-squattings in cold, cheerless rooms" as opposed to "the obvious laws of Hygiene and common sense." But he could not so easily accommodate his second warning about Ahab, this time from old Elijah, whose "ambiguous, half-hinting, half-revealing, shrouded sort of talk begat in me all kinds of vague wonderments and half-apprehensions." He even chided himself for not facing squarely this challenge to his security, but in the busy preparations for the voyage he "said nothing, and tried to think nothing." In such situations, he said, a man "insensibly strives to cover up his suspicions even from himself."

But in spite of himself he was coming ever nearer the vortex. One morning, several days out, "as I levelled my glance toward the taffrail, foreboding shivers ran over me. Reality outran apprehension; Captain Ahab stood upon his quarter-deck." What Ishmael saw for the first time was no Queequeg with his crazy conceits, nor "humbug" Elijah, but a man "with a crucifixion in his face," standing there "in all the nameless regal overbearing dignity of some mighty woe." Ahab had looked on terror, and Ishmael looked on Ahab. Soon he was to stare into it face to face.

Somewhat before this first startling encounter, Melville had begun to shift his method from the narrative mode to the dramatic. It is as if he were confident by now that the bridge was whole and firm between the world of his readers and the tragic world of his imaginings. Ishmael was doing his work; the audience, like him, is almost ready for the full revelation. The "Knights and Squires" of the ship's company have been introduced. Stubb has had his first encounter with Ahab, told not by Ishmael but by Melville as dramatist: Stubb's mild plea that Ahab curtail his nightly deck-walks over the sleeping sailors' heads; Ahab's furious rebuke: "Down, dog, and kennel!"; and Stubb's bewildered ruminations: "He's full of riddles. . . . Damn me, but all things are queer, come to think of 'em." We have met the staid and steadfast Starbuck, "firm in the conflict with seas, or winds, or whales, or any of the ordinary irrational horrors of the world" yet unable (we are told prophetically) to "withstand those more terrific, because more spiritual terrors, which sometimes menace you from the concentrating brow of an enraged and mighty man." We know the "ignorant, unconscious fearlessness" of Flask—"a little waggish in the matter of whales." We have seen Ahab throw away his pipe—his next rejection, after his rebuke of Stubb, of his links with common humanity, which would seek only rest after toil and the solace of creature comforts. We learn of "that certain sultanism of his brain" which the hierarchical situation on shipboard encourages toward "an irresistible dictatorship." We have already accepted the possibility (ch. 16) that out of these old Quaker whalemen might come the "globular brain," the "ponderous heart" the "bold and nervous lofty language," of "a mighty pageant figure"—a Job, an Oedipus, a Lear—"formed for noble tragedies." The stage is set and the characters drawn for "the tragic dramatist" (as Melville now openly calls himself) to present his action.

There is a preliminary lull, but full of portent, in the brief "Mast-head" chapter, when Melville returns the story to Ishmael's consciousness (as, occasionally, he does throughout the action) to show the youthful novitiate's view from the crow's nest, how it induces a mystic, Platonic reverie, providing a kind of "asylum [in the whaling industry] for many romantic, melancholy, and absent-minded young men, disgusted with the carking care of earth, and seeking sentiment in tar and blubber." Here, to the young dreamer at the masthead, the Many merge into One; the watcher, "lulled into such an opium-like listlessness of vacant, unconscious reverie," ceases to watch; the waves blend with his thoughts and the sea with his soul: "he loses his identity." For a moment we hear Ishmael talking: "For one, I used to lounge up the rigging very leisurely, resting in the top to have a chat with Queequeg, or any one else off duty whom I might find there . . ." But it is Melville's voice that dispels this Emersonian dream, the tragic dramatist who prepares for the full revelation. "But while this sleep, this dream is on ye [Melville so addresses the young dreamers], move your foot or hand an inch; slip your hold at all; and your identity comes back in horror. Over Descartian vortices you hover. And perhaps, at mid-day, in the fairest weather, with one half-throttled shriek you drop through that transparent air into the summer sea, no more to rise for ever. Heed it well, ye Pantheists!"

Ishmael was never in greater danger than on his seemingly secure and sunny perch. Here, says the tragic dramatist, was no true wisdom and therefore (in the literal sense) no true poise. Ishmael must return to the common deck and the rigors of whaling. He must know it at its worst as at its best. He must "look in the face of fire." Only then does he learn (in "The Try-Works") that "that mortal man who hath more of joy than sorrow in him, that mortal man cannot be true—not true, or undeveloped." Down from the masthead, on Ahab's own quarter-deck, a major event in Ishmael's development is about to take place.

In the Quarter-Deck scene, when with his demonic eloquence Ahab enticed the crew into his terrifying enterprise, Ishmael was confronted for the first time with a "hero" in action. Ishmael's presence as the percipient narrator is not felt during the scene; we have only his belated comment afterward. In Melville's dramatic presentation Starbuck is given the only role as antagonist to Ahab; but against the "general hurricane" of Ahab's fury, his protest in the name of common sense and respect for God's creatures could not stand. The full drama starts with this thrust of Ahab's against his destiny, against "the unknown but still reasoning thing" (as he sees it) that has worked his woe; and to this heroic fury—terrifying yet somehow appealing—Ishmael could not be a passive witness only. In the turbulent scene, all thought of comic detachment, of being sociable with horror, was for the moment overwhelmed. "I, Ishmael, was one of that crew; my shouts had gone up with the rest; my oath had been welded with theirs; and stronger I shouted, and more did I hammer and clinch my oath, because of the dread in my soul. A wild, mystical, sym-

97

pathetical feeling was in me; Ahab's quenchless feud seemed mine." All of his old, reassuring categories are burst asunder in this first experience of "the dread in the soul."

But, as the voyage progressed, this dread had its abatements for Ishmael—signalizing, perhaps, how sturdy are the "admirable evasions" of average man, loath to admit his failure to domesticate the universe. Ishmael is normal, unpossessed humanity. There are moments of calm when he detaches himself from Ahab's quenchless feud and returns to his philosophizings. They are still cheerful, even if they have a new somber note, as when making mats with Queequeg, he speculates about "chance, free will, necessity," finds them "no wise incompatible—all interweavingly working together." But chance, he concludes darkly, can rule either one, and has "the last featuring blow at events." Later (ch. 49), speculating on "this strange mixed affair we call life," he slips into a sort of "desperado philosophy." In such a mood, he regards the universe as a "vast practical joke," perhaps on himself, but "with nothing to dispirit a man and nothing to dispute." He simply makes his will. "Now then, thought I, unconsciously rolling up the sleeves of my frock, here goes for a cool, collected dive at death and destruction, and the devil fetch the hindmost." Thus, argues the wise youth, if we cannot be merry, we can at least know the universe for the risky thing it is and be prepared for whatever comes. This is not Ahab's feud; it is a stoic rather than a tragic phase. It is as far, except for one other episode, as Ishmael ever gets.

If, as in *The Scarlet Letter,* there is something archetypal of all tragedy in this steady uncovering, layer by layer, of the hard meaning of existence, it is not through Ishmael's consciousness that Melville uncovers it all. Ishmael recedes as Ahab occupies the foreground. The frankly dramatic episodes (for example, The Quarter-Deck, the nine gams, The Forge, The Carpenter, the chases), like much of the whaling lore, are not controlled by Ishmael as narrator (as, for instance, the narrator Marlow controls some of Conrad's stories), nor do they reveal to us any sustained or intense spiritual struggle. A few times only, as Melville develops the "linked analogies" between whaling and human existence, is Ishmael's voice heard unmistakably. The "Monkey-Rope" episode reminds him of the precarious interdependence of human beings, how one man may innocently perish through another's error—Queequeg's, in this instance—and for a moment we hear the young tyro philosophizing again. Squeezing "case" with Queequeg puts him in mind of the friendly pressure of the hands that should bind all men together in "the very milk and sperm of kindness." But is it Ishmael's voice (or Melville's) which thanks God (in "The Fountain") that "through all the thick mists of the dim doubts in my mind, divine intuitions now and then shoot, enkindling my fog with a heavenly ray"? or, in "The Grand Armada," likens the state of his soul, "amid the tornadoed Atlantic of my being," to the calm center in the midst of the vast encircling herd of whales: "But even so . . . do I myself still forever centrally disport in mute calm; and while ponderous planets of unwaning woe revolve round me, deep down and deep inland there I still bathe me in eternal mildness of joy"? Who dichotomizes all men and nations, nay the great globe itself, according to the categories of Fast-Fish and Loose-Fish? All this may be a measure of Ishmael's deepening stoicism or growing philosophic poise; but actually about this time he ceases to be a fictional narrator with an autonomous spiritual development, and merges into Melville the omniscient novelist, commenting and discoursing without regard for Ishmael's fictional status or his personal point of view, and taking us within the personalities of other characters, especially Ahab and Starbuck, where Ishmael as observer could not penetrate.

Only once more before the very end do we see through Ishmael's eyes. In "The Try-Works" he knows for an awful instant what it actually feels like to be "given up" to fire. As helmsman, staring at night into the flaming try-works, he sees in the "tartarean shapes of the harpooneers," as they pitch and pole the hissing masses of blubber, "the material counterpart of [their] monomaniac commander's soul." He sees the "redness, the madness, the ghastliness," and he sees nothing else. He slips into an hypnotic drowsiness; his hold on the helm loosens, and he comes suddenly to consciousness to find himself facing dead astern. Only barely does he save the ship from being brought by the lee and possibly capsizing. He sees in his temporary distraction a sign of Ahab's moral inversion— Ahab who had looked too long on fire. Ishmael, having learned the "wisdom that is woe," now learns the "woe that is madness"; and he learns it this time on his own pulses. He learns that he is not the "Catskill eagle," nor is Ahab, who can dive down into the "blackest gorges" and rise again into the sun. "Give not thyself up, then, to fire [says Melville-Ishmael] lest it invert thee, deaden thee; as for the time it did me."

This is the last of Ishmael's intimate moral revelations. Here, except for the occasional reflections on the likeness of whaling to human life and except for the Epilogue, where he recounts only in the barest fashion the circumstances of his lone survival, we leave him. With "The Try-Works" his main function in the novel is done. He has cast off his green and dreamy youth and brought us to the edge of the vortex. The drama is now Ahab's (with Starbuck the main but ineffectual human antagonist) and Moby Dick's. The necessary probability has been established for Ahab's final plunge into the vortex itself, carrying all but Ishmael to destruction. And not since Job, as Melville's epigraph reminds us, has the destruction been so complete: "And I only am escaped alone to tell thee." All is gone, the whole "Anacharsis Clootz deputation" for the human race so devilishly misled by Ahab. The sea rolls on undisturbed as it rolled five thousand years ago. No angels sing the hero to his rest; no kingdom remains to be restored to order; only one lad just out of his novitiate lives to tell the story. Even the "bird of heaven," pinned to the mast by Tashtego's hammer, "his whole captive form folded in the flag of Ahab," goes down with the ship, which "like Satan, would not sink to hell till she had dragged a living part of heaven along with her . . ."

Such an ending forces to the limit any definition of tragedy comprehending positive values. We look in vain for precedents, certainly among the "Christian" heroes. Dr. Faustus had defied God and ended in hell. But he had defied God not out of hate but out of boredom or curiosity or restlessness, and in the end he had a vision of God's grace and forgiveness none the less real because he could not (or thought he could not) share in them. Lear railed at the universe but sought instruction even in his madness and learned reconciliation and love in unexpected ways. Hester lived out the dark ambiguities of her existence, with no satisfying resolution either way, but grew toward acceptance and humility rather than hate and denial. Ahab hated and denied. The universe had wronged him; he adjudged it evil and defied it. In this phase, he is a demonic, not a tragic, hero; less a Faustus or Lear or Prometheus than (as Richard Chase describes him) [83] a false Prometheus, with destruction not salvation in his heart. Ahab's is no "puritan drama of the soul," a constant tension between the vision of innocence and the accepted guilt. He rejects guilt, both when he puts himself beyond good and evil as lord and master over all the souls on the *Pequod* ("Talk not to me of blasphemy, man; I'd strike the sun if it insulted me . . . Who's over me?") and in his final conception of "this whole act [as] immutably decreed": "I am the Fates' lieutenant." In the first pose, Ahab is more than man—and more than tragic man; he is a self-appointed God. In the latter, he is less than man, a mere agent of destiny. To the extent that the book glorifies Ahab in these two poses and passes no further judgment on him, Melville was right in telling Hawthorne that in *Moby-Dick* he had written "a wicked book." To this extent also, it is no tragedy.

But the indictment fails to do justice to Ahab and to that in the book which is not Ahab. Ahab is an emblem of no absolute order, and the book is not a "hideous allegory" of the triumph of Evil over Good. Like the tragedies which it recalls, it is more an exploration of mysteries than a rejection of mysteries in a sweeping nihilistic gesture. Much has been made of the book as a document in Melville's personal "quarrel with God," [84] and his rebellious accents ring (or so it would seem) unmistakably in passage after passage. But so do Melville's accents sound in Ahab's melting moods, of which there are many, and in Ahab's passages of introspection and self-doubt, as in his confession to Starbuck: ". . . and then, the madness, the frenzy, the boiling blood and the smoking brow, with which, for a thousand lowerings old Ahab had furiously, foamingly chased his prey—more a demon than a man—aye, aye! what a forty years' fool—fool—old fool, has old Ahab been!" Ahab "has his humanities," as Captain Peleg announced to the novitiate Ishmael at the signing on. He understands and admits (as no demonic and few romantic heroes do) his own ruthlessness—toward Pip ("Thou touchest my inmost centre, boy"), toward Starbuck, toward the captain of the *Rachel* who would engage his help in searching for the lost child. He drops his one salt tear into the great Pacific. But more than this, his feud, like Job's and Prometheus' and Lear's, is not entirely his own. He is no Byronic hero kicking himself loose from the moral universe in ironic bitterness. He took upon himself what he conceived to be the burden of humanity. He faced the darkness as he saw it. Starbuck reconciled it with his traditional beliefs; Stubb and Flask laughed it off; Ishmael saw it and adopted his "desperado philosophy." Only Ahab felt what "some deep men feel": "that intangible malignity which has been from the beginning"—whatever it is in nature that makes these hard hearts, whatever oppresses, bewilders, and bears man down. Like Job and Lear, he saw his own misfortunes as a sign of the common lot; and like them he struck back. "He piled upon the whale's white hump the sum of all the general rage and hate felt by his whole race from Adam down; and then, as if his chest had been a mortar, he burst his hot heart's shell upon it."

Should he or should he not have done what he did? Should he or should he not have followed his "fatal pride," as Melville calls it, to the end? If the book is to be read as saying that he *should*, then it is a "wicked" book, justifying monomania, sultanism, blasphemy, and the all-but-total destruction they wrought. But the book neither justifies nor condemns Ahab. Tragedy is witness to the moral ambiguity of every action, and Melville is true to the witness of *Job, Dr. Faustus,* and *Lear* in conceiving of Ahab's action in just this light. Melville keeps the precarious balance in many ways—not only through Ismael's comments and experience and Ahab's brooding awareness of the ethics of his action, which comes to the surface in some of his calmer soliloquies and in his gentler replies to Starbuck, but in the perspective that Starbuck and the visiting captains in the gams give to Ahab's purpose; in the constant reminder, through imagery and (later) direct comment, of the beauty, the goodness, the truth that make (with the vision of evil) the dual vision of tragedy. Indeed, the "monomaniac" Ahab's own statements of this duality are among the most poignant: "I am damned in the midst of Paradise." "There is that in thee, poor lad, which I feel too curing to my malady." "So far gone am I in the dark side of earth, that its other side, the theoretic bright one, seems but uncertain twilight to me."

But having gone thus far in the uncertain twilight, he does not turn back. If it grows ever darker, we are not left in total darkness. He is aware to the end of "the lovely lee-wardings" that he views on his last look from the masthead. Starbuck weeps as he clasps his hand for the last time. "Oh, my captain, my captain!—noble heart . . ." In the end, Ahab goes down "death-glorious" like his ship, "ungodly" yet "god-like," demonic in his own hate and vengeance, yet noble in his sense of the community of all unjust suffering. The book does not pronounce him good or evil any more than *The Scarlet Letter* calls Hester Prynne good or evil. But by carrying him through his fatal action in all its tensions, paradoxes, and ambiguities, the book, like a true tragedy, goes deeply into the mysteries of all moral judgments. All categories are put to the sharpest test, not only Ishmael's, Starbuck's, Stubb's, and Flask's but Ahab's own. We see the nature of each, how far toward good-and-evil each can go. The book leaves us, again true to its tradition, somewhere between pity and terror, faith and doubt, heaven and hell; it leaves us in what Ishmael-Melville calls (in "The Gilder") "manhood's pondering repose of If." But we have seen the conditions of pity and terror, good and evil, heaven and hell, more clearly. "Doubts of all things earthly, and intuitions of some things heavenly; this combination makes neither believer nor infidel, but makes a man who regards them both with equal eye."

Ahab himself never achieved such repose or looked on life so steadily, or if he did it was only momentarily. One other momentary insight comes to him in the frenzy of his final battle with the whale, and in a way it is his climactic insight. The perennial sense of injustice, the cry of Prometheus and Job as of Lear and Hamlet, was also Ahab's. Why do the innocent suffer? "O cursed spite / That ever I was born to set it right." This was the "inscrutable thing" that Ahab hated. Ahab never penetrated the mystery nor came to as full an understanding of the meaning in suffering as did Job or Lear. But in the moment of final conflict he senses a new dimension in his suffering, a relatedness to something other than the sheer malice of the universe, the whiteness of the whale.

As Ahab in his whaleboat watches the *Pequod* founder under the attack of the whale, he realizes that all is lost. He faces his "lonely death on lonely life," denied even "the last fond pride of meanest shipwrecked captains," the privilege of going down with his ship. But here, at the nadir of his fortunes, he sees that in his greatest suffering lies his greatest glory. He dies spitting hate at the whale, but he does not die cynically or in bitterness. The whale conquers—but is "unconquering." The "god-bullied hull" goes down "death-glorious." What Ahab feels is not joy, or serenity, or goodness at the heart of things. But with his sense of elation, even triumph, at having persevered to the end, there is also a note of reconciliation: "Oh, now I feel my topmost greatness lies in my topmost grief." This is not reconciliation with the whale, or with the malice in the universe, but it is a reconciliation of Ahab with Ahab. Whatever justice, order, or equivalence there is, he has found not in the universe but in himself.[85] He is neither "sultan" now nor "old fool." In finally coming to terms with existence (though too late), he is tragic man; to the extent that he transcends it, finds "greatness" in suffering, he is tragic hero.

Melville did not dramatize further this final phase of Ahab's course, and therein lies the peculiarly shocking nature of the book. It is as if we left Job at the end of one of his diatribes or Oedipus at his self-blinding or Lear as he curses his daughters and plunges into the storm. Even with this final insight of Ahab's, the ending seems too dire for tragedy. It seems to deny the future; when the *Pequod* sinks, all seems lost; and there is no further comment, no fifth-act compensations to let in a little hope. The only comment is the action itself, the total action from beginning to end, all the good and the evil it uncovers. There is one survivor of the action: the tragic artist to tell about it from beginning to end. In the chapter called "Brit," Melville writes: ". . . man has lost that sense of the full awfulness of the sea which aboriginally belongs to it"; and the sea, he reminds us shortly, covers "two thirds of the fair world." *Moby-Dick* presents this awfulness relentlessly, even wickedly, as Melville hinted to Hawthorne. It is a cruel reminder of the original terror. If the world it presents is the starkest kind of answer to the Emersonian dream, it is not a world for despair or rejection—as long as there is even one who escapes to tell its full story.

11

THE BROTHERS KARAMAZOV

IDEALLY, tragedy reveals simultaneously, in one complete action, man's total possibilities and his most grievous limitations —all that he should and can do as creator of good, all that he does or fails to do or cannot do as creature of fate, chance, or his own evil nature. Actually, no tragedy can tell the whole truth. All tragedies to this extent only approximate Tragedy, and the stress on one side or the other of the paradox of man differs from one tragedy to another. *Moby-Dick* does not ignore man as creator, but it stresses man as creature, the prey (but not the helpless prey) of mysterious forces within and without, which can lead under certain circumstances to his destruction and which in essence constantly threaten his composure. *The Brothers Karamazov* stretches the definition of tragedy in the other direction. At several points in its action, life is transfigured by a religious vision. Its ending is radiant with reconciliation and hope. But it leaves unanswered many great questions, potent for destruction. All losses are not restored, nor do troubles end.

Like Hawthorne and Melville, Dostoevski also sensed the cultural crisis of his time. "This is a modern case," he had written in *Crime and Punishment,* "an incident of to-day when the heart of man is troubled." [86] What is imaged in the dark forest of Hester's and Dimmesdale's wanderings and in Ahab's furious quest, appeared in *Crime and Punishment* in Raskolnikov's dilemma, in his stinking St. Petersburg and his moldy, tomblike room; and in *The Brothers* it is implicit—this "strange disease of modern life"—in the agonized search for meaning on the part of three young men adrift in a world of "riddles" and "mysteries" and "theories"—as perilous a sea as ever Ahab wandered. The sense of urgency is more immediate in Dostoevski than in the two Americans. The prosecutor at Dmitri's trial broods on "all this tragic topsy-turvydom of to-day." What Hawthorne suggests in his story of a bygone time and Melville in the events of a little-known seafaring industry, Dostoevski gets at through an entirely realistic setting in a typical Russian town of his day ("our town," as he calls it several times) and through a situation involving a typical Russian family—typical enough, at least, to cause at first a general feeling of alarm in its community and (later) throughout the country. Indeed, the situation, when it becomes fully known, is seen to bring into desperate question all the standard and consoling estimates which nineteenth-century Russian humanity had made of itself. "What are these people? What can mankind be after this?" cries a sensitive young observer when the crisis is at its height. To this question (which was also Job's and Oedipus' and Lear's) the book gives no final consoling answer. It presents an action whose large involvement reveals, as seldom in tragedy, man's possibilities for creative and spiritual transcendence, yet shows him, and life itself, as essentially tragic: a dark problem, ambiguous, paradoxical, problematic. "For a long time," wrote Berdyaev, "European society had stayed at the fringes of being and was content with an outward existence." [87] It was Dostoevski who, like Hawthorne and Melville in America, first re-explored the turbulent interior, and in *The Brothers* wrote the definitive tragic analysis of our times.

At first glance, the interior which the book explores seems to reveal confusion worse confounded, with no cheerful Ishmael to lead the way in. It is shocking, bewildering, discordant. We enter a confused area of sadisms and masochisms ("lacerations" is Dostoevski's generic term), of violence, paradox, and the unpredictable. The "grotesque and monstrous" sexual rivalry between Dmitri and his father, which in the first scene ("The Unfortunate Gathering") is revealed as the major

portent of tragic action, is only one sign of a general disintegration of values. The wrangling family is no family, the brothers
share no brotherhood. The church is mocked in Fyodor's un-
speakable displays before Father Zossima. Ivan's devious and
sophistic essay on the ecclesiastical courts shows human
reason at its most corrupt, and his easy formula about morality
and immortality (all is permitted, even crime, to the infidel)
opens at once to Dmitri a terrible possibility: "I'll remember
it," he says suddenly; and shortly after, "evenly and deliberately," hints at his father's death. The unruliness of the opening scene is only a suggestion of what is to come: envy, hatred,
greed in the monastery itself; lust, violence, perversion in likely
and unlikely places. A child hangs cats and buries them with
elaborate ceremony, a young girl relishes the thought of witnessing torture, desires destruction, and slams the door on
her fingers for a full ten seconds by count; a saintly young man
quietly allows a vengeful child to bite his finger to the bone.
Dmitri beats his father bloody and, like Ivan, wills his death.
The parricide, long in the air, is finally committed by Smerdyakov, the illegitimate brother, for no other reason than pure
financial profit.

Such are the visible, surface signs of the Karamazov world.
But they are not in themselves tragic, as mere violence and
perversion (more or less constant in any society) never are.
They take on tragic meaning as we get closer to their source
in the deep spiritual confusion of which they are the symptoms.
Here is the central difference between the world of classical
and Shakespearean tragedy, to which *The Scarlet Letter* and
Moby-Dick refer, and the tragic world, prophetic of our own
day, which Dostoevski envisioned. Gone is the clear purpose,
for right or wrong, of Antigone and Oedipus, Dr. Faustus and
Ahab. Even Hamlet, for all his hesitations and doubts, had a
Hyperion to judge a satyr by; and in her dark forest Hester
Prynne never lost her sense of justification. The modern tragic
problem is not what values or loyalties to choose but the bank-
ruptcy of all values and loyalties, and the consequent disintegration of the individual. This is why the Karamazovs and
many of the lesser folk in their world fling about them so reck-
lessly and probe their inner beings in endless talk; and this is

the meaning of the violence, and of the Freudian gropings, of much contemporary tragic fiction. Lise smashes her fingers to find out who she is, to find her own identity. None of the theories over which Ivan and "the green Russian youth" argue in the "stinking taverns" meets the test of the new experience. The "old moral catechism" has no authority. The echoes that rang in Faustus' ears are all but inaudible, and these latter-day experimenters are fiercely on their own. No classical or Elizabethan hero was ever "lost" in this sense.

Thus the dominant mood of the story (as of much contemporary fiction) is one of disorientation and search, of frantic trial by error, as each of the three brothers tries to find his center out, to find some viable truth among the uncertainties. Each one reaches at times a state of almost unbearable tension which threatens the complete disorganization of personality. Dmitri thrashes about in confusion and disorder. In the crisis, Ivan, the intellectual, "loses his bearings" and almost his mind. Even to Alyosha, the saintly one, the spectacle of his wrangling family and the dark stirrings which, as he grows in knowledge of the world, he feels in himself, pose a fearful question: "My brothers [he confides to Lise] are destroying themselves, my father too. And they are destroying others. It's 'the primitive force of the Karamazovs,' as Father Paissy said the other day, a crude, unbridled, earthly force. Does the spirit of God move above that force? Even I don't know. I only know that I, too, am a Karamazov. . . . Me a monk, a monk! Am I a monk, Lise?" And at a later moment the saintly one himself reaches a point of open rebellion, "with barricades," against a universe, once lovingly accepted, which suddenly loses its meaning for him.

"Does the spirit of God move above that force?" "Am I a monk, Lise?" Each one of the brothers in turn asks questions similar to this, variants of the questions which the pressures of the tragic situation have from the beginning forced to the surface: What is man? What does it mean to be? Only, in the Karamazov world, the problem is complicated as never before. Quick answers abound, each with its own attractiveness and sanction, and each offering an alternative to the questioners. Rakitin, for whom, as Dmitri said, life was "easy," had turned cynic and self-seeker; he had reduced all Karamazovs to "sensualists" (an identity which the goatish Fyodor had permanently and cheerfully accepted) and tried to corrupt Alyosha into following this easy way. Dmitri tried it for a time but found in it unbearable contradictions. Ivan experimented with the rationalist side of cynicism ("Am I my brother's keeper?") until experience (as with Dr. Faustus) changed his mind. Both Dmitri and Ivan honor Alyosha's way of dedicated love (Zossima's teaching), but such are their natures that they can follow no prescribed path, not even one they recognize as good.

This is the gist of the problem for the new tragic hero, a category which Dostoevski may be said to have defined for our time. The only hope for man in his new state of spiritual anarchy is to follow out his nature wherever it leads; he must test his new freedom to the very limit. The measure of the new hero is his capacity for sensing the problem, the dynamic of his searching it out (the risks and the suffering), and the awareness of partial truths gained. This new tragic hero has not the satisfaction of a clear and present opponent—an unjust deity, a plague-stricken city, ungrateful daughters, an oppressive social and religious code, or a Moby Dick. He struggles not so much with a crisis as with a condition; and the condition is the contemporary confusion of values and the dilemma in his own soul. He does not shape events in bold strokes; rather, events to a great extent shape him. His characteristic state is indecisiveness, amounting, in his initial phase, to paralysis of will; and hence the tendency to call him pathetic rather than tragic, a victim rather than a hero. But to the extent to which he senses the dilemma and its full implications, takes positive action of whatever sort, follows it to the end (accepting the consequences in suffering and loss) and in so doing gains new insight into his own being and the human condition, he is still tragic, and a hero. He is characteristically the "lost, violent soul," whose very violence (his only hope) may carry him to a kind of purgation and new insight—as it were, in spite of himself. Of such are Ivan and Dmitri, both "lost" and both violent of soul. Their course through the novel, their world and their head-on collision with it, the infinite involvements of the central action and the meanings dislodged by it, define the area and the central concern of contemporary tragedy.

"The Karamazovs are not blackguards but philosophers," said Dmitri, and we first see him on the way to this insight when, shortly after "The Unfortunate Gathering," he pours out to his younger brother Alyosha the confusions of a distraught mind and heart. His "confession," as he calls it, is the story of his shameful betrayal of the proud and high-spirited Katerina Ivanovna and his choice of Grushenka (his father's inamorata) and the "back-alley." He has been guilty of outrageous behavior, public and private. Besides his threatening remarks about his father in Zossima's cell, he has recently brutalized a drinking companion in public (little Ilusha's father) and carried on scandalous parties with Grushenka, financed by money entrusted to him by Katerina. He has violated all the decencies, and his loathing for his father is a steady, irresistible compulsion. But the very violence of this lost violent soul has had a purgative effect. "Sunk in vilest degradation," as he says of himself, he has made a curious new moral discovery, which he pauses to explain to Alyosha. ("I am not a cultivated man, brother, but I've thought a lot about this.")

In his degradation he has learned what suffering is ("There's a terrible amount of suffering for man on earth, a terrible amount of trouble"). But more than that, he has stumbled onto a baffling contradiction which awakens the philosopher in him. This is the peculiar pride he takes in his excesses and the ecstatic joy, along with the shame, that he feels in them. "I go headlong with my heels up," he tells Alyosha, "and am pleased to be falling in that degrading attitude, and pride myself upon it. And in the very depths of that degradation I begin a hymn of praise." The source of his pride and ecstasy is the beauty he finds in "Sodom," and the contradiction is the coexistence in his own nature of "the ideal of Sodom" and the "ideal of the Madonna," neither of which he can exclude or deny. So far, his course, the bent of his nature, has taken him along the "side-paths, little dark back-alleys behind the main road," where he has found "precious metal

111

in the dirt." The shame is intolerable, the beauty is "mysterious" and "terrible." Is it good or evil? "Yes," he says ruefully, "man is broad, too broad, indeed. I'd have him narrower." "The devil only knows what to make of it," he concludes. "What to the mind is shameful, is beauty and nothing else to the heart." "I go on and I don't know whether I'm going to shame or to light and joy."

So, lured by whatever it is that he calls "precious metal in the dirt," the "beauty in Sodom," Dmitri plunges on in this curious mixture of pride and shame, compulsion and guilt, to find for himself whatever answer he can. He is no mere sensualist on the loose, any more than Dr. Faustus (in Marlowe's conception) was the wicked sorcerer of the medieval story. He is the "new man" with impulses and intuitions he does not understand, knowing none of the restraints of a traditional upbringing in family or school, but conscious that, like Faustus, he must go his own way. He seemed dimly to realize (and this to Dostoevski was the bane as well as the only hope of the new man) that this was his destiny, for better or worse. Dmitri loved and honored Alyosha, but he could not pattern his life on him. "You go your way and I mine," he cries to him in mid-career, "there's terrible disgrace in store for me . . . though I'm perfectly free to stop it. I can stop it or carry it through, note that. Well, let me tell you I shall carry it through . . . The filthy back-alley and the she-devil."

As tension rises in his rivalry with his father for Grushenka, he becomes a man possessed. He beats Fyodor in a jealous rage, makes absurd and pitiful attempts to raise money to pay back Katerina and cries like a child in his frustration. That night, hearing that Grushenka is with his father, he rushes to the place with murder in his heart, only to find the old man waiting for the girl in vain. As Fyodor cranes his neck out the window, Dmitri poises himself for the blow—but it never falls. He flees the spot, and brains the servant Grigory, who tries to stop him. Thoughts of suicide whirl in his head, and he toys with a pistol. But his course is not run, and he knows it. "I was foolish about the bullet! I want to live. I love life!" Learning that Grushenka has gone to join her lover at Mokroe, he hires a carriage and plunges after her. "All was confusion, confusion, in Mitya's soul . . ."

The strange, lacerating orgy at Mokroe is interrupted by the police, who accuse Dmitri of the murder of his father. All the evidence is against him; his sordid rivalry with his father is an obvious motive, and he is stained with Grigory's blood. He fails to stand up under cross-examining, and the more he protests his innocence and "honor" the worse off he is. He is stripped bare, literally and figuratively, before men.

This is his lowest point of humiliation and his moment of intensest suffering. Like Oedipus at the moment of realization, or Lear in the storm, he is pressed to the very limit. Some mysterious new potential in his nature is released, and again he experiences a kind of catharsis. That night he makes a moral discovery in which his old confusions disappear in a new sense of unity and purpose. Exhausted beyond even his immense endurance, he is allowed to rest. He falls at once into a deep sleep and dreams of seeing by the roadside a starving infant in its mothers arms, "its little fists blue from cold." In his dream, which has the power on him of an ecstatic vision, he feels a deep sense of fatherhood toward the little creature and brotherhood toward all suffering mankind. He wakes up to find that some one has put a pillow under his head, an act of brotherliness that touches him deeply. " 'Who was so kind?' " he cries with "a sort of ecstatic gratitude, and tears in his voice. . . . 'I've had a good dream, gentlemen,' " he says, and there is "a new light, as of joy," in his face.

In this new calm of mind, he sees his past and his future in a new perspective. (Later, at the trial, the prosecutor was wrong, of course, when he said that "Karamazov always lives in the present.") "We all make men weep," Dmitri cries to his questioners when the examination is resumed, "and mothers and babes at the breast . . . but of all . . . I am the lowest reptile. . . . I understand now that such men as I need a blow, a blow of destiny. . . . I accept the torture of accusation, and my public shame. I want to suffer and by suffering be purified." Later he tells Alyosha that a "new man" rose up in him at that moment, and in his new insight he speaks in the very words of

113

Father Zossima: "We are all responsible for all," he says. "I go for all, because some one must go for all. . . . I accept it."

This is Promethean and Christlike. But it is a phase only, a momentary calm, in Dmitri's turbulent course. He ends as neither martyr nor religious hero nor (in the old commanding sense) tragic hero. What he has found on his pulses has not the power to sustain; it is only a momentary insight, indicating what might have been but, tragically, is not to be. During the long weeks in prison preceding his trial, he shows fortitude and reflective power. He is repelled by the various suggestions to get him off: of Rakitin, who would prove him the victim of "environment"; of the doctor who would prove him mad; of all the "Claude Bernards" who would prove that "it's all chemistry"; of Ivan who would have him escape to America. He refuses to accept these evasions; he will not "run away from crucifixion." "All these philosophers [he says to Alyosha visiting him in prison] are the death of me. Damn them!" And yet never has life seemed so precious to him: "What a thirst for existence and consciousness has sprung up in me within these peeling walls. . . . I think I could stand anything, any suffering, only to be able to repeat to myself every moment, 'I exist.'" Perhaps, when the opportunity to escape comes, he will decide *à la Bernard*—"'for I believe I'm a contemptible Bernard myself,'" he concludes "with a bitter grin."

By the time of the trial, he has slipped completely from the high moral level. He enters the courtroom looking like "an awful dandy in a brand-new frock-coat." His sudden, intemperate outbursts discompose the court. His final plea to the jury is, not to be allowed to suffer for mankind, but simply to be "spared." The day after his conviction, he falls ill of a "nervous fever" and broods in his hospital room on plans for escape. "I am not ready!" he says to Alyosha in despair, "I am not able to resign myself . . . It's the headstrong, evil Karamazov spirit! No, I am not fit for suffering." Alyosha sees that the cross is not for him, and tries to soothe his troubled spirit: "Only remember that other man always, all your life and wherever you go, and that will be enough for you."

Confused and tormented as he still is ("My God," he cries,

"calm my heart: what is it I want? I want Katya! Do I understand what I want?"), it would be wrong to say that his suffering has been meaningless. It has made a difference, if not the 'heroic' difference of Antigone's or Hamlet's or Samson's, about whose awesome examples a whole society in its "new acquist" could be said to have re-formed, at least a difference in self-knowledge and in a few people who knew him best. Not every one accepted the prosecutor's summary of the trial, which (in one of the great ironic scenes of the book) made a moral story out of a tragic one. It was Kalganov, a young man of twenty, who wept bitterly after the preliminary examination and asked, "What can mankind be after this?" Grushenka, who sensed the complexity of Dmitri's nature and conceived great faith in him, showed signs of a "spiritual transformation . . . a steadfast, fine, and humble determination," even if she had not entirely conquered her old vindictiveness toward Katerina. Alyosha, the closest and most sensitive observer, knew that Dmitri had made a permanent advance, and in this conviction he acquiesces in plans for Dmitri's escape. By refusing that great cross, argues Alyosha, "you will feel all your life an even greater duty, and that constant feeling will do more to make you a new man, perhaps, than if you went there"—to prison in Siberia. With this heightened sense of his moral being, of his very existence ("How I want to live now!"), he will never, as Alyosha tells him, call it "quits." He had conquered the temptation of suicide; he had sensed the shallowness of the materialist philosophies, he had come to see how "dry, dry and flat" the souls of the Rakitins are; and he had found new creative possibilities in his own soul. In the line of tragic heroes, he harks back to the greathearted, passionate, confused ones—the Lears and the Othellos. He had "ever but slenderly known himself," and he never gains Lear's grand composure or Othello's deep and final insight. We leave him still thrashing about, far from the peaks. But he has glimpsed them, and he does not abandon the journey. For one so tried, this is a victory, however ambiguous and incomplete. It is a Karamazov victory, a tragic witness to one aspect of the modern condition.

Ivan's story represents another phase of modern tragic man. If Dmitri's tragic compulsion was the demand of his sensual nature, Ivan's lay in his refusal to accept a universe that failed to square with his penetrating rationalism and in carrying out as far as he could his own rebellious formulation. He functions on a conceptual level far above Dmitri's reach, or Alyosha's. "Ivan is superior to us," Dmitri told Alyosha. He was a brilliant student of the natural sciences, an essayist and critic. He held himself aloof from life, as Dmitri had plunged into it, and was reserved and distant toward his family. Dmitri called him a "tomb," Alyosha a "riddle," and Fyodor "a cloud of dust." The prosecutor at the trial summed him up quickly (and characteristically) as "one of those modern young men of brilliant education and vigorous intellect, who has lost all faith in everything." Ivan himself came closer when he described himself to Alyosha as one of the "green Russian youth" who talk endlessly in the taverns about "eternal questions"—"the existence of God and immortality . . . socialism or anarchism . . . the transformation of all humanity on a new pattern." Alyosha saw him best as one "haunted by a great unsolved doubt . . . one of those who don't want millions but an answer to their questions."

The increasing pressure of events, which forces this wrangling family together in spite of themselves, brought Ivan (like Dmitri before him) into intimate conversation with Alyosha. The question he laid before Alyosha was in essence this: how could life be so lovable and yet so horrible? Dmitri had found contradictions in his own nature, Ivan found them in the nature of things; and in both cases the contradictions were intolerable. He loved life passionately, "the sticky little leaves as they open in spring . . . the blue sky . . . some great deeds done by men." He was no mere intellectualist, nor was he a confirmed atheist. He could accept God as a "hypothesis." What he could not accept was the injustice in the world, the suffering of innocent victims. His problem was as old as Job's (although he never looked upon himself as a victim) and (as the Devil reminds him later) as new as Descartes': he could find no satisfying resolution through his intellect alone. By what reach of faith, he asks, could one resolve into harmony

116

a universe that harbors so hideous an injustice as the torturing of children by their elders—and he chooses this example because it is so "unanswerably clear." He harrows Alyosha with instances, of which he has an impressive collection. Adults, he says, have the compensation, at least, of having "eaten the Apple," but the children have eaten nothing. What is the meaning of "harmony" and forgiveness in such a world? He doesn't want harmony if it would necessitate the forgiveness of the torturers of children. "I would rather be left with the unavenged suffering and my unsatisfied indignation." Even the mother has no right to forgive her child's torturer: she can forgive him *for herself*, perhaps, for the "immeasurable suffering of her mother's heart," but not for the suffering of her child. "And if that is so," he concludes, "if she dare not forgive, what becomes of harmony?" "I must have justice, or I will destroy myself."

Alyosha, of course, tells him quietly that he has forgotten Christ, who, because He shed His innocent blood for all and everything, can forgive "all and for all." In answer Ivan recites his extraordinary "poem," "The Legend of the Grand Inquisitor," depicting a world in which all such questions, and the suffering entailed in them, are absorbed by a small ecclesiastical hierarchy, who rule through "miracle, mystery, and authority." In such a world there would be no freedom, but there would be no agonizing questions. "For fifteen centuries," Ivan's Inquisitor tells the returned Christ, "we have been wrestling with Thy freedom, but now it is ended and over for good. . . . Tomorrow I shall burn Thee."

Thus, cut off as he was from the salutary influence of a father in his own family (Fyodor was a father in name only) and from the fatherhood of God, Ivan had devised intellectually the very opposite, a completely paternalistic society. He makes the rationalist's last desperate attempt to resolve the terrible paradoxes of a universe that can be accepted by a faith like Alyosha's. Ivan knows that it won't work. "It's all nonsense, Alyosha. It's only a senseless poem of a senseless student." And later, in his delirium, when the Devil chides him with his sophomoric attempt, he is "crimson with shame." But it is equally clear that Alyosha's faith is not, as he says, for

117

his "Euclidian earthly mind." "And now you go to the right and I to the left," he says, just as Dmitri had done. Alyosha sees the hopelessness of his brother's position and, with "such a hell in his heart and head," his inevitable collapse into suicide or debauchery. "You will kill yourself, you can't endure it!" he cries, but Ivan knows he can. "There is strength to endure everything," he answers, ". . . the strength of the Karamazovs—the strength of the Karamazov baseness." This is Ivan's tragic compulsion, to live, in spite of his higher knowledge, as a law unto himself, to "drain the cup to the dregs," to live out his own nature in a fatherless and brotherless world ("Am I my brother's keeper?" he had snapped at Alyosha when asked to help with Dmitri)—where, as he puts it in conclusion, "all is lawful."

In the ensuing catastrophe he discovers the limitations of his freedom and makes a new moral discovery. As the tension grows between Dmitri and Fyodor, he becomes involved in spite of himself. He had meant to leave town the day after his talk with Aloysha, to "make a new start and enter upon a new, unknown future," but a strange depression seizes him and he feels fixed to the spot. He is annoyed by the sinister new familiarity of his half-brother, Smerdyakov, who, knowing that they both stand to gain by Fyodor's death, speaks to him in suggestions and innuendoes. He knows that Smerdyakov is slyly daring him to put his theory of "all is lawful" to work—that is, to clear out and let the murder be done. Depression gives place to "intense excitement" and, alternately, to a loathing of Smerdyakov, hatred of himself, even of Alyosha, and an "inexplicable humiliating terror." He feels as if he has "lost his bearings." Late that night, in a moment he later remembers as the "basest action of his life," he gets up from bed, creeps to the staircase, and listens to his father stirring below. "And why he had done all this, why he was listening, he could not have said." Then, coming to a sudden decision, he packs his trunk and next morning announces to Fyodor that he is leaving for Moscow. The old man asks him to do a commission for him at a neighboring town, and Ivan agrees "with a malignant smile." He parts with Smerdyakov as with an accomplice. That night the murder is committed.

Ivan is elated as the train carries him to Moscow. "Away with the past," he cries, "I've done with the old world for ever, and may I have no news, no echo, from it." But for some unaccountable reason he cannot make that clean a break. Five days later comes Aloysha's telegram, and back he goes to the world he thought he had rejected.

His sense of involvement and of guilt grows deeper during the "two dreadful months" preceding Dmitri's trial. He has hallucinations of an alter ego who talks to him in the privacy of his room,. Alyosha, who is convinced of Smerdyakov's guilt, sees the strain Ivan is under and tells him earnestly, " '*it wasn't you* killed father.' 'You've been in my room!" Ivan answers hoarsely. " 'You've been there at night when he came . . . Confess . . . have you seen him, have you seen him?' " He is drawn inevitably to Smerdyakov, who had fallen ill the day after the murder, and in a series of three gruelling conversations Ivan's full responsibility is brought home to him. It was his own cynicism that had infected the lackey-mind of Smerdyakov. " 'Here we are face to face,' " says Smerdyakov, " 'what's the use of going on keeping up a farce to each other? . . . You murdered him; you are the real murderer. . . . Something seemed to give way" in Ivan's brain, and "he shuddered all over with a cold shiver." Like Dmitri, he feels the first shock of Zossima's truth, that we are "all responsible for all" and each for each.

And the truth for a moment sets him free, in a new way. He suddenly decides to make a full confession at the trial the next day. A great burden seems lifted from his shoulders. As he leaves Smerdyakov, "something like joy was springing up in his heart." He rescues a drunken, half-frozen peasant whom he had brutally felled on his way to Smerdyakov and spends a whole hour arranging for his care. He is like Dmitri after the dream.

But, coming back to his room, he undergoes still another transformation. He feels a "touch of ice on his heart" and his sense of gladness and serenity vanishes. He is back again with his past, still unpurged. He feels an increasing physical uneasiness as of approaching delirium, and soon he is in a nightmarish conversation with his familiar alter ego, a very jaunty

Devil, who in a kind of intellectual autobiography confronts him with all the butt ends of his days and ways. At least Ivan sees himself, as the Devil puts it, as "x in an indeterminate equation . . . a sort of phantom in life who has lost all beginning and end. . . . All you care about," chides the Devil, "is intelligence. . . . We are all in a muddle . . . and all through your science. . . . Hesitation, suspense, conflict between belief and disbelief—is sometimes such a torture to a conscientious man, such as you are, that it's better to hang yourself at once." Or else, says the Devil bluntly, "destroy the idea of God in man," get rid of "conscience"—it's only a "habit" anyway—and set up a new morality, a "new man" to whom "all things are lawful." And, with a last turn of the knife, the Devil shows Ivan the utterly cynical side of his position: ". . . If you want to swindle, why do you want a moral sanction for doing it? But that's our modern Russia all over. He can't bring himself to swindle without a moral sanction."

Ivan replies by dashing a glass of tea in the Devil's face. "Ah," cries the Devil, "he remembers Luther's inkstand!" At this point, Alyosha enters, tells Ivan of Smerdyakov's suicide, and tries to soothe the mind now quite distracted. The Devil's words ring in Ivan's ears, "You've not made up your mind [to reveal the truth about the murder and thus free Dmitri]. You'll sit all night deliberating whether or not to go."

The Devil spoke truly; there is no permanent peace for this troubled spirit. Ivan's moment of joy is lost in the confusions of his new self-recognition. If he testifies at the trial, will it be out of pride, the desire to be praised (which the Devil taunted him with), or "to perform an act of heroic virtue"?—but, as the Devil reminded him, "you don't believe in virtue." Out of conscience? But "what is conscience?" asked the Devil, "I make it up for myself. Why am I tormented by it? From habit. From the universal habit of mankind for the seven thousand years." All these thoughts Ivan recognized as his own ("He told me a great deal that was true about myself"), but their truth fails to set him free. "I can't endure such questions," he complains to Alyosha, and in rising bitterness repeats the Devil's final taunt: "You'll go because you won't dare not go. Why won't you dare? You must guess that for

120

yourself. That's a riddle for you!" Confused, insecure, unable (like Dmitri) to solve the contradictions in his nature, he seizes upon this imputation of cowardice. He sees himself despised—even by Lise and Alyosha—and his first response is a protective hate and spite. He curses Dmitri: "I hate the monster! . . . Let him rot in Siberia! . . . Oh, to-morrow I'll go, and spit in their faces!" He even turns on Alyosha, "Now I'm going to hate you again!"

But there is no true release in this outburst. He knows that he is not sufficiently justified. The nightmare-world of his talk with the Devil yields more and more to a kind of Kafka-like trance, or walking dream: "I seem to be sleeping awake. . . . I walk, I speak, I see, but I am asleep," he says plaintively. Alyosha sees that his brother is near collapse; and as he watches over him, at last sunk into actual sleep, he prays for the soul in conflict. "He will either rise up in the light of truth," concludes Alyosha, "or . . . he'll perish in hate, revenging on himself and on every one his having served the cause he does not believe in."

At the trial the next day, Ivan's bitter, insolent confession bears out Alyosha's fears. "It was he [Smerdyakov], not my brother, killed our father," he blurts out. "He murdered him and I incited him to do it . . . Who doesn't desire his father's death?" But he fails to convince anyone and leaves Dmitri in a worse position than before. Soon he loses all control, fells an usher, and is carried screaming from the court. The episode is at once his greatest achievement in courage and his greatest moral failure. In sweeping terms he acknowledges his responsibility; but he is still tragic man—guarding his pride, unwilling to pay the full price in humility and love. We must go back many chapters to Zossima's teaching and his counsel to the "mysterious stranger," who was a murderer in fact, as Ivan was in spirit, as an indication of the road Ivan might have taken. Zossima had read some hard words to his conscience-stricken friend: "Except a corn of wheat fall into the ground and die, it abideth alone: but if it die, it bringeth forth much fruit." But the "evil Karamazov spirit" will suffer no such death unto a new life. Like Dmitri, Ivan is not "ready."

Modern tragic man "doesn't want millions, but an answer to his questions," which, in essence, come to this: "Who am I?" Zossima, in the opening scene of the book, had seen in Ivan a "lofty heart, capable of suffering"; and (to the consternation of the gathering) had knelt at Dmitri's feet even after he had reviled his father. Both boys, in the unfolding action, justify this hint of their heroic stature. Throughout the book, the community, in a sort of choric role, is occupied with their problem as Elsinore is with Hamlet's. Their excesses evoke awe and wonder as the "Karamazov affair" broadens into the problem of modern man. The two brothers, differing from the static figures in the book, possess a spiritual potential capable of forcing a revision of man's conception of himself and his world, like the great tragic recalcitrants of the tradition; and it is this expectation, unarticulated but felt, that keeps the audience at the trial in fascinated attention. The tragically negative ones of the story are Rakitin, for whom "life is easy"; Fyodor, who stands on the "firm rock of his sensuality"; or the sentimental Mme. Hohlakov, who swings like a weathercock to every ideological breeze. Ivan and Dmitri grow as these others do not; they suffer and, in the Aeschylean sense, learn. They live out to a certain degree the old tragic paradox of victory in defeat.

Although the action of the story ends for Alyosha in the reassuring certainty of a religious revelation and hence takes him out of the tragic realm in which his brothers struggle to the end, he too has a dark night of the soul and his final victory is not without its ironical and ambiguous aspects. His nature is not, as it seems at first, all sweet, compliant, and confiding. He is constantly reminded (Rakitin nags him about it) of the Karamazov in him; he is tempted and succumbs to temptation. When he yields for a moment to the persuasiveness of Ivan's humanistic argument about the torturing of children, Ivan catches him up. "You're a pretty monk!" he chides. "So there is a little devil sitting in your heart, Alyosha Karamazov!" Later, when the body of his beloved Father Zossima begins to smell in premature corruption, "in excess of nature," Alyosha is plunged into anguish and doubt, even to questioning the justice of a universe that could permit so un-deserved a wrong. He is haunted by the memory of his con-versation with Ivan and finds himself echoing Ivan's rebellious phrases to Rakitin. "Can you really be so upset because your old man has begun to stink?" asks Rakitin. "I say! you are go-ing it! Why, it's regular mutiny, with barricades!" And with a "revengeful desire to see the downfall of the righteous," Rakitin proposes a visit to Grushenka's. To consort with "this 'dreadful' woman" would in normal times have been unthink-able to Alyosha; but now, with his soul in turmoil and with the same impulse that led his brothers to assert their own compulsions, he agrees to go.

In the ordeal of the visit Alyosha finds new powers within himself. All his terror disappears; "the great grief in his heart" is armor against "every lust and temptation." With a "feeling of the intensest and purest interest" he becomes absorbed in Grushenka and the story of her betrayal. Instead of sensuality and coarseness he finds forgiveness and a loving heart; he too finds "precious metal in the dirt." He returns to the monastery "with sweetness in his heart."

Here he has the vision which, climactic like those of his brothers but of permanently sustaining power, sets the course of his life "for ever and ever." He enters the chambers where the body of Zossima is lying. Half-praying, half-listening to Father Paissy read the Scriptures, he falls into a semiconscious doze. He imagines that Zossima rises from the coffin, speaking to him with reassurance and love. He comes to consciousness feeling that "something firm and unshakable as [the] vault of heaven had entered into his soul." He rises up "a resolute champion" and three days later leaves the monastery to take up his work in the world, as Father Zossima had directed him. Through suffering he has learned who he is.

He goes to work in the world but, ironically, he is far from conquering it. For all his good qualities, he is powerless to prevent the disastrous march of events. His father and his brothers love him, looking to him as their conscience; but they go their own ways as if, in a sense, he never existed. Although he had ample forewarning, the murder happens. He is equally ineffective with his girl, Lise, who tells him to his face, "I am very fond of you, but I don't respect you." When she parades her destructive ideas as if to plague him, he does little more than look sadly into the distance. His only external victory is with that extraordinary group of small boys, centering around the precocious Kolya Krassotkin and little Ilusha, whose role in the book is to present a parallel-in-little to the tragic Karamazovs—an ironic victory in contrast to his larger failure.

In the beginning the brothers were not brothers—even Alyosha had to learn where his true obligation lay—and Fyodor no father. In a larger sense, they all at one time or another question or turn from the fatherhood of God. Kolya Krassotkin, hero of the miniature agon, is fatherless also, in both senses. His prehensile young mind has seized upon all the isms of the day, either picked up in "books unsuitable for his age" or got indirectly from Ivan and directly from Rakitin, who has made a great impression on him. He flaunts his free thought in Alyosha's face ("Of course," he says, "God is only a hypothesis"). He declares himself, at the age of thirteen, a Socialist, scorns all "sheepish sentimentality," and has reached a peak of wisdom from which he sees that "everything is habit with men, everything even in their social and political relations." History, he says, is "the study of the successive follies of mankind and nothing more." "I've read *Candide*," he adds, "in the Russian translation."

Alyosha listens to all this patiently. He had first entered the life of the boys when he protected Ilusha from their stoning and had impressed them all by his amazing forbearance when Ilusha, recognizing him as the brother of Dmitri who had brutalized his (Ilusha's) father, bit his finger to the bone. And now, with Ilusha lying near death, Alyosha is busy restoring a sense of brotherhood to the group to encourage the sick child with friendship and love. He sees that Kolya is the key figure, and he presides with loving forbearance over the pilgrimage of this miniature Ivan. He senses in Kolya the same potentiality Zossima had seen in Ivan. Kolya's bravado, his pet theories and fear of sentimentality, are tested by the illness and death of Ilusha, in which, through Alyosha's quiet mediation, he gradually realizes his own involvement. He goes, as

124

Ivan never quite could, from Descartes' "Je pense donc je suis" to Zossima's "I am and I love." To be sure, he has moments of backsliding. At Ilusha's burial, his small rationalistic intelligence balks at the idea of the funeral dinner. "It's all so strange, Karamazov," he says to Alyosha, "such sorrow and then pancakes after it, it all seems so unnatural in our religion." But then comes Alyosha's pastoral charge to the children and his loving conclusion, "Well, now we will finish talking and go to the funeral dinner. Don't be put out at our eating pancakes—it's a very old custom and there's something nice in that . . . Well, let us go! And now we go hand in hand." Here is fatherhood lovingly extended and willingly accepted, and a brotherhood gladly joined. It is Kolya's shout that is echoed by them all, "Hurrah for Karamazov!" The tragic confusions of Dmitri and Ivan seem far away indeed.

The episode of the boys, especially its conclusion, is not without parallel in the tradition of tragedy. It is as if Dostoevski, in whose tragic view the world as it is remains a dilemma, gives his vision, like Aeschylus in the concluding scene of the *Oresteia,* of the world as it ought to be, when Zossima's teaching becomes practice. It could be said to resolve, theoretically, the entire Karamazov problem. *Theoretically*—but there has been irremediable suffering and loss, and the world as it ought to be is not the world that is.

If the final scene is affirmative and restorative, it is hardly decisive. The clashing antinomies of the Karamazov world have not been resolved. Ivan's question about justice in the world has not been logically answered, any more than Job's. Dmitri still wavers between Sodom and the Madonna, and we leave both brothers stricken with illnesses ("brain fever" or "nervous fever") that are direct symptoms of deep intellectual and spiritual disorder. Each of the three brothers had felt on his pulses the fierce compulsions of the terrible and the holy; had, like Melville's "thought-divers," "gone down five miles or more" and come up "with blood-shot eyes." Such new truth as they found came through the experience of their individual ordeals, and (except for Alyosha's) it had none of the assurance of "the old moral catechism." It is "tragic" truth—that is, fragmentary, tentative, and precarious. It is not Zos-

12

DOSTOEVSKI TO FAULKNER

LITERATURE since Dostoevski that would report faithfully the direful aspects of the human condition has often been appalling witness to the truth of his prophecy. "After Dostoievsky's heroes," wrote Berdyaev,[88] "there is the unforeseeable twentieth century with its promise of a cultural crisis and the end of an era in the world's history." Especially in the two postwar periods, disorientation and violence in human affairs have been the major testimony. Writers such as Ibsen, Conrad, Hardy, Dreiser had reduced the possibility of freedom and transcendence to a minimum. They presented the human struggle against so bleak a cosmic or social background that effort seemed puny indeed in the face of what Conrad called "the fiendish and appalling joke" that is man's lot in the universe—Ivan's irony carried to the bitterest conclusion and redeemed only (in Conrad, for instance) by occasional individual sensitivity to the problem, an increased awareness of the need for human solidarity and responsibility, or (in Ibsen) of the necessity of clinging to the maximal ideal, however futile.[89] "What makes mankind tragic," wrote Conrad,[90] "is not that they are victims of nature, it is that they are conscious of it . . . As soon as you know of your slavery, the pain, the anger, the strife—the tragedy begins . . ." Subsequently the grim Freudian image showed man as slave to the subrational and subconscious, a being who entertained merely "the illusion of psychic freedom"; [91] and the Marxist view pronounced man slave to the great impersonal and external forces of history.[92]

During the decade of the twenties, many observers declared tragedy bankrupt in the general devaluation. In 1924, Macneile Dixon saw no hope for any more "tragedy of the center," by which he meant tragedy (like the Greek and the Elizabethan) which posited freedom and a cosmic order—the "affair with the gods." In 1929 Joseph Wood Krutch's famous essay, "The Tragic Fallacy," [93] denied the possibility of tragedy in the modern world, from which (he wrote) "both the Glory of God and the Glory of Man have departed. . . . Our cosmos may be farcical or it may be pathetic but it has not the dignity of tragedy and we cannot accept it as such." In the critical skirmish that followed Krutch's essay, his assumptions about tragedy were challenged; but the bulk of contemporary "tragic" fiction, both before and after, tended to confirm his views.

But perhaps not for the reasons he alleged: the death of God and the debasement of man in his own eyes—"the enfeeblement [in Krutch's phrase] of the human spirit." "The best that we can achieve," he wrote, "is pathos and the most we can do is feel sorry for ourselves." Granted that the bent of history, especially in the era in which Krutch wrote, was away from tragedy: the disillusioning effects of the first World War, described by Hemingway, for instance, in the weariness and cynicism of *The Sun Also Rises;* or on the other hand the shallow optimisms of the postwar boom (as crippling to tragedy as despair), of technology, and the promises of the social and psychiatric sciences. Granted that contemporary heroes often lack "nobility," actions "magnitude," and that a prevalent tone is despair: "I don't think, I operate," said Rinaldi in *A Farewell to Arms.* Granted also that pathos is a dominant mood in many contemporary would-be tragedies. Indeed, "the drama of pathos" has recently been declared a unique achievement of our theater—and a positive achievement, so the argument runs, of dignity and significance comparable to the tragic achievement of the Greeks and Elizabethans.[94] And granted, finally, the unsettling effects of modern philosophic views of time and space, so that the artist, sensitive to the relativities of

128

his time, and feeling himself estopped from timeless truth, sees himself justified only in snatching a moment from the flux and rendering it vivid in his fictions.

But our era has produced not only artists who saw all this and in the way of Zola (and Thomas Middleton) reported it "without prejudice, without personality" but some who saw around and above it. Indeed, the very attempt to fictionalize it, to give form to the despair and the pity and the flux, is a gesture toward tragedy; it is the first phase of the gesture, or action, of tragedy as we have earlier defined it. In this sense, as it has been said of Joyce's *Ulysses,* many a modern artist is his own tragic hero.[95] The values of tragedy have not disappeared, even if they no longer are embodied in the traditional symbolic figure of the tragic hero. They have been scattered, relocated, distributed. A less dogmatic view than Krutch's would see no blanket capitulation among modern writers. The perceptions are there—even of the nobility, dignity, and magnitude which Krutch found wanting—but he is right that they have nowhere found the synthesis and full development of a realized form.

Apparently there is no want of will on the part of the artists themselves. Although it may be little more than an interesting cultural phenomenon, or of autobiographical meaning only, it is clear that even in this period of the alleged dearth of tragedy artists have consciously striven to realize the form according to whatever notion it was they entertained of it. Neither Hardy nor Conrad called their novels "tragedies," but Hardy had a coherent theory of tragedy, viewed man's lot as "tragic," [96] and Conrad frequently called his characters and situations "tragic." Perhaps, like Ibsen who, after one abortive self-styled verse tragedy (*Catilina*), called his subsequent work "dramas" or "social dramas," Hardy and Conrad realized that their view of man's fate fell too far short of the full tragic affirmation to warrant calling their novels tragedies. Hardy's universe was much like Conrad's "fiendish joke," and he (though less so than Conrad) saw scant value in suffering. ("Error and chance," said Hardy, "rule the world, not justice.") But Dreiser wrote what he called *An American Tragedy;* and O'Neill called himself "a bit of a poet, who has labored . . . to see the transfiguring nobility of tragedy, in as near the Greek sense as one can grasp it" and set out to "develop a tragic expression in terms of transfigured modern values." [97] Hemingway made no such claims (although he once called *A Farewell to Arms* his *Romeo and Juliet*), nor did Fitzgerald; but serious and not unwarranted claims to "genuine tragedy" have been made for them by others. Latterly, in a flurry of interest in the idea of tragedy since World War II, dramatists such as Arthur Miller and Tennessee Williams, articulate about their craft, have freely discussed their own works in the context of traditional tragedy.[98] And it may be significant of a resurgent spirit that the critics seem (for better or worse) more than ever concerned with the label. About every new serious play or novel the question is asked, "Is it a tragedy?" Indeed, the will to tragedy seems so great on both sides of the footlights that there is a general turn toward short cuts. Arthur Miller defends his "common man" as a fitting protagonist in genuine tragedy, and Brooks Atkinson finds Williams' *Summer and Smoke* "a tragedy because its heroine has a noble spirit." [99] In academic circles there is a notable increase (on both sides of the desk) of interest in tragedy and the idea of the tragic—perhaps symptomatic (among students) of a disoriented generation reaching for forgotten values, for a vision of life free from dogma, tonic and positive, however precarious; and (among teachers) of the perennial desire to set the problem of form and meaning in literature in its ultimate perspective—this time by way of an ancient discipline that has latterly known some neglect.[100]

And there has been no want of realization, however partial and fragmented, of genuine tragic values. Hardy is not "dispiriting" in the sense in which cynicism is dispiriting; he depicts people who "refuse to be dwarfed into sluggishness." The stars may shine down on Egdon Heath coldly and impersonally, but they are beautiful. Life is presented in his novels as neither "little, nor cheap, nor easily found out." Ibsen's attitude toward his generation was tragic in many ways; and however he fails to evoke "the original terror" in his dramatic situations, he is acutely conscious of the problem—"tragic" up to a certain point—of the gifted or idealistic individual in the face of a hostile and uncomprehending society. Both Heyst and Lord Jim of Conrad's stories achieved tragic "victories," transcending the pasts which threatened their moral maturity and freedom. If Dreiser and O'Neill misunderstood the Greek idea of fate to imply a denial of human freedom as complete as Marx's and Freud's, their characters have occasional glimpses beyond their bondage; they are sometimes capable (like Clyde Griffiths and Lavinia Mannon) of being schooled in suffering, or (like the wrangling Tyrones) of showing honesty, moral courage, and love which transcend self and the wreckage of their lives. Fitzgerald's Gatsby cherished an ideal, however meretricious; died for it; and brought his choric observer (Nick Carraway) to a new "moral attention." Hemingway's Frederick Henry ends in stoical despair (his universe, too, is "a dirty trick"), but not before he has learned to love—"I don't love," he told the priest at first—and has been moved by pressures of his tragic situation to thoughts, even religious ones, that point to realities beyond the sense of "nothingness" in which he leaves his Catherine's deathbed. Koestler's Rubashov in Lubyanka (*Darkness at Noon*) finally capitulates to the will of the party, but not before he has hearkened to the all-but-forgotten "first person singular" whose reality he denied through forty years of party discipline. He sees the stars shine above the turrets of his prison; perceives what he calls (after Freud?) "the oceanic sense" as the neglected dimension of his party's thinking and as ultimately denying the Marxist promise; and comes (before his capitulation) to Faustus' terrifying realization: "What about the infinite?"

None of these insights, however bracing, will make a tragedy. They are incidental, not powerful enough in their contexts to establish what Henry Myers called the "equivalence" [101] of the good and evil necessary to tragedy. Nor are they incorporated in forms (Conrad is perhaps the closest) which do justice to the full dimensions of tragedy as they have been marked out by the artists of the tradition. Tragedy (as we have seen), coming at the maturity of a culture, has traditionally put to the test of action *all* the formulations, philosophical and religious, which man has shored up against his

to the "genius of comedy" with all the versatility Socrates could have wished; he senses the truth of both—and regards neither as final. But the testimony of his major works—*The Sound and the Fury; Light in August; Absalom, Absalom!*—their concern, method, and purport, are tragic.

With a thoroughness that recalls the great tragedians of the tradition, he presses the "moment," which in his fictions is characteristically a crisis involving extreme violence, the eruption of human passions at their rawest, for its total yield. His patience seems inexhaustible as (so to speak) he lets human nature tell its full story. He sees existence with the "double vision" of tragedy—the goods and the evils forever mixed. At first, he seemed to many to be stopping halfway with an *Inferno*-like report on human vileness and degradation. "This," said an early critic,[105] "is the *reductio ad absurdum* of American naturalism." But as the saga of his mythical Yoknapatawpha County developed, a more positive theme was seen to emerge—a theme which latterly he has made explicit. Thus (to our interviewer): "There isn't any theme in my work, or maybe if there is, you can call it a certain faith in man and his ability to always prevail and endure over circumstances and over his own destiny." But it is only such a faith as we have seen in tragedy—never triumphant or serene, constantly under strain, admitting dire realities and conscious of bleak possibilities.

The "before" and "after" of his stories, to which he refers in such simple terms, are actually by no means simple. To explain the moment, or to prophesy upon it, he ranges wide and deep; no detail of the present, no insight or formulation of the past is irrelevant—classic or modern; Hebraic, Greek, Christian; Freudian or Marxist. His fictional world is the most comprehensive (it might be said) since Dostoevski's. But the method is exploratory, not doctrinaire. Traditional structures are tested in action for whatever life-giving truth they may possess. Starting with the moment, he dips deep into the individual and communal past (his saga of the South resembles the *Oresteia* in this) until the present emerges in a kind of dark luminousness, the characteristic half-light of tragedy. The tone is not consistent. Sometimes (so runs a common charge) the gloom is too unrelieved; the characters, lacking "soul," lacking the power to make conscious and rational choices between good and evil, march to their Greeklike doom under inescapable Freudian compulsion; the horrors they perpetrate or endure have no "cosmic echoes," no source in the secret cause, the true source of tragic terror. Latterly, on the other hand, the redemptive voice has seemed, to some critics, too insistent, the gloom too facilely dispelled. Of his major novels, *Absalom, Absalom!* has, I think, preserved the "dark luminousness" most consistently. It is perhaps his nearest approach to the fully developed form of tragedy.[106]

Although a sense of doom pervades the story of the rise and fall of Thomas Sutpen and his "design" in *Absalom, Absalom!* (a doom that is sealed in the final scene of the smoking ruins of his once proud mansion), more than one escaped to tell of it. In the telling, many meanings are revealed that help explain, partly illuminate, and transcend the ugly surface facts of the saga of Sutpen; his ambition; his two wives, two daughters, and two sons; miscegenation; fratricide; his own dismal end and the end of his line: "and there was only the sound of the idiot negro left." "Violence is just a tool I use," said Faulkner; and here the surface facts are merely the occasion of a long, anguished, "tragic" search for their meaning: like Hawthorne searching out the full meaning of the "certain affair of fine red cloth." "It's just incredible [says Mr. Compson, trying to explain one phase of the story—the fratricide—to his son Quentin]. It just does not explain. . . . We have a few old mouth-to-mouth tales; we exhume from old trunks and boxes and drawers letters without salutation or signature . . . we see dimly people, the people in whose living blood and seed we ourselves lay dormant and waiting, in this shadowy attenuation of time possessing now heroic proportions, performing their acts of simple passion and simple violence, impervious to time and inexplicable— Yes, Judith, Bon, Henry, Sutpen: all of them. They are there, yet something is missing . . . you re-read, tedious and intent, poring, making sure you have forgotten nothing, made no miscalculation; you bring them together again and again nothing happens: just the words, the symbols, the shapes themselves, shadowy inscrutable and serene . . ."

Mr. Compson, who had heard the story from his father, the General, moves as best he can through its intricacies, sees the heroic side of Sutpen, sees his ambition (the "design") as rooted in his boyish sense of injustice and hence "innocence," and, a fatalist himself, tells the story with a fatalist's detachment. Miss Rosa Coldfield, a victim of the "design," tells her side of the story to young Quentin ("Maybe some day you will remember this and write about it")—of Sutpen as "the evil's source and head," of his goal as mere "respectability" and "vain magnificence," of the "accelerating circle's fatal curving course" which brought him to his violent—and (to her) just—end.

But then there is Quentin's version—Quentin a more sensitive and vulnerable Ishmael, for whom the telling (in his cold Harvard study, to his roommate Shreve McCannon) is itself a tragic experience. He cannot enjoy the security of his father's detachment nor the single-minded certainty of Miss Rosa's bitter moral verdict. The story, as he pieces it together from a lifetime of listening to his elders ("his very body was an empty hall echoing with sonorous defeated names; he was not a being, an entity, he was a commonwealth") and as he himself recreates its later scenes in a passionate attempt to bore into its meaning, has a peculiarly intimate, shocking effect on him, testing to the limit his deepest loyalties and beliefs. It is as if the whole burden of the South's (and mankind's) tragic dilemma is suddenly placed on his young shoulders. After the telling, he lies sleepless and anguished in his dormitory room. "I am older at twenty than a lot of people who have died," he says to Shreve at the end.

Indeed, the moment (in Faulkner's term) for which, going back eighty years and three generations, the whole story would account is this full and tragic realization by Quentin of the paradox of his Southern heritage, and the dilemma of man, with which he must somehow come to terms and cannot. ("Nevermore of peace. Nevermore of peace," he thinks to himself on his dormitory cot.) It is as if a son of a lesser Hamlet or of an untutored Faustus were telling his father's story and finding himself unable to live with it. Quentin is no tragic hero; he neither initiates nor is involved in an action of magnitude; he is helpless to do anything about his tragic perceptions except tell about them. The real actors and in this sense the "heroes" of the story are Thomas Sutpen and his son Henry. They initiate the actions but never understand, as Quentin does, their full tragic meaning, nor feel their full tragic impact. They are the furious or possessed or committed ones; they are not (in Dmitri's sense) "philosophers"; they are both "innocent." But their "acts of simple passion and simple violence" provide the impulse, or the first phase, of tragedy—its final phases (the deep spiritual upheaval and knowledge gained) to be realized in Quentin's sensitive and brooding consciousness.

Thomas Sutpen, the son of a migrant, alcoholic hillman, himself descended from the first Sutpen who had probably come to America direct from the Old Bailey, had been reared, barely literate, in a cabin in a mountain cove where "the land belonged to anybody" and "the only colored people were Indians." "So he didn't even know [Mr. Compson told Quentin] there was a country all divided and fixed and neat because of what color their skins happened to be and what they happened to own . . ." At fourteen he had his first brush with property and power. Delivering a message for his father, he was told by a Negro servant at the big house "never to come to that front door again but to go around to the back." It was as simple as that; but his goal from then on was fixed—"which most men [said Mr. Compson] do not begin to set up until the blood begins to slow at thirty or more and then only because the image represents peace and indolence or at least a crowning of vanity." It was not that he was angry, or wanted riches (here Miss Coldfield was wrong) or vengeance—he could have shot the plantation owner, but that was not it. He had to "do something about it [said Mr. Compson] in order to live with himself for the rest of his life . . ." He must "combat them"—and to combat them he had to have what they had—"land and niggers and a fine house."

So he conceived his purpose of "doing something" about it, of achieving through his own courage and shrewdness the values from which he had been excluded, of one day admitting at his own front door "a little boy without any shoes on and with his pap's cut-down pants for clothes" (at least this is the way Quentin imagines it), and thereby righting the injustice he had suffered. He proceeded with Ahab's monomaniac intentness and a kind of Faustian wager with destiny: first to the West Indies to make the money to do it with; then (twelve years later) back to America and Yoknapatawpha County, where he arrived looking as if he had been through "some solitary furnace experience which was more than just fever," with a French architect and a handful of West Indian slaves—his "twenty subsidiary demons." A sense of something a little less than justice seemed to compel him as he tore from the wilderness what was to be the crowning symbol of his design, the largest and finest mansion in the county. He connived, enslaved, brutalized whenever he found it necessary to the design. He had abandoned his Haitian wife and child when he saw them as fatal to it. He took another wife and got other children to fulfill it, with the same shrewdness with which Ahab manipulated the crew of the *Pequod* to his purpose. When they too failed him, he tried a third time to found a line. He proposed to Miss Rosa Coldfield, his dead wife's sister and thirty-eight years his junior, that "they try it; and if it's a boy, we'll get married." And he finally perished at the hands of a poor white underling and drinking partner (Wash Jones) who hacked him to death with a rusty scythe for getting Jones' sixteen-year-old granddaughter with a child who Sutpen hoped would be his son and heir (Miss Rosa having refused his offer). But the child turned out to be a girl.

Sutpen comes to us, for all his dreary end, with some of the qualities and many of the trappings of a tragic hero. Even Miss Rosa admitted his extraordinary power of will and his bravery ("I have never gainsaid that"), though she denied him (wrongly) pity and honor. He had impressive qualities of leadership—like the "authority" that Kent recognized in Lear. In Haiti, on the eighth night of the rebelling sugar-workers' siege of the plantation house, when all seemed lost, Sutpen put down his musket, "had someone unbar the door and then bar it behind him, and walked out into the darkness and subdued them"—how, Mr. Compson is not sure: "maybe by yelling louder, maybe by standing, bearing more than they believed any bones and flesh could or should . . ." Rearing his mansion in the Mississippi wilderness, he led his "twenty demons" with the same mysterious (and this time quiet) power; General Compson told Quentin's father that, "while the negroes were working Sutpen never raised his voice at them, that instead he led them, caught them at the psychological instant by example, by some ascendancy of forbearance rather than by brute fear." It is by this same curious ascendancy that he enlisted into his design Mr. Coldfield, Rosa's father, the Methodist steward of "immaculate morality," first by getting him to sign his very dubious bond and then by persuading him (again, no one knew how) to let him marry Ellen, Rosa's older sister, by whom he intended to become respectable and found his line. ("He had marked down Miss Coldfield's father with the same cold and ruthless deliberation with which he had probably marked down the French architect" who had been essential to the building of the house itself.) In the same way he subdued the town which he had "marked down" for his purpose. He outfaced the crowd of townspeople (by this time restless as well as suspicious) who came to disrupt his wedding—"standing there motionless, with an expression almost of smiling where his teeth showed through the beard, holding his wild negroes with that one word," leading his bride to the carriage, while the crowd "vanished back into the region from which they had emerged for this one occasion like rats." In the War he became a colonel, and returned with a citation for bravery signed by Lee himself. He set about restoring his house and plantation with the same "fierce constant will" with which he originally built it—and from which nothing could deflect him, not even the deputation of Klansmen whom he refused to join when they put to him the "friend or enemy" question. "This may be war," they told him; and he answered, "I am used to it."

But he is more than a strong and determined man, of whom (said Quentin's grandfather) "anyone could look at him and say, *Given the occasion and the need, this man can and will do anything."* To many, he seemed something more (or less) than human—to Miss Rosa "fiend, blackguard and devil," "the evil's source and head"; to Shreve as he listened, a "Faustus . . . demon . . . Beelzebub"; to Wash Jones, whose idol he was for long, *"A fine proud man. If God himself was to come down and ride the natural earth, that's what He would aim to look like."* Shreve, when he had heard more, imagined him (had the design succeeded) an Abraham, who, full of years, could say, " 'Praise the Lord, I have raised about me sons to bear the burden of mine iniquities . . .' " Or (as Faulkner suggests by the title of the book) he was David, the favored one of God, lamenting his son Absalom. If to Miss Rosa, his face was "like the mask in a Greek tragedy," always ogre-like, he had another and more important affinity with the classic heroes. "His wild braggart dream," as she saw it, provoked "the very dark forces of fate" and spelled his inevitable doom: death at the hands of poor, forlorn Wash Jones, "brute instrument [as Miss Rosa described him] of that justice which presides over human events . . . which, by man or woman flouted, drives on like fiery steel and overrides both weakly just and unjust strong . . ." Quentin's father spoke of "that entire fecundity of dragons' teeth" Sutpen had sewn, and of the irony, suggesting something more than mere coincidence, of Charles Bon's appearing after twenty-seven years at Sutpen's Hundred—his own son to court his own daughter— and bringing the collapse of all that he had hoped and worked for.

Thus there is at once a whiff of sulphur about him and a touch of the superhuman, a man out of the ordinary in whom the Fates themselves seemed concerned. The dimension lacking, of course, is what made Oedipus suffer twice—"once in the body and once in the soul"; the fearful echoes that thundered in Faustus' ears; that which in Job and in Lear made them long for "instruction"; which made Ahab see himself as "a forty years' fool"; and what Dmitri meant when he called the Karamazovs philosophers. "Sutpen's trouble was innocence," Quentin tells Shreve, summarizing the judgment handed down from his grandfather. But it was more than the innocence of the evil of property and caste and exploitation—

the innocence with which in Haiti (that "theatre for violence and injustice and bloodshed and all the satanic lusts of human greed and cruelty") he believed the earth to be "kind and gentle and that darkness was merely something you saw," not knowing that "what he rode upon was a volcano . . ." It was more even than his naively innocent view of morality whose ingredients were "like the ingredients of pie or cake and once you had measured them and balanced them and mixed them and put them into the oven it was all finished and nothing but pie or cake could come out." It was an innocence which overlooked the moral relationship of means and ends and with which he could view the collapse of his design, not as retribution, not as "fated," not even as bad luck, but simply the result of a "mistake." "You see [he told Quentin's grandfather], I had a design in mind. Whether it was a good or a bad design is beside the point; the question is, Where did I make the mistake in it . . ."

"According to the old dame," said Shreve, meaning Miss Rosa, "he never had had a soul" to begin with; and the question implicit in the narrations of the others (especially Quentin's) is the extent to which he ever developed one. Doctor Faustus knew he had a soul but thought it was his own to bargain with, until experience changed his mind. Sutpen's innocence never comprehended "soul." At least, we are not shown that it did. He is described as a man in action, "on the way," in the sureness of his cause not harassed by the tragic hero's doubts or self-doubts. And yet there is sufficient ambiguity about him to give pause, as it did, agonizingly, to Quentin. To be sure, he saw nothing wrong in his design or his methods, and had scarcely a twinge of conscience about abandoning his first wife and child. By concealing the fact of her Negro blood, she had cancelled, so he thought, whatever responsibility he might have had for her; and even then he made generous provisions for her welfare. "Grandfather [Quentin told Shreve] said there was no conscience about that." Then for nearly thirty years the course of his design ran smooth. Only Bon's arrival at Sutpen's Hundred threatened it and presented him with a moral problem not to be settled by the swift Yes or No of an unclouded purpose. It brought him as near an actual spiritual struggle as he ever came.

His question was whether to keep Bon's identity undisclosed and (he told Quentin's grandfather) "let matters take the course which I know they will take and see my design complete itself quite normally and naturally and successfully to the public eye, yet to my own in such fashion as to be a mockery and a betrayal of that little boy who approached that door fifty years ago and was turned away, for whose vindication the whole plan was conceived and carried forward to the moment of this choice . . ." How real he felt his dilemma to be, to what extent it opened up for him those dark areas of the soul which tragic heroes know, we are not told. "He left for Virginia that night," and for the War. Quentin and Shreve (now caught up in the narrative), as they dramatize between them the meeting of father and son at night in a tent in a Carolina bivouac, throw Sutpen's renunciation in a suddenly tragic light—Sutpen's fatherly embrace, his "Henry— My son . . . I have seen Charles Bon . . . You are not going to let him marry Judith, Henry" and his final revelation of the Negro blood. "So he got his choice made, after all," Shreve said. "He played that trump after all."

What it cost him in spiritual anguish, what he learned, is not dramatized. He returns from the War a hero, still furious in his determination to try for his design once more, but this time in corrupted innocence. He ages rapidly, gets fat, fraternizes with Wash Jones, and bullies his women. Miss Rosa quits the place after his preposterous proposal; and his betrayal of Wash's granddaughter, Milly, leads to his swift (and to Miss Rosa) just end. Miss Rosa, forty years later, watches the decaying symbol of his design, the mansion, go up in smoke, taking the last survivors (except one) with it: "and there was only the sound of the idiot negro left." The spiritual ordeal of this hero, the "war in the cave" from which Job (and Oedipus and Faustus and Hester Prynne) emerged with calmer mind and deepened insight, is only hinted at and its results never articulated. It is not that Sutpen had "forgotten the infinite"; he never knew it. His downfall is a reminder of whatever is grave and constant in human suffering; but, in

142

spite of Miss Rosa's ready-made notions of doom and fate (part Greek and part Old Testament), there is nothing secret about its cause. His fall, like Agamemnon's, was moral, not tragic.

The tragedy is Quentin's. The action he is involved in extends through four months. It begins when Miss Rosa summons him, one September afternoon a few days before he is to leave for Harvard, to listen to her story and thus get him to escort her, that same night, to Sutpen's Hundred to find out if her suspicion is true that Henry (now in his sixty-first year) is in hiding there—still a murderer in the eyes of the law. After supper that night, while waiting for the time to go with Miss Rosa, his father fills out the story, recounting what *his* father, the General, had told him, and showing Quentin the letter of proposal that Bon had written Judith from the front. Later, when it is quite dark, Quentin and Miss Rosa make the trip and find Henry in the stripped and crumbling mansion, wasting with fever on his deathbed, tended by old Clytie, Sutpen's daughter by a Negro slave. Three months later, Miss Rosa brings ambulance and attendants to the mansion to rescue Henry, only to have Clytie mistake them for the police and touch off the blaze which, by prearrangement with Henry, had been prepared for three months. In mid-January Quentin hears from his father of Miss Rosa's death and that night tells the story to Shreve.

The course of Quentin's four-month action shows him becoming ever more deeply involved. At first he had been a little bored with those "stubborn back-looking ghosts," his elders, who seemed obsessed with the past and curiously insistent on imposing their memories on him. "But why tell me about it?" he asked his father after the first session with Miss Rosa. "What is it to me that the land . . . the earth or whatever it was got tired of him at last and turned and destroyed him? What if it did destroy her family too? It's going to turn and destroy us all some day, whether our name happens to be Sutpen or Coldfield or not." During that sultry September afternoon, he had listened politely, with an occasional "Yessum" or "No'me" to prove his attention; but in spite of himself the story soon penetrates his youthful indifference and easy fatalism—reminiscent of Ishmael's before he saw horrors he could not be social with. During his "day of listening," first to Miss Rosa and then to his father, he not only becomes caught up in the story but finds himself visualizing its scenes with almost painful reality. Of the fratricide, for instance, "it seemed to Quentin that he could actually see them [Henry and Bon], facing one another at the gate," young, gaunt, on two gaunt horses, the pistol lying across the saddle bow, the quiet command and the refusal; and then the shot and "the running feet on the stairs . . ." Often his mind leaps beyond the narrator's version (his father's or Miss Rosa's) to speculate or build upon it, living it through more fully in his imagination, trying it out on his pulses.

Following this first sense of involvement, which is a kind of commitment, comes the increasing pressure of the story's meaning. It is Shreve who touched off the final phase, that January evening at Harvard, when, wondering at Quentin's curious concern over the news of Miss Rosa's death—an "old dame" and no kin to him—he puts his flippant request: *Tell about the South. What's it like there. What do they do there. Why do they live there. Why do they live at all—*" As Quentin tells the story, Shreve himself goes through something of a transformation, though not a permanent one. He tends to vulgarize and simplify (the architect, he suggests, fled because he wanted a woman; Sutpen "chose lechery" or—a little higher level—"So he just wanted a grandson. That was all he was after"). Halfway through the narrative Shreve explodes, "Jesus, the South is fine, isn't it. It's better than the theatre, isn't it. It's better than Ben Hur, isn't it. No wonder you have to come away from it now and then, isn't it." But he himself is drawn in, though never as Quentin is, and the two boys together, now one talking, now the other, re-create for themselves the final scenes of the story. Shreve never comes out from "that protective coloring of levity behind which the youthful shame of being moved hid itself"; but, coming to Henry's part of the story, both boys talk themselves, as it were, out of themselves, out of their cold room: "Because now neither of them were there. They were both in Carolina and the time was forty-six years ago . . . and both of them were

Henry and both of them were Bon, compounded each of both and yet either neither, smelling the very smoke which had blown and faded away forty-six years ago . . ."

Although, the story told, Shreve could return to his detachment—interested, perplexed, honestly (not flippantly) trying to understand, Quentin had lost his forever. During the narrative he had grown increasingly tense and morose. Shreve becomes more voluble as the night wears on, taking more part in the narrative— "Now let me play awhile," he says at one turn in the story. Shreve bundles up in the growing chill of the room (though he forgets his breathing exercises), while Quentin sits huddled, wan, "brooding," his overcoat forgotten on the floor. He answers Shreve's questions tersely, as if deep in a personal anguish he cannot share with his friend. "Wait. Listen," says Shreve. "I'm not trying to be funny, smart. I just want to understand it if I can . . . What is it? something you live and breathe in like air?" "You can't understand it," replies Quentin. "You would have to be born there." To Shreve, the South, and this story of the South, had presented little more than a problem, as Hamlet's situation was a problem to Horatio. To Quentin it had become a matter almost of survival—a test of the most vital kind. We witness his increasing tension, the growing "tomb-like" chill of the room, his irrepressible trembling, his long, long thoughts as he broods over the enigma of the tale just told: " 'And she waited three months before she went back to get him,' Shreve said. 'Why did she do that?' Quentin didn't answer. He lay still and rigid on his back with the cold New England night on his face and the blood running warm in his rigid body and limbs, breathing hard but slow, his eyes wide open upon the window, thinking, 'Nevermore of peace. Nevermore of peace. Nevermore Nevermore Nevermore.' "

It is as if Quentin, through this saga of Sutpen and his son, had, like Ishmael, looked in the face of fire. These acts of simple passion and simple violence—Sutpen knowing no restraints (but one) to the fulfillment of his design, Henry acting out the role of the Southern chevalier in killing his friend to save his sister's honor—proved not so simple after all. To Quentin they were dragon's teeth. "What is it to me . . ." he had asked his father after the talk with Miss Rosa; and four months later in far-off Massachusetts he began to find out. It was partly the move to the North, with the sudden, sharp change of perspective; partly Shreve's prodding, which made him retell (and relive) the story all but against his will: *"Am I going to have to hear it all again* he thought . . . *I shall have to never listen to anything else but this again forever . . .",* as if he dreaded confronting face-to-face the hidden and desperate meanings which he had begun to sense on the September afternoon with Miss Rosa. He feels the "cursed spite" of Hamlet's fated involvement, is irritated at Shreve's insistence, and talks often as if to himself, staring down at the letter (about Miss Rosa's death) on his desk. Unlike Hamlet, he never speaks of his shattered illusions nor passes judgment. All we know is that the story in some way found him out, laid a question on his plate that he could not live with in peace. Was it Sutpen's ambition, furiously ambiguous, symbolic of an era and of all eras? Was it Henry's fatal predicament? Miss Rosa's wasted life? Was it the South's tragic dilemma, seen by him clearly for the first time—and, since the South's, his own? Perhaps it was all these questions and many more, plus the image of a certain kind of heroism against which he could not help measuring himself, that made him feel suddenly older "than a lot of people that have died." He has found unacceptable what he once accepted on boyish faith, and yet he cannot wholly reject it; these very living ghosts are his and he cannot renounce them. " 'The South,' Shreve said. 'The South. Jesus. No wonder you folks all outlive yourself by years and years and years.' " At the very end, Shreve, "the child of blizzards and cold," had one more question: " 'Now I want you to tell me just one thing more. Why do you hate the South?' 'I dont hate it,' Quentin said. . . . *I dont hate it* he thought, panting in the cold air, the iron New England dark; *I dont. I dont! I dont hate it! I dont hate it!*' "

This is as far in the tragic course as Quentin goes—that is, barely through initiation. He is like young Kalganov after witnessing the first shocking revelation of the Karamazov tragedy: "What are these people? What can mankind be after this?" In *Absalom, Absalom!* we never see what happens to

Quentin after the first shock. He is never called upon, as Hamlet was, to act, and so we never know what he might become. Though heavy with a past, the situation in this sense lacks a future; and we are left, as after the sinking of the *Pequod*, in doom and despair. But, as with *Moby-Dick*, the very shock sends us back to the full story, to all that has been recounted and revealed about the possibilities in humankind for good and evil; and again we see that life has been presented as neither trivial nor base nor unlovely. Both Sutpen and Henry had great capacities, though not for self-analysis and self-knowledge. They had crude but vital principles for which they were prepared to take the ultimate risk—each swore, in his own way, "a pact with mankind." Even Miss Rosa, cherishing her hate for forty-three years, insisting "out of some bitter and implacable reserve of undefeat" that her story be told, had heroic qualities. Shreve suggests that in the end she even conquered her hate and went with ambulance and doctors to save Henry—or at least, knowing what might happen, was willing to risk losing "for his sake" this object of hate which like a drug had kept her going all these years. As the various narrators recount their versions of the story, or, like Quentin and Shreve, re-create its scenes in their own imaginings and become vicarious participants in it, the ugly surface facts are distanced and transcended. They are brought into the perspective of a whole community of values and shown to be rooted deep not only in time but in the timeless, in the ancient feud of man with his own nature and his destiny. The truth of Sutpen's story comes to us not as One but as Many—many-faceted, ambiguous, a sum of irreconcilables. This is the source of its terror for Quentin, the glimpse it gives him into the abyss. The novel never specifies his future, or ours, but it leaves open many possibilities, for evil and for good. The total vision is neither of doom nor redemption, but of something tantalizingly, precariously in between. We have no hope, yet we hope. It is tragic.

14

THE TRIAL

WE HAVE seen how the novel, in the absence of a viable
tragic theater, brought into tragic focus the lives of "little
people," not the kings and counselors of the earth but an
erring woman in a small New England town; an old hunks of
a sea captain involved, as the world goes, in a minor industry;
and a family of Russians living obscurely in an all but nameless Russian town. That these people achieve tragic stature—
anything but "little"—is due in large part to their capacities,
developed through suffering, to understand themselves, judge
themselves, and see in their lot an image of the universal.
Hester imagined herself a "destined prophetess" in the tradition of the sainted Anne Hutchinson; the Karamazovs, in
Dmitri's words, "aren't blackguards but philosophers"; Ahab
took upon himself "the sum of all the general rage and hate
felt by his whole race from Adam down." Similarly, Faulkner
gave his small-town Mississippian, Quentin Compson, qualities of introspection and vision that, as he brooded on his
family's past, led him to tragic conclusions about his whole
race and kind. Though all these characters, in worldly terms,
were inconspicuous, or unimportant, they were seized by or
were witness to mighty passions. The situations or actions
they were involved in were the sort that function in the greatest tragedies: adultery, revenge, parricide.

By contrast, the area of life and the central action of
Kafka's *The Trial* seem humdrum indeed. A sentence from
the early pages of Tolstoi's *The Death of Ivan Ilych* might
serve as an epigraph for *The Trial:* Ivan's life, wrote Tolstoi,

was "most simple, and most ordinary and therefore most terrible." It was Tolstoi's genius, and Kafka's, to see the terror in the commonplace, in the daily, unimaginative, unexamined routine of lives whose aim is worldly success and prestige. It was only Ivan's long and agonizing illness that at last stirred him out of his complacence, caused him to see his life in all its hollowness, and brought him to a final moment of enlightenment. "Such men," as Dmitri said, "need a blow." But it was not the blow of a violent action undertaken in a crisis of passion; rather, Ivan's illness came from a trivial accident when he was hanging curtains in his fashionable new house.

So it was with Josef K. in *The Trial*. He was quietly arrested one fine morning in his quarters, for no reason at all, so far as he could see. He had done nothing wrong. He had no enemies. His life was in perfect order. He was thirty years old, a bachelor, and well along in a promising career in the Bank. His daily routine started with breakfast at eight, brought to him in bed. Then promptly at nine he would take up his duties at the Bank, with their own supportive routine. He made weekly visits to a certain waitress named Elsa, who worked in a cabaret most of the night and "during the day received her visitors in bed." [107] Nothing gross, simply routine. There were occasional invitations, much to his satisfaction, from one of his superiors at the Bank. His first response that morning when, instead of breakfast, two warders and an Inspector came to arrest him, was irritation. It was absurd that such a thing could happen to a man of his consequence. He could get no explanation from the warders. If only, he said to himself, he could have "a few words with a man on my own level of intelligence." But all he could get from the Inspector, of whom he had more hope, was an evasive, "Think less about us and of what is going to happen to you, think more about yourself instead."

The meaning of the novel could be said to hinge on this simple exhortation.[108] One can hear an echo of Mephistophilis's portentous reply to Doctor Faustus's early arrogance about hell's being "a fable": "Think so still till experience change thy mind." The day of Josef K.'s arrest marks the first of his year-long struggle to find out what the charges are against him and, whatever they are, to establish his innocence. The question the novel puts is, to what extent does he follow the Inspector's advice? Does he "think about himself" to any redeeming end? If the novel is to be saved for tragedy and not to be consigned to the literature of despair, the answer to these questions must in some degree be positive.

At first glance, the answer seems dubious. Like Tolstoi's Ivan Ilych, Josef K. appears as the "unauthentic man" of the modern world, faced with a sudden disruption of his smooth and superficial life—and ending it (as he says himself) "like a dog." He tries to accommodate his arrest to his neat little rationalistic scheme of things. Even his landlady, Frau Grubach, as he describes to her what happened that morning, sees something mysterious in it, something "learned," as she says, that she can't understand. "There's nothing learned about it," Josef K. replies. "It's completely null and void. I was taken by surprise, that was all." If only, he goes on, it had happened in the Bank:

> "In the Bank . . . I am always prepared, nothing of that kind could possibly happen to me there, I have my own attendant, the general telephone and the office telephone stand before me on my desk, people keep coming in to see me, clients and clerks, and above all, my mind is always on my work and so kept on the alert, it would be an actual pleasure to me if a situation like that had cropped up in the Bank."

In one fleeting moment that morning, the idea of suicide comes to him—to end the whole stupid business quickly. He thinks of simply walking out. Would the warders dare hinder him? But he is not the man for such heroics: "To take his life [he argues reasonably] would be such a senseless act"; and if it came to a tussle, he would lose whatever advantage he had over the warders. The thought comes to him that perhaps the whole affair is a practical joke—it was his thirtieth birthday—and to take it seriously would only reveal his obtuseness. "He had always been inclined to take things easily, to believe in the worst only when the worst happened, to take no care for the morrow even when the outlook was threatening." Like Melville's Ishmael, he would like to be "social" with horrors—to "settle the matter amicably," as he says to the Inspector, holding out his hand in a friendly gesture. But, unlike Ishmael, who was "quick to perceive a horror" even in the days before he boarded the *Pequod,* Josef K. sees no horror at all. He says to the Inspector:

> ". . . it can't be an affair of any great importance. . . . I argue this from the fact that though I am accused of something, I cannot recall the slightest offense that might be charged against me. But that even is of minor importance, the real question is, who accuses me? What authority is conducting these proceedings? Are you officers of the Law? . . . I demand a clear answer to these questions, and I feel sure that after an explanation we shall be able to part from each other on the best of terms."

The Inspector, ignoring Josef K.'s hand, merely says: "How simple it all seems to you!"

But even in this poor start, there are some redeeming elements. Though startled and confused at first, Josef K. shows signs of following the Inspector's advice. When the wardens offer to take charge of his personal possessions, he pays no attention to such petty, practical matters: ". . . far more important to him was the necessity to understand his situation clearly." If, as we can see in retrospect, the series of questions he addresses to the Inspector leaves out the most important matter of all—the possibility of his guilt—he at least shows a certain courage and persistence. He is much relieved when he learns that being under arrest does not prevent his going to the Bank that morning and resuming his usual routine. "Then being arrested isn't so very bad," he concludes. It is notable, however, that he does not use his freedom to escape; he accepts the arrest as a fact; and he turns down a flattering invitation from the Deputy Manager of the Bank in order to keep his appointment with the Court the following Sunday. ". . . the case was getting under way and he must fight it."

His progress during the year-long fight is presented in a series of discrete episodes and encounters, each one replete with ambiguities and paradoxes. His twistings and turnings, his decisions and indecisions, his many weaknesses and few strengths seem the opposite of the heroic, certainly of the heroes encountered in our study. And yet, as in the episode of the Arrest, there are redeeming elements in Joseph K.'s character that in the end culminate in a moment of self-awareness reminiscent, however slightly, of the great ones.

On Sunday, instead of attending the Deputy Manager's yachting party, he goes to his first Interrogation. Although, as he realizes later, he is completely deluded about the nature of the Court he addresses, and although he still basks in his sense of superiority and detachment, as an innocent man, from the proceedings, what he says to the Court has a certain resonance for the reader of tragedy. He speaks with courage and authority:

> "What has happened to me is only a single instance and as such of no great importance, especially as I do not take it very seriously, but it is representative of a misguided policy which is being directed against many other people as well. It is for these that I take up my stand here, not for myself."

This is hardly Ahab; nor is the following bit of rhetoric Job: ". . . innocent persons [he continues] are accused of guilt, and senseless proceedings are put in motion against them. . . ." But in Josef K.'s stand for humanity, however specious Kafka intended his eloquence to be, there is the faintest echo of both. He cannot be denied a hint, at least, of the heroic. In the nightmarish episode of the Whipper, when the warders are being punished for misappropriation of Josef K.'s clothes, his compassion for these men, who are suffering because of him, almost overcomes his concern for his status at the Bank (the warders are actually clerks at the Bank and the whipping is done in the basement). Almost, but not quite. He reasons his way out of his better impulse;

> . . . he was really anxious to get the warders off; since he had set himself to fight the whole corrupt

152

administration of the Court, it was obviously his duty to intervene on this occasion. But at the moment when Franz began to shriek, any intervention became impossible. K. could not afford to let the dispatch clerks and possibly all sorts of other people arrive and surprise him in a scene with these creatures in the lumber-room. No one could really demand that sacrifice from him.

He even thinks of offering himself to the Whipper as a substitute but, again, finds reasons against it. He resolves, however, not to hush the matter up but to bring the real culprits, the "high officials," to account—a resolve that comes to nothing. All we learn is that, for a while at least, Josef K. is capable of an authentic emotion.

The succeeding episodes show him increasingly independent in his struggle with the Court. A bit of his old snobbery returns when his uncle, his former guardian—"the family skeleton," Josef K. calls him—tries to help him and succeeds, at least, in getting him to go for help to Huld, the lawyer. But after long frustration Josef K. fires Huld and undertakes his case himself. By now, "the thought of his case never left him." He considers writing an account of his life to submit to the Court (an echo of Job's "Oath of Clearance"?). He would examine his life and measure it: ". . . and when he came to an event of any importance explain for what reasons he had acted as he did, intimate whether he approved or condemned his way of action in retrospect, and adduce grounds for the condemnation or approval." He goes to Titorelli, the painter, to hear what he has to tell about the Court, only to learn that it is everywhere, that everything belongs to it, that it "never forgets anything," and that its procedures are so infinitely redundant as to make acquittal practically impossible. He feels faint in the stuffy air of Titorelli's attic and leaves, tottering.

Josef K.'s persistent appeal for clarification, his longing to learn what he has been charged with and by whom, has been compared with other "mythic searches for information": Telemachus for his father, Job for the reasons for the disasters visited upon him, Doctor Faustus for the limits of human knowledge.[109] His persistence and his occasional show of courage lift him above the grovelling and hopeless defendants who crowd the lawyer's office. Little man that he is, he is better than the others. His uncle thought only of family prestige. Huld, Titorelli, and Block (the commercial traveler) become part of the corruption of the Court or linger on in all but hopeless litigation. Leni, the lawyer's corrupt secretary, urges Josef K.—like Job's counselors—to admit his fault and have done: ". . . you can't put up a resistance against this court." Huld goes even farther. There is no sense in wasting time and energy trying to reform the Court: "The only sensible thing was to adapt oneself to existing conditions."

In the penultimate episode, "In the Cathedral," Josef K. is granted the nearest approach to a hearing he achieves. However remote the parallel, one is reminded of Job's final vision. The priest whom he encounters in the vast, darkening interior calls him by name, comes down from his pulpit, extends his hand, and agrees to give him "as much time as you need." The priest, actually the prison chaplain, knows all about Josef K.'s trial and is impatient with him when he protests his innocence. To clear up his "delusions" about the nature of the Court, he tells him the legend of the door-keeper who guarded the door of the Law from the man from the country. The interpretations and counterinterpretations of the legend leave Josef K. weary and discouraged: ". . . the trains of thought into which it was leading him were unfamiliar. . . . The simple story had lost its clear outline, he wanted to put it out of his mind. . . ." But till then he had held his ground in the argument with the priest, and in one important particular he agrees with him: that the man from the country (whose predicament the priest likens to that of Josef K. himself) is superior to the door-keeper because he sees "the radiance that issues from the door of the Law," while the door-keeper with his back to the door, does not.

The point is crucial. All the other people in the novel now appear as door-keepers, standing between Josef K. and the radiance of the Law. The Bank, with its hierarchy and routine, is the corporate symbol for them all. As Josef K. gropes his way, with the help of the priest, through the dark cathedral, he trumps up an excuse for leaving. "Do you want to leave already?" asks the priest.

> Although at that moment K. had not been thinking of leaving, he answered at once: "Of course, I must go. I'm the chief clerk of a Bank, they're waiting for me, I only came here to show a business friend from abroad round the Cathedral." "Well," said the priest, reaching out his hand to K., "then go."

At this climactic moment, when the priest—though a part of the Court but not, one feels, of its corruption [110]—is ready and willing to talk further and to explain more, Josef K. fails him. Like the man from the country, like Ivan Ilych, he is destined to ask the right question only at the point of his dissolution. Josef K. is aggrieved at the priest's sudden indifference:

> "Don't you want anything more to do with me?" asked K. "No," said the priest. "You were so friendly to me for a time," said K., "and explained so much to me, and now you let me go as if you cared nothing about me." "But you have to leave now," said the priest. "Well, yes," said K., "you must see that I can't help it."

But he knows he *can* help it—"he could quite well stay longer." He is not the man for the heroic decision or the ultimate vision. Following the priest's direction he gropes his way to the door of the cathedral in the dark.

In the tragic analysis, much depends on the reading of the final episode when Josef K., on his thirty-first birthday, is executed in the quarry at the outskirts of the city. "In all literature," Maurice Blanchot writes, "the narratives of Kafka are among the blackest, among those most riveted to absolute disaster . . . [that] most tragically torture hope. . . ." [111] The death of Josef K. seems among the blackest, and bleakest. What is the meaning of those last words—"Like a dog!"— spoken as the life goes out of him? The tragic heroes of the tradition die, but they do not die like dogs. Lear dies in an ecstasy of love. Ahab, spitting defiance at the whale, achieves at least in his own mind his "topmost greatness." Even the suicides of Antigone, Othello, of Antony and Cleopatra are gestures of assertion, done in full self-knowledge. Has Josef K. simply come to the end of his endurance? Has he nothing to say? In refusing to use the knife on himself—an opportunity offered him by his executioners—he is guilty, says the narrator, of his "last failure," the last of the long series beginning with the warders that fateful morning and culminating in the cathedral, when the priest's angry "Can't you see anything at all?" seems to sum up Josef K.'s moral blindness. When, following K.'s "Like a dog!", the narrator says, in the final sentence in the book, "it was as if he meant the shame of it to outlive him," we get a suggestion, at least, of a moral judgment. But whose shame? K.'s own? The Court's? The executioners'? The world's? "This final noun of the novel," writes Walter Sokel, "not only emphasizes a desperate negativity in contrast to the tragic affirmation with which the earlier punitive fantasies ended [*The Penal Colony* and *The Metamorphosis*]; it also expresses a total ambiguity, which makes it impossible to decipher the final meaning of *The Trial*." [112]

This is blackness indeed. All tragedies end in a certain degree of ambiguity. Was Ahab right or wrong to pursue his quenchless feud? Melville never answers definitively—one reason, perhaps, why he told Hawthorne that he had written "a wicked book" yet felt "spotless as a lamb." Antigone, Hamlet, Oedipus, Lear—all have their dark sides which we do not forget even as they transcend them. But in the face of *total* ambiguity, the Muse of Tragedy walks out.

A parallel from a quite different source may be instructive. When Conrad's Marlow, the narrator of *Heart of Darkness,* is at the bedside of the dying Kurtz, he hears him utter four words: "The horror! The horror!" Unlike Kafka's hesitant narrator, Marlow interprets his hero's last words with complete confidence: "He had something to say. He said it. This is the reason why I affirm that Kurtz was a remarkable man. . . . It was an affirmation, a moral victory paid for by innumerable defeats, by abominable terrors, by abominable satisfactions. But it was a victory!"

Unauthentic men do not live in our imaginations; they are

not "remarkable," at least in the sense Marlow gives the word. Until his final moment, Kurtz's life has been a travesty, a hideous lie. To the impressionable Marlow, his last words redeem him. Kafka allows Josef K. no such redemption; he is no changed man; there can be no cry of victory. The meaning of *The Trial*, Cyrena Pondrom writes, "must remain ambivalent—not because the novels fails to make itself clear but because its very ambivalence is part of its clarity: the novel as a whole, like the 'Legend of the Doorkeeper,' stands as a symbol of man's intrinsic inability to know completely or to judge finally." [113] It is true that Josef K. learns no more about the Law than does the man from the country, although he is impressed by what the priest says about its radiance. But in the final moments in the quarry he has insights and asks questions—the right ones at last. He reaches out in ways of which the snobbish rationalist of the opening scene would have been incapable. Does he, like Kurtz, pass moral judgment on himself, or are we left in total ambiguity?

To be sure, he carries his inadequacies and banalities to the end. He persists in looking to women for help (the priest had chided him for this); he had taken a guide book, not a prayer book, to the cathedral (the priest told him to throw it away); his old snobbery returns as he scrutinizes the executioners when they come to take him away: "Tenth-rate old actors they send for me. . . . They want to finish me off quickly." As they proceed to the quarry, he clings to his old habits of thought: "the only thing for me to do is to keep my intelligence calm and discriminating to the end." (This is the very fallacy the Devil had warned Ivan Karamazov against: "You think intelligence is everything!") But in the next sentence something in Josef K. is operating beyond intelligence. It is closer to vision, or insight, a glimpse into himself, a moment akin to the characteristic, often final, phase of the tragic hero's experience; that is, perception.

> "I always wanted to snatch at the world with twenty hands, and not for a very laudable motive, either. That was wrong, and am I to show now that not even a whole year's trial has taught me anything? . . . I

157

am grateful for the fact that these half-dumb, senseless creatures have been sent to accompany me on
this journey, and that I have been left to say to myself all that is needed."

This is not the first time the idea of learning, or being
"taught," has entered Josef K.'s thoughts in this last episode.
On the way to the quarry he catches a glimpse of (he thinks)
Fräulein Bürstner entering the square from a sidestreet. Leading the two executioners, he follows in her direction, "not that
he wanted to overtake her or to keep her in sight as long as
possible, but only that he might not forget the lesson she had
brought into his mind." We can only guess what the lesson
was. The relationship between the two (sketched briefly in
the episode of the Arrest) had failed, ending with Josef K.'s
animal-like embraces and her weary departure. Later, through
her friend Fräulein Montag, she had refused to see him again.
What had she taught him? That it was futile to ask for help
from others, that he must depend on himself? Did her sudden
appearance, a human being he had once conversed with and
embraced, remind him of all that had been left out of his life?
Then, as the executioners pass the knife between them in
their "odious ceremonial of courtesy," humanity intrudes again.

His glance fell on the top story of the house adjoin-
ing the quarry. With a flicker as of a light going up,
the casements of a window there suddenly flew open;
a human figure, faint and insubstantial at that distance and that height, leaned abruptly far farward
and stretched both arms still farther. Who was it?
A friend? A good man? Someone who sympathized?

During the many months of pleading his case, insisting on his
innocence, keeping his intelligence always active, Josef K. had
not thought this way. It is as if the greatest truth of all had
just dawned on him. To be sure, his intelligence is still working: he wonders whether some "arguments in his favour had
been overlooked." He immediately assures himself that "there
must be." But in the next breath he calls in question the very
adequacy of "argument": "Logic is doubtless unshakable," he

says, "but it cannot withstand a man who wants to go on living." (One is reminded of Alyosha's urging his brother Ivan "to love life more than the meaning of it.") A rush of questions follows. "Where was the Judge whom he had never seen? Where was the High Court, to which he had never penetrated?" The tone of these questions seems very different from the contempt and frustration with which he had viewed the Court so far. Had the talk with the friendly priest, with his story of the man from the country and the radiance of the Law, somehow enlarged Josef K.'s spirit? In his last gesture, he may be reaching out toward those hands stretched out from the window—a longing for human contact he has never known—or it may be that he is reaching out, in a new longing, for a spiritual reality he has never known. Kafka only describes the gesture: "He raised his hands and spread out all his fingers."

But, if the gesture implies a new vision, a perception, it comes, as in many of the great tragedies, too late to save the hero. The knife goes into Josef K.'s heart. The executioner turns it twice. Josef K. has strength only for his last summing up, "Like a dog!" It is his final insight, his final self-judgment. The shame is *his;* he knows it; and we are back again at one of the first and one of the greatest affirmations of tragedy, twice spoken by the Chorus in Aeschylus's *Agamemnon:*

> Zeus, who guided men to think,
> . . . has laid it down that wisdom
> comes alone through suffering . . .

and later, with even mightier emphasis,

> Justice so moves that those only learn
> who suffer . . .   [trans. Richmond Lattimore]

The degree and quality of the wisdom Josef K. learned from his year-long ordeal may be questioned; but it is enough, I think, to reject the notion that the novel ends in "total ambiguity," which (as I see it) would cancel everything out to zero. The pattern is familiar: Job's exemplary life had blinded him to certain values; in his years of power, Lear had "ta'en too little care of this" (the wretchedness in his own kingdom);

159

Ivan Karamazov learned that "the intellect isn't everything" because (as Zossima saw) he had "a heart capable of suffering"—and of learning from it; Tolstoi's Ivan Ilych learned through intense physical suffering to cherish certain human values he had ignored in the days of his prosperity. Josef K. had "snatched at the world with twenty hands" and he saw at the end that it was wrong. "He had something to say." The progression in the novel is toward values, not toward a denial of them or toward the no-decision of total ambiguity. The function of tragedy as the critical and creative approach to the mystery of man's suffering has been fulfilled. Fresh from the masterworks of our study, we may feel that Josef K.'s perception is meager indeed, that the final scene is too dismal for tragedy, the mystery only deeper. But Kafka's "little man," to whose unheroic nature Kafka's is scrupulously true to the very end, somehow becomes bigger. It is Josef K. who controls the final scene, not the executioners. For a few moments he goes beyond himself. He reaches out—and the gesture is tragic.

15

LONG DAY'S JOURNEY INTO NIGHT

WHAT KEEPS *Long Day's Journey into Night* from "dwindling to a sorrowful tale" is this same capacity for suffering—and for learning from it—on the part of the four Tyrones, the name O'Neill gives his own family in this autobiographical play. (They are: James Tyrone, the actor-father; Mary his wife, far gone in dope; Jamie, the older, wastrel son; and Edmund, O'Neill himself at twenty-three, the would-be writer and incipient consumptive.) Each one, during the long day of the play, goes through a kind of agon, not the lonely ordeal of the hero but inseparable from the ordeal of the family, so inextricably—and fatefully—are these four lives woven. No one dominates the scene; there is no Jobian figure to confront whatever it is that has brought this family to the point of dissolution. One is reminded of the wrangling Karamazovs; but there is no Father Zossima to define the evil and send out his Alyosha to do battle. The fog that thickens during the play is, in one sense, a fitting symbol: these are the "fog people" (as Edmund calls them, including himself), individually all but lost in the fog of temperament until, interacting much as had the Karamazovs, in the very torture of their interaction they have glimpses through the fog to new truth.

The play brings up vividly the question of the involvement of the tragic artist in his own fictions, a quality in contrast to the so-called detachment of the satirist or ironist. The closer to modern times, the more such involvement can be documented. O'Neill made his own involvement poignantly clear. To his wife Carlotta on their twelfth wedding anniversary, he wrote:

> Dearest: I give you the original of this play of old sorrow, written in tears and blood. A sadly inappropriate gift, it would seem, for a day celebrating happiness. But you will understand. I mean it as a tribute to your love and tenderness which gave me the faith in love that enabled me to face my dead at last and write this play—write it with deep pity and understanding and forgiveness for *all* the four haunted Tyrones.
>
> These twelve years, Beloved One, have been a Journey into Light—into love. You know my gratitude. And my love! [114]

"To face my dead at last." This confrontation, the "facing," had a long beginning. (O'Neill was sixty-three when he completed the play.) It was as surely a quest for meaning as any of the great ones of our study. The pattern is familiar: out of the welter of experience, out of the suffering, comes the tragic question, "Why?" In his afflictions, Job sought meaning: "Teach me and I will hold my tongue, and cause me to understand wherein I have erred." Lear asked, "Is there any cause in nature that makes these hard hearts?" And Kalganov, weeping over the degradation of Dmitri, asks, "What can mankind be after this?" When O'Neill calls his family the "four haunted Tyrones," he suggests his own sense of the mystery. Writing the play was the result of his forty-year attempt to pierce it—to "understand" it, as he wrote to Carlotta, and "pity" and "forgive." The "tears and blood" suggest the suffering it cost him.[115]

Each of the Tyrones, as if in turn, indicates the take-off point of ONeill's quest and, had it not been for the play, the end of it—in fatalism, despair, bitterness. Mary sees them all as prisoners of the past: "None of us can help the things life has done to us. . . . He [Jamie] can't help being what the past has made him. Any more than your father can. Or you [Edmund]. Or I." Edmund would simply deny the problem: "Who wants to see life as it is, if they can help it? That's what I wanted—to be alone with myself in another world where truth is untrue and life can hide from itself." Toward the end, Mary asks a question for them all: "What is it I'm looking for? I know it's something I lost," and we see her husband James "trying to shake off his hopeless stupor." "It's no good, Papa," says Jamie, and quotes Swinburne:

> There is no help, for all things are so,
> And all the world is bitter as a tear.

Or, as Job's wife advised, "Curse God, and die."

But no one curses God, and no one commits suicide. The very stamina of these people is awesome as they survive hour after hour (or so it seems) of the often furious exchange of blame and counterblame. The long day is very long, reaching far into the night. Edmund's "fog people" hardly does justice to their emotional capacity—the bursts of temper, the clashes of temperament, the excruciating self-revelations, and (most impressive) the love and loyalty that, for all the bickering, keep them from disintegration, as individuals and as a family. If none of the characters in the play achieves the "deep pity and understanding and forgiveness" of the note to Carlotta, they all have moments of redemptive insight. This is not to say that the family (or any member of it) is redeemed. There is no assurance that the next day might not be a repetition of this long one; but the play shows, clearly and powerfully, how it might have been. The ultimate perception was O'Neill's: "the faith in love that enabled me to face my dead."

The play opens on an August morning in 1912 with the Tyrones in their New London home near the sea. We are confronted at once with the precariousness of the family situation. As Tyrone and Mary emerge from breakfast, their mood seems happy and loving: Tyrone gives Mary a "playful hug" and calls her "a fine armful." But she is clearly on edge, and she jokes a bit caustically about Tyrone's huge appetite and his inept business dealings. They worry about Edmund's illness and Jamie's failure. When the boys come in, the discords mount, and Tyrone's forced good humor is seen for what it is.

Immediately there is a tiff between Tyrone and Jamie, a prelude to the pattern of encounters to come: blame, counterblame, uneasy truce. It starts with Mary's seemingly innocent remark about Tyrone's snoring; then Jamie's "The Moor, I know his trumpet"; then Tyrone's "If it takes my snoring to make you remember Shakespeare instead of the dope sheet on the ponies, I hope I'll keep on with it." Jamie wants out: "What's all the fuss about? Let's forget it." But one word borrows another: "Yes, forget!" says Tyrone. "Forget everything and face nothing. It's a convenient philosophy if you've no ambition in life except to——." Mary steps in and changes the subject. Truce.

Soon the family is laughing over Edmund's story of old Shaughnessy and his pigs and millionaire Harker's ice pond. But the mood doesn't last. Tyrone suspects the boys, with their "damned Socialist anarchist sentiments," of wanting to get him in trouble with Harker. Mary tries to soothe him. Edmund, in "sudden nervous exasperation," leaves the room; and Mary, "with a strange obstinate set to her face," goes to confer with Bridget the cook. Another truce.

Tyrone and Jamie are left alone, and the stage is set for their first major encounter. The theme, as usual, is guilt. Jamie blames Tyrone for Edmund's illness: he was too stingy to pay for "a real doctor" when Edmund first got sick. Tyrone counters with the terrible accusation that Jamie, out of jealousy, corrupted Edmund to undermine his health. "That's a lie!" Jamie shouts. "I won't stand for that, Papa! . . . Oh, for Christ's sake, Papa! Can't you lay off me!" For a moment the two touch bottom: the charges could hardly have been worse. But then something new happens. It is as if both men have been shocked into their senses by what they have said—and shocked into their better natures. Tyrone's thoughts turn to Mary and the bad luck that Edmund's illness should come at a time when her own state is so precarious. His voice "grows husky and trembles a little": "It's damnable she should have this to upset her, just when she needs peace and freedom from worry. She's been so well in the two months since she came home. It's been heaven to me. This home has been a home again. But I needn't tell you, Jamie." The two suddenly see eye to eye. A stage direction makes it explicit: "His son looks at him, for the first time with an understanding sympathy. It is as if suddenly a deep bond of common feeling existed between them in which their antagonisms could be forgotten." Jamie says ("almost gently"): "I've felt the same way, Papa."

But, being what they are (O'Neill seems to be saying), they cannot sustain this mood for long. Within seconds they are quarreling again. Jamie picks up the theme of his mother's illness and blames it on Tyrone: he was too stingy to hire a proper doctor at the time of Edmund's birth. Tyrone's furious "That's a lie!" seems likely to lead to violence except for Mary (again), whose unexpected entrance brings about another truce.

And now Mary herself has her turn. She brings Act I to a close in a flurry of accusations and self-pity. She pours out her heart to Edmund. Everything is Tyrone's fault. He was too stingy to give the family a decent home, with an automobile and nice friends. She is lonely. She is worried about Edmund's health. The family doesn't trust her—they keep spying on her. Edmund's "Mama! Stop it!" is unavailing, and he goes, leaving her alone. As the curtain falls, she is "terribly tense . . . seized by a fit of nervous panic," on the point of another fix. When she reappears in Act II (noon of the same day), "Her eyes are brighter, and there is a peculiar detachment in her voice and manner. . . ." While the others find momentary release in temper and (later) alcohol, she finds it in the detachment of morphine. "The only way," she tells Edmund, "is to make yourself not care," and it is here that she slips into the fatalism that relieves everyone of blame and puts it all on "Life."

But neither she nor the others can rest long in such an evasion. This is important to the student of tragedy; for suffering we can call tragic is not to be resolved that easily. There is an echo here of the tragic Dostoevskian ethic, so clear with the Karamazovs, that there may be salvation in following one's nature, however violent or however extreme in other ways, to

165

the very end—as Dmitri found "precious metal in the dirt."
So it is that violence "becomes" these Tyrones. Mary's com-
bative nature soon reasserts itself, and in the ensuing scenes
none of the men escapes. Tyrone, she says, never wanted a
home; he should have been a bachelor, with his barrooms and
his cheap hotels. Jamie's alcoholism is all his fault, and now
he lets the invalid Edmund take a drink: "Do you want to kill
him?" she snaps. She turns on Jamie, accusing him of killing
her second baby by deliberately exposing him to measles—
again, out of jealousy.

Then, alone with Edmund, her favorite, she turns on *him*
as the source of all her troubles. It was her illness at his birth
that led to the quack doctor who prescribed the morphine.
And now it's her worry over his health that has driven her to
it again. Suddenly she checks herself, as if shocked by what
she has said. She cries ("distractedly"), "But that's no excuse!
I'm only trying to explain. It's not an excuse!" ("She hugs him
to her—pleadingly.") "Promise me, dear, you won't believe I
made you an excuse." But all Edmund can say ("bitterly") is,
"What else can I believe?"

And now, in her near-panic, comes her moment of insight
and gentleness. She confesses her lies and her guilt. "I don't
blame you," she says to Edmund:

> "How could you believe me—when I can't believe
> myself? I've become such a liar. I never lied about
> anything once upon a time. Now I have to lie, espe-
> cially to myself. I've never understood anything about
> it [her dependence on morphine], except that one
> day long ago I could no longer call my soul my own."

Once started, she experiences a tiny epiphany, a vision of a
better time to come. It is as if O'Neill, in his quest, were uncovering in his family unsuspected areas of truth (and beauty
and goodness). "Lowering her voice to a strange tone of whispered confidence," she pictures for Edmund a time when she
might regain her soul, be forgiven, and be believed.

> "But some day, dear, I will find it again—some day
> when you're all well, and I see you healthy and

happy and successful, and I don't have to feel guilty any more—some day when the Blessed Virgin Mary forgives me and gives me back the faith in Her love and pity I used to have in my convent days, and I can pray to Her again—when She sees no one in the world can believe in me even for a moment any more, then She will believe in me, and with Her help it will be so easy. I will hear myself scream with agony, and at the same time I will laugh because I will be so sure of myself."

But this mood doesn't last, either, and like all such moments in the play it is ambivalent. It may have been partly a pose for Edmund's sake. He "remains hopelessly silent," and she concludes curtly, "Of course, you can't believe that, either." Alone a moment later as the scene ends, she is glad the others are gone, glad "to get rid of them." "Then Mother of God," she asks, "why do I feel so lonely?" Pose or no pose, she speaks the plain truth here: she can't get along without her family. Nor can they get along without her.

One simple criterion of tragedy lies in the question, How does our first view of the protagonist (in this case the family) differ from what we see at the end? Has there been a gain, if only minimal, in humanity, self-knowledge, wisdom, insight—all that we have subsumed under the notion of perception? What has been won from "the fine hammered steel of woe"?

When, at the end of Act II, the Tyrones disperse for the afternoon, there seems no good reason, except food and shelter, why they should ever assemble again. Each has said enough, one would think, to make further relations impossible. It is no wonder that when Tyrone and Edmund reappear at dinner time (Act III) they have had a lot to drink. (When Jamie shows up at midnight, in Act IV, he is drunk.) Hearing their voices, Mary says, "Why are they coming back? They don't want to. . . ." And only a few moments later, when the bickering starts all over again, Tyrone says, "Oh, for the love of God! I'm a fool for coming home!" But here they are, together again. As the two men come in, Mary says to herself that she'd "much rather be alone" but in the next breath ("pathetically relieved and eager") adds, "Oh, I'm so glad they've come! I've been so horribly lonely!" What is it at the very end of the play, when the three men sit in silence during Mary's long soliloquy, that gives the scene, as here in this reunion for dinner, a power that goes beyond pathos? How in the last two acts and especially in the final scene does the family transcend itself, leaving us not so much in tears as in awed silence?

The progress, or "journey," of the play is toward a deeper understanding of each others' nature on the part of the four Tyrones. What they go through—what they put themselves through—is hardly heroic suffering. There are no Jobian afflictions, no state is threatened, no fear (except Edmund's illness) for life or limb. What takes place is all *within*—within the confines of the Tyrone living room, within a single day, within the family (Cathleen, the maid, is the only outsider and has no idea of what is going on). The only intrusions from the outside world are the doctor's verdict on Edmund and the sound of the foghorn and the fog itself, which intensifies the fierce concentration of the scene. "It hides you from the world and the world from you," Mary says. The last two acts reiterate the themes already stated—Tyrone's tightfistedness, Mary's addiction, Jamie's jealousy of Edmund, the strange mixture of emotions each member of the family has for the others: pride and shame, love and hate, contempt and admiration. What is new is the degree of understanding each of them achieves. The climax comes in the alcoholic unburdenings of the men and in Mary's dope-induced finale at the end, but not before the old recriminations have gone back and forth in bitterness and (twice) in physical violence. It is as if the truth has had to wait until every other route (and they themselves) has been exhausted. They have had to find out that the endless blame-laying was a dead-end, that there would be no release until they could look within themselves and be honest to what they saw. This is the true within-ness of the play, the true suffering.

It is here that the magnitude of the play—and of the characters—lies. Nothing would have happened had they not been capable of submitting themselves to each other, of undergoing the agony not only of self-disclosure but of listening to the disclosures of the others. No one walks out and slams the door. They bear it out to the end—and the end is not bitter.

The sequence begins, as we have seen, with Mary's confession to Edmund, who listens in silence. What he learns comes out later as he and his father talk about Mary's condition during their never-finished game of cards at the beginning of Act IV. Edmund stumbles on a major insight:

> "The hardest thing to take [he tells his father] is the blank wall she builds around her. Or it's more like a bank of fog in which she hides herself. Deliberately, that's the hell of it! You know something in her does it deliberately—to get beyond our reach, to be rid of us, to forget we're alive! It's as if, in spite of loving us, she hated us!"

There is a moment of calm as Tyrone "remonstrates gently": "Now, now, lad. It's not her. It's the damned poison." But the damned poison, Edmund points out ("in bitter accusation") is not her fault: "I know damned well she's not to blame! And I know who is! You are! Your damned stinginess! . . . Jesus, when I think of it I hate your guts!" Then comes more vindictive rage until he, too, near bottom, comes to his senses—and to the same insight he had about his mother: that human beings are capable of loving and hating at the same time. "I didn't mean it, Papa. I'm like Mama, I can't help liking you, in spite of everything." Later in Act IV, after Jamie's shocking confession that it was indeed true that he had intentionally corrupted Edmund, he too finds himself saying, "But don't get the wrong idea, Kid. I love you more than I hate you."

As the card game goes on, we realize that the bottom has not quite been reached. It is not until Edmund, "bursting with anger," his "voice trembling with rage" and "shaken by a fit of coughing," accuses his father of wanting to save money by sending him to a state institution that Tyrone himself is shocked into his better nature. Now, as "his head bows" and "he stares dully at the cards on the table," he talks "without resentment": "A stinking old miser. Well, maybe you're right." And he launches into a long confession in an attempt to explain himself—his poverty-stricken youth in Ireland, the struggle to establish himself in America, his early years in the theater and his "good bad luck" in finding "the big money-maker" (*The Count of Monte Cristo*).[116] The stage directions indicate the mixture of "guilty contrition," "self-contempt," "drunken peevishness," "grim humor," even sentimental nostalgia ("He wipes the tears from his eyes"), and (finally) bitterness: "What the hell was it I wanted to buy, I wonder, that was worth—Well, no matter. It's a late day for regrets." Edmund is "moved, stares at his father with understanding," and says ("slowly"), I'm glad you've told me this, Papa. I know you a lot better now."

One by one, each member of the family goes through the same harrowing process. Now it's Edmund's turn. "You've just told me some high spots in your memories," he says to his father. "Want to hear mine?" What follows is a long, lyric reminiscence of his life at sea. He recalls two episodes when, "for a second," there was "meaning." The first was on a square rigger bound for Buenos Aires, driving along at fourteen knots under a full moon in the Trades. "I became drunk with the beauty and singing rhythm of it," he says, "and for a moment I lost myself—actually lost my life." He became one with the "white sails and flying spray," he *became* "beauty and rhythm . . . moonlight and the ship and the high dim-starred sky." He felt "peace and unity and wild joy." He "belonged . . . to Life itself! To God, if you want to put it that way." The second moment was on a steamship of the American Line, on lookout in the dawn watch—a "moment of ecstatic freedom . . . the peace, the end of the quest, the last harbor, the joy of belonging to a fulfillment beyond men's lousy, pitiful, greedy fears and hopes and dreams!" In such moments it seems as if a veil were drawn back: "For a second you see—and seeing the secret, are the secret." But the veil drops back again and "you are alone, lost in the fog again, and you stumble on toward nowhere, for no good reason!" At this point, "he grins wryly" by way of ironic comment on his ultimate confession:

170

"It was a great mistake, my being born a man.
I would have been much more successful as a sea-
gull or a fish. As it is, I will always be a stranger
who never feels at home, who does not really want
and is not really wanted, who can never belong, who
must always be a little in love with death!"

Bitter as his conclusion is, he is blaming no one but himself, and his candor brings him and his father to a moment
of understanding. Tyrone "stares at him—impressed." "Yes,
there's the makings of a poet in you all right." Then, "pro-
testing uneasily": "But that's morbid craziness about not being wanted and loving death." Edmund, perhaps noting the
uneasiness of his father's protest, ignores the morbidness and
picks up the matter of the poet:

"The *makings* of a poet. No. . . . I couldn't touch
what I tried to tell you just now. I just stammered.
That's the best I'll ever do. I mean, if I live. Well, it
will be faithful realism, at least. Stammering is the
native eloquence of us fog people."

Whether O'Neill actually thought this about himself at
age twenty-three, and the way his career belied it, are matters
that go beyond the play. What happens in the play is that the
moment of harmony between father and son is interrupted by
Jamie, who comes in drunk. "Get him to bed, Edmund," says
Tyrone. "I'll go out on the porch. He has a tongue like an
adder when he's drunk. I'd only lose my temper."

The scene that follows is Jamie's. It's his turn now. No
great nature is revealed, but there are surprises, like Dmitri's
parting words to Alyosha, "Love Ivan!" He is more than the
"drunken hulk" his father calls him. His course during the
scene is uneven, but it follows the pattern made familiar by
the others. From the moment he enters ("Oh, hello, Kid. I'm
as drunk as a fiddler's bitch") he is refreshingly honest. He
talks frankly but compassionately about his whore, Fat Violet,
and, drunk as he is, he is concerned about Edmund: "I know,
Kid, it's been a lousy day for you." And then "in vino veritas"
(he uses the phrase), it all comes out: his jealousy of Edmund
from the first—"Mama's baby and Papa's pet!"; his deliberate

171

attempt to pull Edmund down with him: "Mama and Papa are right. I've been a rotten bad influence. And worst of it is, I did it on purpose"; his love-hate of Edmund; and finally his own explanation, which lays blame on no one but himself: "Can't help it. I hate myself. Got to take revenge. On everyone else. Especially you."

Jamie doesn't repent or promise to reform. He warns Edmund to be on his guard—he'd still stab him in the back "at the first chance I get." He simply tells the truth: "Remember I warned you—for your sake. Give me credit. Greater love hath no man than this, that he saveth his brother from himself." And finally, before sinking into a drunken doze: "Don't die on me. You're all I've got left. God bless you, K.O."

Tyrone, having overheard the last part of the talk, comes in from the porch. "His face is stern and disgusted but at the same time pitying." Looking down on Jamie "with a bitter sadness," he says, "A sweet spectacle for me! My first-born, who I hoped would bear my name in honor and dignity, who showed such brilliant promise!" Edmund, who has hardly noticed Tyrone's entrance, finally breaks his silence: "Keep quiet, can't you, Papa?"

Pity touched with awe is the mood of the final scene. The family has resisted all the forces that would pull it apart. Mary, who has been moving about upstairs for some time and causing anxious remarks from the men, is heard playing the piano, awkwardly, like a schoolgirl. She suddenly appears "in a sky-blue dressing gown," carrying her wedding dress. She is lost in morphine. Jamie's sardonic comment, "The Mad Scene. Enter Ophelia!" infuriates the other two. Edmund slaps him across the mouth, and Tyrone blurts out, "The dirty blackguard! His own mother . . . I'll kick him out in the gutter tomorrow, so help me God." But Jamie's quick admission— "All right, Kid. Had it coming. But I told you how much I'd hoped—" and his sobbing breaks the anger of his father, who pleads, "Jamie, for the love of God, stop it!" It is Mary's quiet, girl-like, detached presence that quiets the men. The rest of the play, save for Jamie's lugubrious quotations from Swinburne, is Mary's. She has, quite literally, the last word.

She moves about the stage like a sleepwalker, talking to

herself, ignoring the others. Tyrone, "in anguish," gently takes the wedding dress from her, which she relinquishes "with the shy politeness of a well-bred young girl toward an elderly gentleman who relieves her of a bundle." The men, for all their drinking, are strangely sober. When Mary speaks, "they freeze into silence again, staring at her." Their first reaction, as she proceeds to act out "the mad scene," is hopelessness, and it is here that Jamie says, "It's no good, Papa," and quotes Swinburne. Tyrone gives up: "Oh, we're fools to pay any attention. It's the damned poison. . . . Pass me that bottle, Jamie. And stop reciting that damned morbid poetry. I won't have it in my house."

This turns out to be the last skirmish. They all pour drinks. As they are about to drink, there is an important stage direction: "Tyrone lifts his glass and his sons follow suit mechanically, but before they can drink Mary speaks and they slowly lower their drinks to the table, forgetting them." From here on, the men are under her spell. She "stares dreamily before her. Her face looks extraordinarily youthful and innocent." She reminisces about her days in the convent, about her talk with Mother Elizabeth, "so sweet and good," about praying to the Virgin and finding "peace again because I knew she heard my prayer." The men sit motionless and silent.

There is nothing "great" here, but there is a vision, dope-induced as it is, of the good (and true and beautiful). At least we see what might have been—and recall Alyosha's pastoral charge to the boys at the end of *The Brothers Karamazov*, which, if nothing else, made clear the values missing in that family. Neither Alyosha nor Mary brings about radical change. But when Alyosha talked, the boys stopped quarreling; and when Mary begins her soliloquy, the men put down their drinks and listen. Mary's final sentences end the play in a kind of ironic benediction: "That was in the winter of senior year. Then in the spring something happened to me. Yes, I remember. I fell in love with James Tyrone and was so happy for a time." As the curtain falls, only Tyrone "stirs in his chair."

Such was the situation in the O'Neill family, the play says, in "August, 1912." What "haunted" them? Nothing, surely, like the Curse on the House of Atreus, or a regicide, or the ancestral sins that so haunted Hawthorne. No one killed an albatross or was dismembered by a whale. Perhaps O'Neill's word "haunted" is to be explained mainly by the facts of inherited temperament—the family Irishness, of which he makes a good deal: the bursts of temper, the moodiness, the sudden extremes of emotion, the flamboyance and love of talk, the touch of the visionary in each of them, even Jamie. But temperament isn't all; it doesn't determine everything. O'Neill makes it clear that the fault (Tyrone quotes the passage) is not in their stars. And like all tragic faults (or flaws) it involves the exercise of the will.

Tragedy, to O'Neill, ennobled in art what he called man's "hopeless hopes." [117] If life in 1912 seemed hopeless, something in him—the dream, the vision, the hope, the very Irish vitality that is awesome in the play—kept him going, with the results we all know.[118] There is something here of the hopeless hope that kept young Quentin Compson burrowing into the story of his family in an attempt to understand and perhaps forgive; but we know that in *The Sound and the Fury* Faulkner has his young hero, unable to bear the burden, commit suicide. O'Neill bore it out to the end. He was once reported as saying, "I couldn't ever be negative about life. On that score you've got to decide YES or NO. And I'll always say YES." [119] There was a good deal of the Greek in him, as well as the Irish. "To O'Neill tragedy had the meaning the Greeks gave it, and it was their classic example that he tried to follow. He believed with the Greeks that tragedy always brought exaltation, 'an urge [he once said] toward life and ever more life.' " [120] Tragedy, he said, brought men "to spiritual understandings and released them from the petty greeds of everyday existence." Whatever it was that haunted his family—and him—he found release in his lifelong dedication to the tragic drama, to the dream, he said, that kept man "fighting, willing—living."

Notes and References

1. Thus the reader of tragedy, and of books on tragedy, must guard against the notion that the two modes (or any other modes, for that matter) exist in a chemically pure state and are mutually exclusive. The comic and the tragic, of course, may deepen and intensify each other in a single work. The problem of the writer of tragedy, as Aldous Huxley shows in an amusing essay, "Tragedy and the Whole Truth," *Virginia Quarterly*, April 1931, is to maintain the integrity of his tragic world against too great an intrusion of comic irony and irrelevance—and hence tragedy cannot tell "the whole truth." The problem of the reader of tragedy is to be sensitive to the delicate interactions of the modes; and so he must understand comedy, too. For a perceptive study of the values of comedy and tragedy, back to back, see Albert Cook's *The Dark Voyage and the Golden Mean*, Cambridge, Mass., 1949. Hawthorne's paradox is to the point when he speaks in *The House of the Seven Gables* (chap. 11) of "the tragic power of laughter." Did the Greeks have some such idea in mind when they presented satyr plays after the tragedies—a device which the more variegated Elizabethan tragedies were not felt, apparently, to require?

2. This issue has occasioned much spirited criticism. Croce once denounced all talk of the "genres" as alien to the artistic process and to the nature of the work of art ("Aesthetics," *Encyclopedia Britannica*, 14th ed., 1929). But talk of the genres, especially tragedy, has persisted —in modern times from Hegel and Nietzsche on. In our own century it has come in distinguishable flurries: In the early years, notably W. L. Courtney, *The Idea of Tragedy in Ancient and Modern Drama* (1900) and A. C. Bradley, *Shakespearean Tragedy* (1904). In the 1920's, Macneile Dixon, *Tragedy* (1924); F. L. Lucas, *Tragedy in Relation to Aristotle's Poetics* (1928); and the critical skirmishes occasioned by Joseph

Wood Krutch's essay, "The Tragic Fallacy," in his *The Modern Temper* (1929). During the 1930's and 1940's, the developing "New Criticism" was the central preoccupation, at least in America, although specific attention to tragedy appeared in Maxwell Anderson's *The Essence of Tragedy* (1939), in William Van O'Connor's *Climates of Tragedy* (1943), and in Moody Prior's *The Language of Tragedy* (1947). Since World War II (and partly because of it?) there has been perhaps the most notable resurgence of interest: Herbert Weisinger, *Tragedy and the Paradox of the Fortunate Fall* (1953); Eugene H. Falk, *Renunciation as a Tragic Focus* (1954); Henry Alonzo Myers, *Tragedy, a View of Life* (1956); Herbert J. Muller, *The Spirit of Tragedy* (1956); T. R. Henn, *The Harvest of Tragedy* (1956); William G. McCollom, *Tragedy* (1957); and two anthologies of essays on tragedy: *Tragic Themes in Western Literature*, ed. Cleanth Brooks (1955) and *The Tragic Vision and the Christian Faith*, ed. Nathan Scott (1957). In the last decade, also, the work of Kenneth Burke, Francis Fergusson, Northrop Frye, and R. P. Blackmur, to mention only a few, has touched upon tragedy at many points. The list is far from complete; my indebtedness to it and to many other monographs and essays bearing on our subject can be only partly indicated in the formal acknowledgments in the pages to follow. The significance of this concern for tragedy in our time I shall remark upon in due course. For now, it proves the vitality and, in spite of Croce, I should say the legitimacy of the discussion of the genres. See Laurence Michel's apt reply to D. J. Enright's disinclination to "haggle over literary categories," in *Essays in Criticism* (Jan. 1955), pp. 81–8.

3. Cf. Laurence Michel, "The Possibility of a Christian Tragedy," *Thought*, Autumn 1956, and see n. 47 below.

4. This summary treatment of Shelley's play, as of others mentioned in this quick survey, needs a word of comment, if only tentative and anticipatory. At times in the preface to *The Cenci* Shelley comes close to the heart of the matter. In dramatizing this "fearful and monstrous" story (as he calls it), he hopes to illuminate "some of the most dark and secret caverns of the human heart . . . all the feelings of those who once acted in it, their hopes and fears, their confidences and misgivings, their various interests, passions and opinions." He disavows "moral" or "dogmatic" purpose. But at once he sees the story as capable of "awakening and sustaining the sympathy of men"; he would "bring it [the story] home to their hearts"; he sets out to "increase the ideal, and diminish the actual horror of the events, so that . . . pleasure which arises from the poetry may mitigate the pain of the contemplation of moral deformity . . ." What is "tragic" is Beatrice's sad or pathetic fate, and the cause of it is clear: moral deformity. Manes Sperber once noted (*New York Times Book Review*, June 3, 1951, p. 1) that, in the romantic era "an individual's unhappy end was substance for tragedy. . . . In our age only Man's can be." This is portentous; but it points to what I think will emerge, as we proceed, as the parochial nature of Shelley's tragedy.

5. See Erich Heller's illuminating discussion of "Goethe and the

Avoidance of Tragedy" in his *The Disinherited Mind*, Cambridge, Mass., 1952.

6. F. O. Matthiessen, *American Renaissance* (New York, Oxford University Press, 1941), p. 184, writes: "How an age in which Emerson's was the most articulate voice could also have given birth to *Moby-Dick* can be accounted for only through reaction." The reaction of both Melville and Hawthorne was explicit, as Matthiessen shows. Richard Chase's recent treatment of Hawthorne and Melville in *The American Novel and Its Tradition*, Garden City, Doubleday, 1957, puts them in the tradition of the American "romance-novel," which he opposes to the English novel, following "the tendency of tragic art and Christian art." I think, however, with Matthiessen, that these authors, in *Moby-Dick* and *The Scarlet Letter*, are in the direct tragic line. Why I think so the rest of this book, especially Chs. 9 and 10, should make clear.

7. Miguel de Unamuno's *The Tragic Sense of Life*, tr. J. E. C. Flitch, London, 1921, republished Dover Publications, 1954, is a landmark in the discussion of tragedy comparable to Nietzsche's *The Birth of Tragedy* (1870-71). It directed attention not so much to the literary form of tragedy (Unamuno makes but one reference to Aeschylus, none to Sophocles and Euripides, one to Shakespeare and Marlowe) as to the complex of attitudes, ideas, feelings we call tragic, what I have elsewhere, following R. P. Blackmur's idea of "the form behind the forms we merely practise," called "the tragic form" ("The Tragic Form," *Essays in Criticism*, Oct. 1954) and what Murray Krieger calls "thematics" (Tragedy and the Tragic Vision," *Kenyon Review*, Spring 1958). In the present study I find the term "vision" an increasingly useful one, for all its ambiguities. I use it in what might be called its plenary sense: to indicate the total vision of the artist (insofar as we can reconstruct it from the evidence of the fulfilled form, the tragedy itself) of the nature and destiny of man. Krieger uses "the tragic vision" to refer to what I see as only one phase—what he calls the romantic, rebellious, demonic spirit, which needs (he writes) "the ultimate soothing power of the aesthetic form which contained it—of tragedy itself—in order to preserve for the world a sanity which the vision itself denied." To him, the tragic vision is "errant," "Dionysian" without the salutary restraint of the "Apollonian." Unamuno's "tragic sense" is but one phase, too, of the tragic vision as I use the term: the "furious hunger for being" as it is denied by the ineluctable fact of nonbeing, death. This may be one phase only, but it is the one from which all else springs.

8. Walpole's famous remark was made in a letter to Horace Mann on Dec. 31, 1769. The whole passage reads: "I have often said and oftener think that this world is a comedy to those who think, a tragedy to those who feel—a solution of why Democritus laughed and Heraclitus wept."

9. Murray Krieger (see n. 7 above) regards this attitude, often tinged, as he says, with the demonic, unruly, and destructive, as the essential,

177

"protestant," tragic vision. I regard it as one phase only, but never (in tragedy) wholly absorbed, resolved, or "soothed."

10. I first heard this term put to good use by Ralph Harper in his lectures on tragedy in the Institute for Religion in Independent Schools at Yale University in the summer of 1956. Since I put it to so much use myself, a word about its history is appropriate. (Here again I am indebted to Ralph Harper.) Karl Jaspers has used the phrase since 1919, obviously inspired by his reading of Kierkegaard. It has had some currency, notably in Paul Tillich, *The Protestant Era*, University of Chicago Press, 1948: "The human boundary-situation is encountered when human possibility reaches its limit, when human existence is confronted by an ultimate threat" (p. 197). See also a similar formulation in Erich Frank, *Philosophical Understanding and Religious Truth*, New York, Oxford University Press, 1945, where the existential man "at the limits of his sovereignty" finds the consolations of philosophy no longer effective.

11. To involve the artist in the "boundary-situation" of his created fiction is of course arbitrary. We can never know whether the Poet of Job or Sophocles or Shakespeare was thus involved. We can merely say that it seems as if they were, and point to evidence of such involvement that many latter-day writers have left on record: Hawthorne, Melville, Hardy, Conrad, Kafka, Dostoevski. Indeed, it has been pointed out that, in the modern age, when the symbol of the hero as the dominating center of the play seems to have lost its power with artist and audience, the artist becomes his own tragic hero. The "action," the suffering, and the perception are not objectified in the hero's ordeal, but seem to be the artist's own. At any rate, the distinction is one way of pointing to the difference between the tone of tragedy and the Olympian distance of Meredithian comedy, the harmony of the final phase of Dantesque comedy, or the ironic detachment of satire. Nietzsche noted the difference between the Dionysian (or tragic) artist and "the poet of the dramatized epos . . . the calm, unmoved embodiment of Contemplation, whose wide eyes see the picture before them" (*Birth of Tragedy* in *Works*, ed. O. Levy, Edinburgh and London, 1909, 3, 96). For further discussion of "involvement," see below, nn. 62, 73, 80.

12. The genetic studies of tragedy—anthropological, archaeological, and mythographic—further confirm the sense of involvement. See the work of Francis Cornford, Jane Harrison, and Gilbert Murray. Latterly, Herbert Weisinger has contributed notably to this study (*Tragedy and the Paradox of the Fortunate Fall*, 1953, and "The Myth and Ritual Approach to Shakespearean Tragedy," *The Centennial Review of Arts and Sciences,* Spring 1957). For the "propitiatory" theory of the origin of tragedy, see Helen Adolf, "The Essence and Origin of Tragedy," *Journal of Aesthetics and Art Criticism*, Dec. 1951. Hovering behind this paragraph is Willard Farnham's definition of tragedy as "the artistic and critical approach to the mystery of man's suffering on earth" in the preface to *The Mediaeval Heritage of Elizabethan Tragedy* (Berkeley, University of California

Press, 1936), p. xi. His treatment (in ch. 1) of the relation of tragedy to religious ritual and folk drama, though done with special reference to Elizabethan tragedy, recapitulates illuminatingly, I think, the perennial process.

13. *The Tragic Sense of Life*, p. 17.

14. Since I shall put it to frequent use, here is the whole of this much quoted passage from *A Portrait of the Artist as a Young Man* (New York, B. W. Huebsch, 1916, p. 239): "Pity," explained Stephen Daedalus to his friends at the university, "is the feeling which arrests the mind in the presence of whatsoever is grave and constant in human sufferings and unites it with the human sufferer. Terror is the feeling which arrests the mind in the presence of whatsoever is grave and constant in human sufferings and unites it with the secret cause." Louis L. Martz put the idea of "the secret cause" to good use in his "The Saint as Tragic Hero," *Tragic Themes in Western Literature*, New Haven, 1955.

15. Paul Weiss, "The True, the Good, and the Jew," *Commentary* (Oct. 1946), p. 315.

16. For a discussion of the realistic and skeptical aspects of the Hebraic temper, see Duncan B. Macdonald, *The Hebrew Philosophical Genius*, Princeton, 1936. A comparative study of Hebrew, Egyptian, and Babylonian world-views, emphasizing the distinctions I am asserting here, is in *The Intellectual Adventure of Ancient Man*, Chicago, 1946 by H. and H. A. Frankfort, John A. Wilson, Thorkild Jacobsen, and William A. Irwin.

17. Lecomte de Noüy once remarked that in the Fall of Man was the first creative expression of the tragic idea.

18. Simone Weil, "The Iliad or, The Poem of Force," 1940–41, tr. Mary McCarthy, *Politics*, Nov. 1945.

19. Quotations are from the Authorized Version unless otherwise noted. Concerned only with *Job* as it has come down to us traditionally, I am ignoring, of course, the vexed problem of multiple authorship.

20. *Moby-Dick*, ch. 96 ("The Try-Works").

21. R. P. Blackmur, "Anna Karenina: the Dialect of Incarnation," *Kenyon Review*, Summer 1950, quotes this phrase from Jung's *Psychology and Religion* (New Haven, Yale University Press, 1938), p. 55. The experience which Jung discusses in this passage is the religious experience as he defines it—the direct confronting of the "powers" ("spirits, demons, gods, laws, ideas, ideals"), the "dynamic factors" in our lives—"powerful," "dangerous," "helpful," or "grand, beautiful and meaningful enough to be devoutly adored and loved" (p. 5). He is speaking specifically of the Protestant who, lacking the mediation of the dogma and ritual of an "absolute" Church, "is defenseless against God and is no longer shielded by walls and communities" (p. 62). Jung, of course, is concerned with the terrifying effect on the individual of his discovery in himself of all the "forces waiting for liberation in the unconscious mind" (pp. 59–60). What tragedy reveals is the "terrifying ambiguity" of the forces both within and without—in the individual, in society, in the universe. It presents these forces *immediately*, or "unmediated."

179

22. This translation (or close variations of it) of 13:15 is generally accepted. See *A Commentary on the Bible*, ed. A. S. Peake, London, 1919, article "Job," by R. S. Franks. Cf. Moffatt's translation: "He may kill me —what else can I expect?"

23. Wallace Fowlie ("Swann and Hamlet: A Note on the Contemporary Hero," *Partisan Review*, May–June 1942) finds this a distinguishing characteristic of the tragic as opposed to the romantic hero. The romantic hero, he says, is preoccupied with the "intermittences" of his own heart; the tragic hero moves beyond them to make "a pact [with the world] that is unremitting and sealed" (p. 202).

24. T. S. Eliot, *The Family Reunion*, Pt. II, sc. 1. Copyright 1939 by T. S. Eliot. Reprinted by permission of Harcourt, Brace:

> "To rest in our own suffering
> Is evasion of suffering. We must learn to suffer more."

William Van O'Connor, *Climates of Tragedy* (Baton Rouge, University of Louisiana Press, 1943), p. 48, discusses this quotation in connection with tragedy's affirmation of the possibility of "awareness and dignity through suffering." And see below, n. 27.

25. *Moby-Dick,* ch. 41 ("Moby Dick").

26. As Captain Peleg tells Ishmael before the *Pequod* starts its journey, *Moby-Dick*, ch. 16 ("The Ship").

27. The place and quality of suffering in tragedy is a central theme of this study. It is treated passim, mostly in connection with specific fictional contexts. See especially pp. 36–7 and 47 below, and my treatment of it in "The Tragic Form," which includes the following formulation: ". . . tragic man would not define himself, like the man of corrective comedy or satire, 'I think, therefore I am'; nor like the man of achievement (epic): 'I . . . conquer, therefore I am': nor like the religious man: 'I believe, therefore I am': nor like the man of sensibility [the romantic]: 'I feel, therefore I am.' Although he has all these qualities (of thought, achievement, sensibility, and belief) in various forms and degrees, the essence of his nature is brought out by suffering: 'I suffer, I will to suffer, I learn by suffering; therefore I am.' The classic statement, of course, is Aeschylus': 'Wisdom comes alone through suffering' (Lattimore's translation); perhaps the most radical is Dostoevski's in *Notes from Underground*, B. G. Guerney's translation: 'Suffering is the sole origin of consciousness'" (*Essays in Criticism*, Oct. 1954, p. 354).

28. *Moby-Dick* ch. 16 ("The Ship").

29. Again the AV has been emended (19:25). See R. S. Franks in Peake's *Commentary*. Cf. Anthony and Miriam Hanson, *The Book of Job*, Torch Bible Commentaries (London, SCM Press, 1953), p. 70: "Fortunately there is one important thing that does stand out of this appallingly confused passage: Job still hopes somewhere (whether in the body or out of the body, we know not) for vindication before God."

30. As with suffering, the place and treatment of pride in tragedy is a major theme of this study. Tragic pride is not to be equated with sin

or weakness. The Counselors, and the Chorus, invariably argue against pride, urging caution and moderation, because they see it as blasphemous or presumptuous, and most surely leading to suffering; but tragedy does not prejudge it. Speaking of "the tragic flaw" in much these same terms, Arthur Miller ("Tragedy and the Common Man," *New York Times Theater Section*, Feb. 27, 1949, p. 1) shows how it can on occasion transfigure the "common man" and make him a fit subject for tragic treatment: "It is not peculiar to grand or elevated characters. . . . Nor is it necessarily a weakness. . . . [It] is really nothing . . . but [the hero's] inherent unwillingness to remain passive in the face of what he conceives to be a challenge to his dignity, his image of his rightful status."

31. The translation of 36:15 is from the American Standard Version.

32. This translation of 37:13 is from the American Standard Version.

33. See Hanson, *The Book of Job:* The "poem . . . clearly shows itself to be the vision of a great and daring mind. . . . We have the feeling of reaching darkness rather than light. A mystery has been probed, little help given, and the unconvincing conclusion only deepens the mystery . . . [pp. 16–17]. For an approach to the problem of innocent suffering that can be of comfort and solace to the Christian in trouble, it is not wise to look to the Book of Job . . ." (p. 20). The Hansons, however, true to the fundamentally religious nature of *Job* as a whole, shift the emphasis from the problem of innocent suffering to Job's "encounter with the Living God."

34. Reinhold Niebuhr (*The Nature and Destiny of Man*, New York, Charles Scribner's Sons, 1941), speaking of "the air of melancholy" which hangs over Greek life, writes: "Neither Greek nor Roman classicists had any conception of a meaning in human history. History was a series of cycles, a realm of endless recurrences" (p. 10). Later (p. 24) he speaks of "the Hebraic sense of a meaningful history, in contrast to the meaningless history of the Greeks."

35. Charles Seltman, *The Twelve Olympians* (London, Pan Books, 1952), p. 23.

36. Ibid., p. 22.

37. "In the end," writes Simone Weil, "the very idea of wanting to escape the role fate has allotted one—the business of killing and dying—disappears from the mind:

> *We to whom Zeus*
> *Has assigned suffering, from youth to old age,*
> *Suffering in grievous wars, till we perish to the last man.*

Already these warriors, like Craonne's so much later, felt themselves to be 'condemned men.'" (*The Iliad or, The Poem of Force.*)

38. *The Iliad*, Bk. 24 (Achilles to Priam).

39. *The Iliad or, The Poem of Force*, p. 27.

40. Ahab to the crew of the *Pequod* in "The Quarter-Deck," ch. 36.

41. Such traditional readings of the play, and some not so traditional, are critically treated in several recent studies of *Oedipus*, five of which (although they emphasize different aspects and disagree on important

issues) I have found helpful: the chapters on *Oedipus* in H. D. F. Kitto, *Greek Tragedy: A Literary Study*, London, Methuen, 1939; in C. M. Bowra, *Sophoclean Tragedy*, Oxford University Press, 1944; and in Cedric Whitman, *Sophocles: A Study of Heroic Humanism*, Cambridge, Harvard University Press, 1951; the notes on *Oedipus* in Cleanth Brooks and R. B. Heilman, *Understanding Drama*, New York, Henry Holt, 1945; and, most recently, Bernard Knox, *Oedipus at Thebes*, New Haven, Yale University Press, 1957. Bowra stresses the predetermined nature of Oedipus' actions and his faults of character too much to suit Whitman, who insists on his freedom and the "innocence" of his actions both before and during the play. Whitman finds in the play "unmitigated pessimism"—"a detailed picture of the irrational and unjustifiable evil inwrought in the texture of life, against which the greatest natural and moral endowments struggle in vain" (p. 127). Knox, also stressing Oedipus' freedom and innocence, goes back to Kitto's emphasis on the play as demonstrating a logos, or order, in the universe—where prophecies however dire and cruel at least *come true*; the play, that is, represents an attack on fifth-century Greek rationalism, a view which Brooks and Heilman also stress. My own reading stresses the ambiguity in Oedipus' character and actions—and resists resolving the questions of man's nature and destiny, and of the nature of the gods, which Sophocles, it seems to me, leaves open. Whitman himself speaks truly, I think, both of Sophocles and of tragedy in general when he says in a final note (p. 282) ". . . these tags [pessimism, optimism] are meaningless to an intellect such as Sophocles'." (Many modern scholars, including Bernard Knox, reject the Chorus' final speech as not a part of Sophocles' original text; I am concerned here, however, with the play as it has come down to us traditionally.)

42. E. F. Watling's translation (as throughout my discussion) in *Sophocles, The Theban Plays*, London, Penguin Classics, 1947.

43. Kitto, *Greek Tragedy* (2nd ed., 1950), pp. 139–40.

44. *Oedipus at Thebes*, pp. 147–58. The mathematical metaphor, by which Oedipus, who was first "equated" with the gods and finds in the end that he is "equated" only with himself, is one of the many metaphors which Knox traces through the play, each one deepening and extending the tragic meaning of the central action.

45. Though the affirmation that suffering brings knowledge seems clearly one of the constants of tragedy, it is by no means true of life in general. All suffering does not lead to knowledge. Suffering leads often to a complete collapse of the personality; it can degrade and benumb. Alberto Moravia's striking article, "The Sterility of Suffering," *Yale Review*, Winter 1958, points this out in connection with the "epoch of suffering" in Russia that began in 1917 and resulted in the deadening of sensibility and failure of compassion even among the intellectuals and artists of the time. And compare Arthur Koestler, *The Age of Longing* (New York, Macmillan, 1951), p. 22: "Why has all this made him so nasty and quarrelsome? thought Hydie. What about the famous purifying effect of suffering? Some people suffer and become saints. Others, by the same experience, are turned into brutes thirsting for vengeance. Others, just into neurotics. To

draw spiritual nourishment from suffering, one must be endowed with the right kind of digestive system. Otherwise suffering turns sour on one. It was bad policy on the part of God to inflict suffering indiscriminately. It was like ordering laxatives for every kind of disease." The distinction to emphasize is between suffering in general and what tragedy says about it: that on occasion, perhaps on rare occasion, it can lead to knowledge.

46. See Roy Morrell, "The Psychology of Tragic Pleasure," *Essays in Criticism*, Jan. 1956. This article contains many illuminating distinctions about the effect of tragedy. It does away nicely with the sadistic and masochistic theories—and with the cant which would exalt "catharsis" into a pseudoreligious conversion ("The action must end in disaster. More than a bare hint of the 'rebirth' or renewal theme is dangerous," p. 37). Mr. Morrell refers to Freud's account of the treatment of shell-shock victims during the war—"not by removing the patients to the quiet of the country, trying to make them forget, but rather by reminding them of the battlefield, supplementing their imaginings by noises of bombardment and by additional shocks" (p. 24). "The effect of Tragedy," Morrell concludes, "is courage; not mere toughness, nor bravado, nor the will to display power, but simply calmness and readiness, the discovery that even in the harshest experiences there is, to quote Richards, 'no difficulty'; the difficulty arises from the illusions and subterfuges by which we seek to dodge reality, and which we unconsciously fear are going to betray us" (p. 31). Although I know of no tragedy that left me in a state of "calmness" (if by that word he means spiritual tranquility or ease of mind about the human lot) I accept the "readiness" and agree wholly with his final comment: "But in the tragic end of the hero, and of the hopes we had in him, there is nothing defeatist . . ." (p. 37). And [earlier] ". . . his experiences [have increased] our capacity for living" (p. 36).

47. In one of the most vigorous recent attacks on the problem of Christianity and tragedy, Laurence Michel ("The Possibility of a Christian Tragedy") puts the case even more bluntly: "Christianity is intransigent to tragedy; tragedy bucks and balks under Christianity" (p. 427). Nothing in literature, he points out, can be both Christian and tragedy at the same time. He finds the true stuff of tragedy in the Old Testament, especially in *Job*, and points truly to the developing sense of tragic "dualism" in the story of the Creation: "Immediately we are confronted with actuality and existence, with the word 'good,' and in very short order with life, knowledge of good and evil, commandments, sorrow, fear, sin, death. . . . From the very outset, in a creative act there are elements of destruction and danger and hardship; but somehow at the end there is life abundantly, and blessedness, and rest. And this is a view of things in which the tragic sense can flourish" (pp. 410–11). But it is otherwise with the religion of Christianity. For anyone who "takes the reality of the Incarnation seriously" (and the doctrines of Atonement, Sin, and Grace), the incompatibility of tragedy and Christianity is inescapable (p. 419). Michel rightly deplores the careless use of the term "Christian Tragedy," and shows how, if we allow such subdivisions (like Domestic Tragedy, Heroic

183

Tragedy, the Tragedy of Revenge, the Tragedy of Blood, etc.) the word Tragedy itself becomes so diluted and distorted that our search for its underlying essence and form is "obstructed rather than fostered" (p. 423). I agree with this, and hence have avoided proliferating such distinctions in this book. It will be seen in the following discussion, however, that I cling to the term "Christian tragedy"—but only as a useful way of referring to tragedy written in the Christian era which bears the mark of Christian thought and feeling, however short it falls (and to be tragedy, it always does) of the doctrines of the Church. Michel shows truly that the "neo-realist" Protestant theologians point to the "somber side" of Christianity— "fear and trembling, dread, anxiety, despair, the absurd . . . not peace but the sword . . . hard-kept faith . . . the Crucifixion as well as the Eucharist . . ." (pp. 418–19). It is from such a matrix as this that "Christian tragedy" springs. Since Job and Prometheus, tragedy has always been "protestant," restless, anxious.

48. Paraphrasing Rousseau's views on the relation of the "true" Christian to the state, Ernest Hunter Wright (*The Meaning of Rousseau*, London, Oxford University Press, 1929, p. 88) says: "To the true Christian nothing matters in this vale of tears. States may come and states may go, battles may be lost or won, and tyrants may oppress and torture; let him be but pure in heart, and all will be well with him in a little while, his very resignation to the present evil making his reward to come the surer. If the danger appear fanciful, it is only because there are so few real Christians; but we are speaking now of such alone, having just considered other kinds."

49. M. Adriani, in *Apocalisse e Insecuritas*, 1954, as quoted in *Cross Currents* (Fall 1955), p. 374. But I do not mean to confuse the issue, so sharply stated by Michel. Adriani is not a "tragic theologian," nor does tragedy know the Revelation of which he speaks. Christian tragedy, to put it briefly, is not Christian; if it were, it would not be tragedy. But there is much that is "tragic" in Christian thought and feeling.

50. Walter F. Otto, *The Homeric Gods*, tr. Moses Hadas (New York, Pantheon Books, 1954), p. 177. In an earlier passage (p. 10) he writes: "The ancient Greek religion comprehended the things of this world with the most powerful sense of reality possible, and nevertheless—nay, for that very reason—recognized in them the marvellous delineations of the divine. It does not revolve upon the anxieties, longings, and spiritual broodings of the human soul: its temple is the world . . ." A passage in Nicholas Berdyaev's *Dostoievsky* (tr. Donald Atwater, London, Sheed and Ward, 1934, p. 74) gets at this same distinction and suggests some of the tensions introduced by Christianity which we shall discuss further in the chapter on *Doctor Faustus*: "Liberty in revolt, tumultuous aspirations without end, the irrational element in life, these are phenomena of the Christian world, and the uprising of human personality against world-organization and control is an interiorly Christian manifestation. Greek tragedy and the best Greek philosophy had shown the need to pull down the barriers and shut their world in and thus pointed the way towards the new Christian dispensation; but neither the drama nor the philosophy

of the Greeks knew anything about the soul of Faust and its awful freedom."

51. Otto, *The Homeric Gods*, p. 174.

52. Kierkegaard's discussion is in "Problem II" of *Fear and Trembling*, tr. Walter Lowrie, New York, Anchor Books, 1954.

53. Cf. Henri de Lubac, *Aspects of Buddhism*, tr. George Lamb (New York, Sheed and Ward, 1954), p. 37: "The essential thing, the thing that puts a gulf between Buddhist charity and Christian charity, is that in Christianity the neighbour is loved for himself. In Buddhism this is impossible . . . since in Buddhism the ego is entirely illusory, or exists only to be destroyed, [and hence] it can hardly be loved for itself. . . . 'The insignificance of the individual is for the Buddhist a fundamental axiom, like the infinite value of the human soul for the Christian.' This remark is made by Keyserling in support of the Christian. It nevertheless states a truth, and one of capital importance." Another difference, essential to tragedy, is brought out in a remark of Thoreau's in *A Week on the Concord and Merrimack Rivers:* "The Brahman never proposes courageously to assault evil, but patiently to starve it out . . ." Willard Farnham, commenting (in *The Mediaeval Heritage of Elizabethan Tragedy*) on the Chinese and Sanskrit cultures, says that they "have never so far as we know produced what men of the European tradition would call full-formed tragedy." In the classic *No* drama of Japan, he writes, "which at times can move us as does our own tragedy and which uses certain of the Greek methods to a highly remarkable degree, apparently by independent discovery . . . we are apt to find the tragic note ill sustained" (p. 1).

54. F. M. Powicke, *The Christian Life in the Middle Ages* (Oxford University Press, 1935), p. 7: "By paganism I mean a state of acquiescence, or merely professional activity, unaccompanied by sustained religious experience and inward discipline. It is not a state of vacancy and scepticism. It is confined to no class of persons, and is not hostile to, though it is easily wearied by, religious observance. It accepts what is offered without any sense of responsibility, has no sense of sin, and easily recovers from twinges of conscience. At the same time, it is full of curiosity and is easily moved by what is now called the group-mind. It is sensitive to the activities of the crowd, is often emotional, and can be raised to those moods of passion, superstition, and love of persecution into which religion, on its side, can degenerate." And later, p. 10: "It was all very interesting: the Church gave them very much, and yet they were at the same time inside the Church. They were both spectators and actors. They got wonderful buildings, pictures, plays, festivals, stories full of apocryphal detail about Biblical heroes and saints; but they could themselves help to build, paint, perform, repeat. They gibed incessantly at the clergy with their hypocrisy, venality, immorality, yet they had a good deal of sympathy with them, for they were of their own flesh."

55. This is to suggest, of course, that in ages when the dominant trend is the other way the tragic spirit often finds expression in lesser forms (see below, p. 83). The significance of the tragic ballads in this respect is not

often noted, except for passing references to their "Greeklike" spirit and even form. For instance, Martin Jarrett-Kerr, *Studies in Literature and Belief*, New York, Harper, 1954, sees in the ballad called "Babylon" (or "The Bonnie Banks of Fordie") "the normal five acts of tragedy, quite undeliberately reproduced" (p. 33). He quotes L. C. Wimberly's study, *Death and Burial Lore in English and Scottish Ballads*, University of Nebraska, Studies in Language, Literature and Criticism, No. 8, 1927, p. 9, as noting the similarity between the tragic ballads and the "sombre, fatalistic outlook, the same crushing imminence of death and disaster . . . the awareness of and insistence upon the darker side of human experience" of the early tragic Northern poetry—the Beowulf, certain of the Eddic lays, and the Nibelungenlied. But there is, too, in the tragic ballads, the relish of things of this life—sex, food and drink, color, jewels, fine clothes, physical beauty in nature and in man and woman—which creates a tension we have found to be true of formal tragedy. In these ballads death does not lose its sting; life is affirmed. There is sometimes suggested a typically tragic development of character, from "purpose" through "passion" to "perception," as in "Barbara Allen," where Barbara repents too late her failure to understand young Jemmy Grove's love for her, learns humility, and joins him in death. The American ballad "John Henry" shows in its hero a man fated from infancy— "Steel will be the death of me"—yet persevering in his purpose (the pride of his young manhood) against the competition of the steam drill and losing his life in the struggle—and the struggle presented with nice ambiguity. (This now famous description of the tragic hero's course—"purpose," "passion," "perception"—is Francis Fergusson's translation of Kenneth Burke's original formulation in *A Grammar of Motives*, pp. 38 ff., "*poiema, pathema, mathema*." See Fergusson's *The Idea of a Theater*, ch. 1, "The Tragic Rhythm of Action.")

56. In *The Mediaeval Heritage of Elizabethan Tragedy*, pp. 117–18: "So far as man's free will and validity were concerned, there was little to choose, theoretically speaking, between the old fatalism and the new [divine] determinism." I have followed in many points Farnham's analysis of the Renaissance "regaining of the world."

57. *The Prince*, tr. T. G. Bergin (New York, F. S. Crofts, 1947), ch. 25, p. 75.

58. "The Christian Tragic Hero," *New York Times Book Review*, Dec. 16, 1945. I agree with Laurence Michel (see above, n. 47) that tragedy is not Christian and never can be, and that such terms as "Christian tragedy" involve dangerous ambiguities. But (to repeat): the term is permissible and, I think, useful, to indicate the new dimensions and tensions introduced into human life by Christianity and which perforce entered into the Elizabethan tragic synthesis. Tragedy puts to the test *all* the formulations of a culture and comes out committed to none. What Auden describes as the Greek "tragedy of necessity" actually shows the extent to which man is free in the midst of fate; and what he calls the Christian "tragedy of possibility" shows the old sense of fate in the midst of the new freedom. I use this much-quoted remark from his *New York*

Times essay merely to point to the central stress (not new but more exigent) of Elizabethan tragedy.

59. Cf. Theodore Spencer, *Death and Elizabethan Tragedy* (Cambridge, Harvard University Press, 1936), p. 232. To the Elizabethans, "Death, indeed, *was* tragedy; a tragedy was a play which ended in death." Death was feared as "the end of accomplishment"; it destroyed beauty, power, wealth—all the good things of life. Spencer suggests (to anticipate for a moment) that the increasing number of tragedies during the early years of the seventeenth century was due in part, at least, to a kind of national preoccupation with death during Elizabeth's last years and following her death. "There is more than merely biographical importance in the fact that Shakespeare stopped writing comedies in [these years]. He simply expressed better than anyone else the trend of contemporary thought . . . He began to contemplate life tragically" (p. 233). (One is reminded of Dr. Johnson's remark [19 Sept. 1777]: "Depend upon it, Sir, when a man knows he is to be hanged in a fortnight, it concentrates his mind wonderfully.")

60. "Tragedy and the Common Man," *New York Times Theater Section*, Feb. 27, 1949. Miller here stresses what I regard as only the first phase of the tragic hero's experience, the romantic or rebellious phase: Faustus, that is, as he embarks on his course.

61. Indeed, as Herbert Weisinger suggests (*Tragedy and the Paradox of the Fortunate Fall*, E. Lansing, Michigan State College Press, 1953, p. 10), the doctrine of the *felix culpa* springs from the same archetypal experience. Just as the primitive king or hero—and later, the Savior—taking upon himself the sins of the people, died sacrificially, was reborn and brought new life, so the tragic hero in his pride "sins," dies, and brings us "new life." Weisinger sees the secularization of the paradox of the fortunate fall as "the substance out of which tragedy, and particularly Shakespearean tragedy, is made."

62. Paul H. Kocher, in his introduction to *Doctor Faustus* (Crofts Classics ed. New York, Appleton-Century-Crofts, 1950, p. viii), sees this, on whatever authority, as related directly to Marlowe's personal experiences: ". . . his imagination leaped to the wonder and terror of the deeds of magic, and the religious conflict drew powerfully on feelings which he was undergoing in his own life. It was for him the perfect theme." It is worth noting, now that we have reached in our study the era of modern drama when biographical information accumulates, that such suggestions —they can seldom be more than that—about the "involvement" of the artist in his fictions increase. Berdyaev, for instance, makes them repeatedly about Dostoevski: "The destiny of his characters is his own, their doubts and dualities are his, their iniquities are the sins hidden in his own soul." (*Dostoievsky*, p. 32).—My quotations from *Doctor Faustus* are from the Crofts Classics edition throughout.

63. E. M. W. Tillyard, *The Elizabethan World Picture*, New York, 1944, and Theodore Spencer, *Shakespeare and the Nature of Man*, New York, 1945, present the view summarized in the following.

64. The text follows the Everyman Library edition of Marlowe's plays.

65. Here, as throughout, my quotations follow the text of the Yale Shakespeare, ed. Tucker Brooke and William Lyon Phelps, New Haven, Yale University Press, 1947.

66. In an informal address at Silliman College, Yale University, 1948, Tillich described the plight—which he called "tragic"—of many intellectuals he had met during a recent visit in Germany. They felt that World War II had been "fated"—a part of German's destiny—and yet they felt deeply "guilty."

67. F. L. Lucas, *Tragedy in Relation to Aristotle's Poetics* (New York, Harcourt, Brace, 1928), p. 58.

68. Sylvan Barnet, "Some Limitations of a Christian Approach to Shakespeare," *Journal of English Literary History,* June 1955, presses this point vigorously, and gives some striking examples. "The rigidly Christian interpretation," he concludes, "forces a tragedy to fit ideas which Shakespeare doubtless held but did not dramatize. It is of value in explicating some puzzling lines and in emphasizing the moral tone of the plays. But it turns Othello into a villain . . . and it gives a comic ending to every tragedy, for it insists that the good are rewarded and the bad punished. It shifts the focus from this world to the next, muting the conflict of the tragic hero. . . ." (p. 92).

69. See Martin Steinmann, Jr., "Tragedy or 'Tragedy,'" *Essays in Criticism,* July 1955, who urges this more positivistic approach: searching out "a definition or definitions of what the word 'tragedy' has in fact been used to mean" (p. 281). Although such an approach would lead (and has) to interesting essays in cultural history, I see in it little gain toward answering the ultimate question. His strictures on the method of my article, "The Tragic Form," contain a salutary warning, however, and have in part influenced the method of this book, which proceeds, insofar as this is possible, from "tragedies" to "tragedy."

70. This and the following quotations from *The Duchess of Malfi* are from the Crofts Classics text, ed. Fred B. Millett, New York, Appleton-Century-Crofts, 1953.

71. Una Ellis-Fermor, *The Jacobean Drama,* London, Methuen, 1936, makes frequent use of this quotation from Webster's *The White Devil:*

> While we look up to Heaven we confound
> Knowledge with knowledge.

It not only sums up (she writes, pp. 17–18) "the content of his own great tragedies, but [is] the most nearly universal comment that was made upon the world of chaotic thought behind the Jacobean drama." What has happened is that "the outer and the inner worlds have become two," with the inevitable "loss of a spiritual significance from within the revealed world of fact and event. . . . In the world of Marston, Chapman, Middleton, Tourneur, Webster, Beaumont, Fletcher, Ford, there is crime and suffering, often of Aeschylean depth, but no hint of the Aeschylean resolution of evil through the education that suffering brings. If there is any comment (and often enough the tragedy ends in a crash of hardy and unmoved defiance) it is at most a thin, wavering doubt, a wandering scent blown for a moment on the tempest across the dark action of the final catastrophe."

72. Farnham (*Shakespeare's Tragic Frontier*, Berkeley, University of California Press, 1950) finds the Jacobean tragic view characteristic of the late tragedies of Shakespeare—*Timon of Athens, Macbeth, Antony and Cleopatra, Coriolanus*. In them "there is less of the medieval drama of good and evil" (p. 8), with its sharp and clear contrasts. The heroes are more deeply flawed; "they all are at times made ridiculous, and all are frequently enough subjected to ridicule at the hands of associates" (p. 11). There are no villains; the evil is within the heroes themselves. As with Antony, their "taints and honours wag[e] equal" with them, and we are left with a paradox and a mystery. This is a tragic frontier beyond which no author can go "without deserting tragedy" (p. 2). The "tragic emotions and the essential simplicities of tragic understanding are in constant danger of being overwhelmed by paradox" (p. 2). Although I agree as to the tendency, the "simplicities" do not seem so simple to me even in the middle tragedies, or in any tragedy, nor do I think that in *Antony* Shakespeare has left us in doubt about his sympathies.

73. Eliot expands this observation, which Una Ellis-Fermor uses to begin her own discussion of Middleton in *The Jacobean Drama*, in his essay, "Thomas Middleton," *Selected Essays 1917–1932*, New York, Harcourt, Brace, 1932: "Of all the Elizabethan dramatists Middleton seems the most impersonal . . . He has no point of view, is neither sentimental nor cynical; he is neither resigned, nor disillusioned, nor romantic, he has no message" (pp. 140, 141). In his tragedies as in his comedies he exhibits "the same steady impersonal passionless observation of human nature" (p. 145), ". . . he is merely a great recorder" (p. 148). Here is an example, relevant to our study, of what strikes at least one reader as the *de*involvement of the artist; and the example comes from a time when tragedy is clearly on the wane.

74. And, according to Robert Warshow, in the gangster film. The context of his observation, with its implications concerning tragedy in a period (which he conceived the late 1940's to have been) when the "organs of mass culture" seem bent on maintaining optimistic or "positive" social attitudes, is worth giving in some detail: "Even within the area of mass culture, there always exists a current of opposition, seeking to express by whatever means are available to it that sense of desperation and inevitable failure which optimism itself helps to create. Most often, this opposition is confined to rudimentary or semi-literate forms: in mob politics and journalism, for example, or in certain kinds of religious enthusiasm. When it does enter the field of art, it is likely to be disguised or attenuated: in an unspecific form of expression like jazz, in the basically harmless nihilism of the Marx Brothers, in the continually reasserted strain of hopelessness that often seems to be the real meaning of the soap opera. The gangster film is remarkable in that it fills the need for disguise (though

189

not sufficiently to avoid arousing uneasiness) without requiring any serious distortion. From its beginnings, it has been a consistent and astonishingly complete presentation of the modern sense of tragedy" (pp. 240–1). ("The Gangster as Tragic Hero," *Partisan Review,* Feb. 1948.) Warshow's prime example is the film, *Little Caesar.*

75. This and the following quotation from *An Essay on Man* (Epistle II and Epistle I), which follow the text of *The Best of Pope,* ed. George Sherburn, New York, Thomas Nelson and Sons, 1931, illustrates Whitehead's remark in *Science and the Modern World* (Mentor ed., Macmillan, New York, 1953), p. 82: "But the real point to notice is that Pope as well as Milton was untroubled by the great perplexity that haunts the modern world." Although William Van O'Connor's *Climates of Tragedy* is primarily concerned with periods, like those of fifth-century Greece and Elizabethan England, in which the "climate" was favorable to tragedy, the book makes an illuminating analysis, to which I am indebted, of climates *un*favorable to tragedy. Eighteenth-century England is a case in point.

76. "The Editor's Table," *Russell's Magazine* (Charleston, S.C.), *1,* Apr.–Sept. 1857), 279–80.

77. George E. Woodberry noted in Hawthorne this questioning, exploratory method, which seems true of tragic artists in general. Hawthorne's habit, he writes, was "to let the story tell itself from within according to its impulses, and not to shape it from without by his own predetermined purpose" (*Nathaniel Hawthorne,* Boston, Houghton Mifflin, 1902, p. 148). Similarly, Conrad tells in the preface to *Lord Jim* how the episode which he originally contemplated as the basis of a short story grew, as he explored its implications, into the substance of a full-scale tragic novel. Faulkner has made much the same comment to a recent interviewer (Jean Stein) about the origin and genesis of *The Sound and the Fury:* "I wrote it five separate times, trying to tell the story, to rid myself of the dream which would continue to anguish me until I did. It's a tragedy of two lost women: Caddy and her daughter. . . . It began with a mental picture. I didn't realize at the time it was symbolical. The picture was the muddy seat of a little girl's drawers in a pear tree, where she could see through a window where her grandmother's funeral was taking place and report what was happening to her brothers on the ground below. . . . I realized it would be impossible to get all of it into a short story and that it would have to be a book" (*Writers at Work,* ed. Malcolm Cowley, 1958, p. 130). The sentence, *"I didn't realize at the time it was symbolical,"* and Faulkner's subsequent comment, illustrates not only how symbolism works as a "way of knowing," a means of getting at meaning, but the symbolistic nature of the tragic artist's procedure in general. Thus, the Poet of Job, Aeschylus, Sophocles, Shakespeare saw the old stories they found at hand as richly symbolic and pressed the symbols for whatever meaning they could extract. Cf. Charles Feidelson's discussion of symbolism and of Hawthorne as symbolist in *Symbolism and*

American Literature, University of Chicago Press, 1953. Symbolism, he says, unlike allegory, does not "beg the question of absolute reality" (p. 8). The question, open to begin with, is left open at the end.

78. "Emily Dickinson," *On the Limits of Poetry* (New York, The Swallow Press and William Morrow, 1948), p. 200. Though admittedly stating the Emersonian doctrine in its extreme terms, Tate attributes the prevailing and (for us) nontragic mood of mid-century America to his influence: ". . . the Lucifer of Concord, he had better be called hereafter, for he was the light-bearer, and was fearfully blind. . . . [For Emerson] man is greater than any idea and, being himself the Over-Soul, is innately perfect; there is no struggle because . . . there is no possibility of error. There is no drama in human character because there is no human fault." Tate quotes Robert Penn Warren's remark that "after Emerson had done his work, any tragic possibilities in that culture were dissipated."

79. Rudolph Von Abele, "The Scarlet Letter: A Reading," *Accent* (Autumn 1951), p. 222, indicates the recurrence of the adjective "dark" and its synonyms throughout the novel. "In such a dim world," he writes, "light comes mostly in feeble or transient gleams . . ."

80. Henry James, *Hawthorne* (New York, 1880), p. 96. This remark appears in a passage which anticipates what I have just quoted from Allen Tate: "Emerson," wrote James, "as a sort of spiritual sun-worshipper, could have attached but a moderate value" to this cat-like faculty of Hawthorne's. Elsewhere he contrasted the two in similar vein: "Hawthorne's vision was all for the evil and sin of the world: a side of life as to which Emerson's eyes were thickly bandaged." (From James' review of *The Life of Emerson,* in *Macmillan's Magazine,* New York, 1887, as quoted in Peter Buitenhuis, *James and America,* unpublished Yale dissertation, 1955.) But James refused, and quite rightly, to view Hawthorne as the "dusky and malarious genius" (*Hawthorne,* p. 46) which some have taken him to be. James is impressed by what is generally true of Hawthorne—his fine artistic detachment: "He is no more a pessimist than an optimist," he is "to a considerable degree ironical . . . but . . . neither bitter nor cynical—he is rarely even what I should call tragical" (pp. 58, 59). James made these remarks in his discussion of the *Twice-Told Tales.* Later, speaking of *The Scarlet Letter,* he notes more involvement and more of the "tragical": "The work has the tone of the circumstances in which it was produced. If Hawthorne was in a sombre mood, and if his future was painfully vague, *The Scarlet Letter* contains little enough of gaiety or of hopefulness. It is densely dark . . ." (p. 106). That Hawthorne was one of James' literary models is clear enough; surely this phase of Hawthorne was one of the sources of James' own sense of the "tragical."

81. F. O. Matthiessen quotes this remark early in his discussion of Hawthorne (*American Renaissance,* p. 192). His account of the literary affinities between Hawthorne and Melville includes much that is true not only of their place in mid-nineteenth-century America but in the tragic tradition in general. See especially the opening paragraphs of his

chapter, "The Vision of Evil" (pp. 179–80). Later (p. 189) he says that it was Melville's meditation on Shakespeare that "brought him to his first profound comprehension of the nature of tragedy." What Melville liked in Hawthorne, writes Matthiessen, was "the same kind of 'short, quick probings at the very axis of reality' that had so impressed him in Shakespeare."

82. In *The Melville Log*, ed. Jay Leyda (New York, Harcourt, Brace, 1951), there is the following entry under March 23, 1850 (*Moby-Dick* was begun Feb. 1, 1850): "M. acquires another Bible . . . In *Job* . . . Chapter 13 he scores and underscores: 15 Though he slay me, yet will I trust in him: *but I will maintain mine own ways before him*." My attention was called to this entry by Laurence Michel.

83. Chase's treatment of Ahab ("An Approach to Melville," *Partisan Review*, May–June 1947) is surely true of one phase of his character. Ahab, says Chase, undergoes "transfiguration, not into the image of Prometheus, but into the image of the Beast-Machine. . . . Caught in the final violence of the whale hunt, Ahab is transfigured into the 'impersonal,' into the mechanical monster with blood on his brain" (p. 290). But this does not seem to me definitive of our total image of Ahab or even of the Ahab of the whale hunt.

84. This is the theme (though disputed) of Lawrance Thompson's *Melville's Quarrel with God*, Princeton, 1952. Merrell Davis comments truly, I think, in his review of the book in *Review of English Studies*, July 1954: "In *Moby-Dick*, dealing with the problem of evil, Melville naturally uses the theological categories—and there is, of course, irony at the expense of Presbyterian orthodoxy—but, finally, Ahab is moving in the true tragic zone which is neither Christian nor Atheist . . ." (p. 327).

85. Henry Alonzo Myers, in *Tragedy: A View of Life* (Ithaca, Cornell University Press, 1956), ch. 3, "The Tragic Meaning of *Moby Dick*," calls this "Ahab's great discovery and the key to the tragic meaning of *Moby Dick*" (p. 72). He goes on: "The end of Ahab is not unrelieved defeat, but victory in defeat; and the main point of *Moby Dick* is that any great human action will show that the heavens and the deeps, eternal symbols of man's triumphs and disasters, are merely the limits of his experience, related to each other through that experience and dependent upon each other and upon him for their meaning" (p. 73). Ahab, "neither saint nor sinner" but with a "grand passion to do and to know," discovered in the end that "the only compensations for his fate are to be found in himself, in the nature that is capable of an exaltation exactly equal to his grief. . . . Ahab's victory equals his defeat, his joy equals his sorrow" (pp. 74–5). Although there is much in this, and in this fine essay, which seems to me true, I find it difficult to accommodate Myers' idea of exact equivalence into what I think this tragedy (and tragedy in general) says. *Does* Ahab's final joy equal his sorrow? Like Job, Ahab never got an answer to his question. He never "penetrated the mask." The metaphor of "equivalence" suggests, I think, too neat and precise an equation. The metaphor of pre-

carious and imperfect balance, to which I have had occasional recourse in this study, is none too satisfactory; but it suggests the constant opposition of forces, the unremitting tension, which I find true of tragedy.

86. Throughout this chapter, I have followed the Constance Garnett translations as they appear in the Modern Library editions of *Crime and Punishment* and *The Brothers Karamazov*. The quotations are used by permisison of William Heinemann, Ltd.

87. *Dostoievsky*, p. 227. This book, one of the most perceptive studies of Dostoevski, is justly famous also for its insights into the modern tragic situation.

88. *Dostoievsky*, p. 75.

89. See Konstantin Reichardt, "Tragedy of Idealism: Henrik Ibsen," in *Tragic Themes in Western Literature*.

90. In a letter to R. B. Cunninghame Graham, Jan. 31, 1898 (G. Jean-Aubry, *Joseph Conrad, Life and Letters*, Garden City, Doubleday Page, 1927, *1*, 226.) Conrad's novels and letters abound in remarks that reveal a view ranging from a subtragic pessimism to a view which, by counter-thrust of spirit, is redeemed for tragedy. He may speak (in *Lord Jim*) of the "fiendish joke" of existence, of the "burlesque meanness" of the "Dark Powers," and have Marlow say of Jim's case, "There was not the thickness of a sheet of paper between the rightness and the wrongness of this affair." Again, at one point he suspects that "the aim of creation cannot be ethical at all." In another letter to Cunninghame Graham he writes: "Life knows us not and we do not know life. . . . Faith is a myth and beliefs shift like mists on the shore: thoughts vanish: words once pronounced, die: and the memory of yesterday is as shadowy as the hope of tomorrow . . ." And yet he can regard life as "a spectacle for awe, love, admiration, or hate . . . but . . . never for despair." (Quoted by W. Macneile Dixon, *The Human Situation*, New York, Longmans, Green, 1937, p. 239.) Morton D. Zabel's Introduction to *The Portable Conrad* (1952) is a sensitive treatment of this central aspect of Conrad's thought.

91. Sigmund Freud, *A General Introduction to Psychoanalysis*, (Garden City Publishing Co., 1943), p. 45. Stanley Edgar Hyman's article, "Freud and the Climate of Tragedy," *Partisan Review*, Spring 1956, which touches our study at many points, makes a sharp distinction between the "gloomy, stoic, and essentially tragic" Freudian view and the "optimistic and meliorative" (p. 201) interpretation of it by the "revisionists," Horney, Fromm, and Sullivan, who see man (says Hyman) as "fundamentally good, innocent, and unfallen" (p. 207). But in declaring his belief that "the writings of Sigmund Freud once again make a tragic view possible for the modern mind" (p. 201), he seems to be identifying the tragic view with the "gloomy" and the "stoic." The "discovery," or "perception," of tragedy is to him merely man's awakening to the grim facts of his own nature and to the fact that life "is nasty, brutish, and short" (p. 214). This, says Hyman, is what "the great philosophers and the great tragic writers have always said." His strictures upon the revisionists are well taken in regard to tragedy. In their brand of "cultural determinism" in

which "whatever is is no individual's fault" (p. 211), tragedy is impossible. But the great tragic writers have said more about life, of course, than that it is nasty, brutish, and short. The crux of the matter, I think, is Freud's view of psychic freedom as illusory. Later in *A General Introduction* (p. 252) he writes: "But man's craving for grandiosity is now suffering the third and most bitter blow [after Copernicus and Darwin] from present-day psychological research which is endeavouring to prove to the 'ego' of each one of us that he is not even the master in his own house, but that he must remain content with the veriest scraps of information about what is going on unconsciously in his own mind." If man is not in some degree the master in his own house, who can be held responsible for anything, where is guilt, and where is tragedy?

92. What happens to tragedy under statism of any kind is well illustrated in George Orwell's *1984* (New York, Harcourt, Brace, 1949), p. 31, where the protagonist reminisces in this vein about his mother's death: "The thing that now suddenly struck Winston was that his mother's death, nearly thirty years ago, had been tragic and sorrowful in a way that was no longer possible. Tragedy, he perceived, belonged to the ancient time, to a time when there were still privacy, love, and friendship, and when the members of a family stood by one another without needing to know the reason . . . [His mother] had sacrificed herself to a conception of loyalty that was private and unalterable. . . . Today there were fear, hatred, and pain, but no dignity of emotion, no deep or complex sorrows."

93. In *The Modern Temper* (New York, Harcourt, Brace, 1929), ch. 5. A vigorous reply to this essay came in Mark Harris, *The Case for Tragedy*, New York, G. P. Putnam's Sons, 1932. Questioning Krutch's "absolute" requirements for tragedy, Harris set up a sociological, or relativistic, theory based on the concept of the democratic, "representative individual," (p. 163) whose values the audience shares. The "tragic response" is elicited when these values are jeopardized. Although demonstrating effectively that Krutch had not the last word in this controversy, Harris' theory depends too much, I think, on the "response" of the audience. It speaks more of what tragedy *does* than what it *is*. He does not question the nature of the values shared by hero and audience.

94. Preston T. Roberts, Jr., "Bringing Pathos into Focus," *University of Chicago Magazine*, Feb. 1954, p. 7: "The first and most distinguishing mark of modern plays is their pathos." The Greek plays, like *Oedipus*, says Roberts, are preoccupied with "what is simply and purely tragic about life," and "Christian plays like *King Lear*" with "what is redemptive or more than tragic in life . . ." *A Streetcar Named Desire* and *Death of a Salesman* are typical modern plays "distinguished by their absorption with what is pathetic or less than tragic and incapable of redemption in experience. They seem to be peculiarly concerned with those aspects of experience which lie below the conscious mind or active will . . ." The question, of course, is what *is* "simply and purely tragic." Does Roberts mean that there is no redemption of any kind in *Oedipus*, and is the idea of redemption so powerful in *Lear* as to raise it "above" tragedy? I hope

194

my previous analyses have made my answers to these questions clear.

95. F. L. Lucas, in *Tragedy in Relation to Aristotle's Poetics* (pp. 57–8), makes this point, which I have already alluded to (see above, n. 11): "Complaining of the want of great personalities in this play or that, they [the critics] forgot the author. For the characters may be poor in spirit and feeble in desire, and the play remain tragic in spite of it, if we feel that the author is himself none of these things and has never cheated or paltered in his picture of men as they are." I am doubtful how far one can carry this view without accepting mere reportage, however stark and "honest," as tragedy. If all his characters are "poor in spirit and feeble in desire," how and where can the author dramatize the transcendence, the perception, the "knowledge" indispensable to the full vision of tragedy? Tragedy cannot stop with the realist's picture of men "as they are."

96. See Helen Garwood, *Thomas Hardy: An Illustration of the Philosophy of Schopenhauer* (Philadelphia, The John C. Winston Co., 1911), ch. 3, for a perceptive exposition of Hardy's views on tragedy. The quoted remarks on Hardy in the following paragraphs are from her study. In general, Hardy saw no tragedy where the individual is able to help himself; there is "tragedy," he felt, only when the individual is helpless and blameless, a victim of the "blind irrationality" of the universe. "So we get characters," writes Helen Garwood, "who are not aggressive nor strenuous, who seldom take the initiative, who do not demand much, who do not challenge life, who scarcely aim at all, much less at the stars . . . and above all [are] capable of endurance. Placed, against their will, in a world not to their liking, they are resigned to it and will make the best of it" (p. 68).

97. See Sophus Keith Winther, *Eugene O'Neill: A Critical Study* (New York, Random House, 1934), p. 220, who quotes the passage from Arthur Hobson Quinn's *History of the American Drama*, (New York, F. S. Crofts, 1943), 2, 199. The extent to which O'Neill succeeded in achieving in his plays "the transfiguring nobility of tragedy" has been variously argued. See for instance Herbert Muller's sympathetic but, in the end, dissenting view in his section on O'Neill in *The Spirit of Tragedy* (New York, Alfred A. Knopf, 1956), pp. 311–19. "He was in fact," writes Muller, "closer in spirit to Greek tragedy than any other modern dramatist. His high aim may therefore make one more painfully aware of his limitations, both as thinker and as poet." Muller points in a general way to some of these limitations—the "sometimes limp" colloquial dialogue, the "sometimes crude" and labored psychology stemming from "a secondhand Freudianism learned by rote." They are more specifically illustrated in Doris M. Alexander's study of *Mourning Becomes Electra* (the play which invites most immediate comparison with Greek tragedy) in "Psychological Fate in *Mourning Becomes Electra*," *PMLA*, Dec. 1953.

98. I have already referred to Miller's essay on "Tragedy and the Common Man" (see n. 60 above). He made another statement of his ideas on tragedy in "The 'Salesman' Has a Birthday," *New York Times Theater Section*, Feb. 5, 1950. See also his Introduction to *Arthur Miller's Collected*

Plays, New York, Viking Press, 1957, where he makes some pungent remarks on academic definitions of tragedy. Of *Death of a Salesman* he says: "I set out not to 'write a tragedy' in this play, but to show the truth as I saw it. However, some of the attacks upon it as a pseudo-tragedy contain ideas so misleading, and in some cases so laughable, that it might be in place here to deal with them" (p. 31). It might be said that any writer, at this late date, who sets out to "write a tragedy" is as vulnerable as the critic who attacks a play because "it is not a tragedy." The crux of the matter is the nature of the truth revealed in the play, and one may properly ask whether it is "tragic," or "pseudo-tragic," or something else. For now, it is enough to say that these are questions that seem to be of increasing concern to us, and it is well that it is so. To my knowledge, Tennessee Williams has never discussed his craft as fully as Miller, but see his brief prefatory notes to *The Glass Menagerie*, Norfolk, Conn., 1949, and *27 Wagons Full of Cotton*, Norfolk, Conn., 1953. Above all, see Elia Kazan's notes on *A Streetcar Named Desire* in *Directing the Play*, ed. Toby Cole and Helen Chinoy (New York, Bobbs-Merrill, 1953): "This is like a classic tragedy," writes Kazan. "Blanche is Medea or someone pursued by the Harpies, the Harpies being *her own nature*" (p. 301).

99. Atkinson reviewed Williams' play in the *New York Times*, April 25, 1952.

100. Perhaps, among other reasons, because of the influence on teaching of the methods introduced by I. A. Richards' *Practical Criticism* (1930) and the development of the New Criticism? This was true, certainly, in many academic communities in America. In some quarters the current interest in tragedy is seen as a reaction against the so-called formalistic approach, with its sharp focus on the inner harmonies and structure of the single work, particularly the lyric poem. Herbert Muller makes this a minor polemical theme of his *The Spirit of Tragedy*, though he makes exceptions: "The language of a poem is a continuous reference to things outside itself. Its meaning is never intact, self-contained, self-explanatory. Hence a sensitive reader like Cleanth Brooks, who is most insistent on the necessity of staying inside the poem, is usually carried further afield than most readers just because he finds poetry more profoundly suggestive" (p. 13). The danger, of course, is that the student of tragedy, concerned as it is with such momentous issues, may go too far afield and forget that he is dealing with works of art. The two disciplines are complementary— or should be. The "tragic analysis" as I have tried to illustrate it in this book—its focus on "the vision of evil: the vision of the good"—is never complete until the last metaphor and the last structural relationship are explored for their full meaning.

101. See above, n. 85.

102. I am not alone in this view, of course; but I would call attention to a particularly early recognition of Faulkner's distinction in this regard in an article by Warren Beck, "Faulkner and the South," *The Antioch Review*, Spring 1941. "Faulkner," he writes, "is chronologically of that generation which went to the first World War when they were barely

out of their teens, but he rapidly transcended the view which narrowed and paralyzed some of them, that this catastrophe was unique, a special fate victimizing them as no other men before them had been victimized" (p. 83). Though recognizing "the dark shape of doom" (a phrase from *Sartoris*) as "eternal and omnipresent," Faulkner achieved a "dynamic tension," Mr. Beck wrote, (not true of the "inverted aestheticism" of the postwar school) between "his realistic discernment of fact and the demands of his indomitable idealism" (p. 84). The tension, that is, at the heart of tragedy.

103. Ernest Hemingway, *A Farewell to Arms* (New York, Charles Scribner's Sons, 1929), p. 196.

104. Cynthia Grenier, "The Art of Fiction: An Interview with William Faulkner—September 1955," *Accent* (Summer 1956), p. 171.

105. Harry Hartwick, *The Foreground of American Fiction* (New York, American Book Company, 1934), p 160. Faulkner's "cosmos," wrote Hartwick, is "ghastly and anarchic," his universe "bereft of authentic proprieties and the accents of logic," where "violence is the only source of emphasis and intensity left in fiction." His deeds of "crime, perversion, and sadism . . . never transcend the level of bare perception. There is nothing, we feel, behind his atrocities, no cosmic echo . . ." (p. 161). Hubert D. Saal protested this judgment in an early essay, "Faulkner: Chronicler and Prophet," *Yale Literary Magazine*, Dec. 1947.

106. I wish to preface my analysis of *Absalom, Absalom!* by mention of two studies: Cleanth Brooks, "*Absalom, Absalom:* the Definition of Innocence," *Sewanee Review*, Autumn 1951, and Ilse Dusoir Lind, "The Design and Meaning of *Absalom! Absalom!*," *PMLA*, Dec. 1955. Both place the novel squarely in the tragic tradition. "In *Absalom, Absalom,*" concludes Brooks, "it is tragedy that [Faulkner] has given us" (p. 558). Ilse Lind's introductory remarks sum up my purpose in devoting to this novel my final chapter, in which I would like to think that all the themes and motifs of the previous pages are recapitulated in one final demonstration. "Broadly stated," she writes, "the intention of *Absalom! Absalom!* is to create, through the utilization of all the resources of fiction, a grand tragic vision of historic dimension. As in the tragedies of the ancients and in the great myths of the Old Testament, the action represents issues of timeless moral significance. . . . Events of modern history, here viewed as classic tragedy, are elevated through conscious artistry to the status of a new myth. . . . Only by considering form and meaning in organic interrelationship can we hope to discover the conception underlying this vast and strangely compelling tragic vision" (p. 887). (Quotations from the novel by permission of Random House, Inc. Copyright, William Faulkner.)

107. Throughout this chapter I have followed the translation by Willa and Edwin Muir, revised by E. M. Butler, in the paperback edition published in 1968 by Schocken Books, New York.

108. This, to many, will seem a very large statement indeed, assuming as it does that the "meaning" of *The Trial* is that accessible.

Recent criticism (see *Twentieth Century Interpretations of The Trial,* ed. James Rolleston, Prentice-Hall, Inc., 1976, for an excellent selection) stresses the ambiguities in the novel that defy simplistic reduction. My own reading most closely follows that of Ingeborg Henel, "The Legend of the Doorkeeper and Its Significance for Kafka's *The Trial*" (*Twentieth Century Interpretations,* pp. 40–55), which sees guilt and self-knowledge as the theme of the novel. I am also indebted to Murray Krieger's discussion of *The Trial* in his *The Tragic Vision* (1960). Rolleston's *Introduction* (pp. 8–9) contains a salutary warning. Although every interpreter of Kafka, he says, is "a free man," he must contemplate the possibility that his interpretation is doomed ultimately "to be absorbed with hardly a trace in the restless silence of the text." But much the same could be said of every masterwork, and still we press on.

109. Cf. Cyrena Norman Pondrom, "Kafka and Phenomenology: Joseph K.'s Search for Information," in *Twentieth Century Interpretations,* pp. 70–85.

110. Cf. Erich Fromm, *The Forgotten Language* (1951), pp. 261–62. Fromm sees Joseph K.'s ultimate error in his failure to understand that "the moral law represented by the priest and the law represented by the court are different." He "had a chance to look into himself and to ask what the real accusation was, but . . . he was interested only in finding out where he could get more help" (p. 260).

111. "Reading Kafka," trans. Glen W. Most, *Twentieth Century Interpretations,* p. 19.

112. "The Opaqueness of *The Trial,*" *Twentieth Century Interpretations,* p. 58.

113. *Twentieth Century Interpretations,* p. 85.

114. *Long Day's Journey into Night* (Yale University Press, 1956), p. [7].

115. The play has been much discussed in its dramatic, aesthetic, and autobiographical dimensions. I have found the following most helpful: Doris V. Falk, *Eugene O'Neill and the Tragic Tension* (1958); Travis Bogard, *Contour in Time: The Plays of Eugene O'Neill* (1972); Leonard Chabrowe, *Ritual and Pathos—The Theater of O'Neill* (1976); Arthur and Barbara Gelb, *O'Neill* (1960); and Louis Shaeffer, *O'Neill: Son and Playwright* (1968).

116. This is the play, a version of the Dumas romance, that brought fame and fortune to James O'Neill; but as Arthur and Barbara Gelb point out (p. 48), ". . . it put a strict limitation on his career. It became a trap from which he never escaped and into which Eugene O'Neill was born."

117. This and the following remarks by O'Neill on tragedy are quoted in Arthur and Barbara Gelb, *O'Neill,* p. 5.

118. The Gelbs pay this tribute to O'Neill's achievement: "For over a quarter of a century he had battled to lift American drama to the level of art and keep it there, to mold a native, tragic stage literature.

The first American to succeed as a writer of theatre tragedy, he had continued shattering Broadway convention and made possible the evolution of an adult theatre in which such playwrights as Thornton Wilder, Tennessee Williams and Arthur Miller could function" (p. 5).

119. *Time*, October 21, 1946. Quoted in Chabrowe, *Ritual and Pathos—The Theater of O'Neill*, p. 198.

120. Arthur and Barbara Gelb, *O'Neill*, p. 5.

Index

The primary aim of this index is to make available to the reader at a glance the major ideas, concepts, and themes developed in the discussions of the particular works, thus reversing the method of the book as a whole. Since many themes or aspects (e.g., "Action," "Freedom") are too pervasive for complete listing, references are given to the passages where they come most conspicuously to the surface.

Abbreviations: *BK* for *The Brothers Karamazov; AA* for *Absalom, Absalom!; LDJ* for *Long Day's Journey into Night.*